MORGAN
Sweeps the Board

MORGAN
Sweeps the Board
The Three-wheeler Story

Dr. J. D. Alderson and D. M. Rushton

Foulis

Haynes

ISBN 0 85614 050 3

A FOULIS Motoring Book

First published, by Gentry Books Ltd, 1978
Revised edition, published 1984

© J Alderson and D Rushton 1978, 1984

All rights reserved. No part of this book may be reproduced or transmitted in any form or by any means, electronic or mechanical, including photocopying, recording or by any information storage or retrieval system, without permission of the publisher.

Published by:
Haynes Publishing Group
Sparkford, Yeovil, Somerset BA22 7JJ, England

Distributed in North America by:
Haynes Publications Inc.
861 Lawrence Drive, Newbury Park,
California 91320, USA

To
the memory of
HFS Morgan
and his supporters

Contents

Acknowledgments	8
Foreword by Peter Morgan	9
Introduction	11
The Pioneering Days	13
Events Galore	39
Still Faster	89
The Three-speeder Era	163
The Four-wheeler Era	207
Records Held by Morgans 1912-1930	239
Index	251

Acknowledgments

We would like to thank the following people and companies for their tremendous help in the production of *Morgan Sweeps the Board:* Peter Morgan, A Allard, CE Allen, R Baker, J Bayley, H Beart, W Boddy, L Bolton, J Breyer, The Brooklands Engineering Co, The Brooklands Society, ES Brownbill, T Bryant, RD Caesar, R Chapman, G Church, L Creed, R Currie, C Curtis, B Davenport, SCH Davis, Mrs Dawes, Dunlop Ltd, G Fairburn, Ford Motor Co, G Goldsmith, WA Goodall, J Gosney, K Green, C Hale, P Hartley, GM Hawkes, FP Heath, J Hooper, RT Horton, EP Huxham, IPC Business Press Ltd, RR Jackson, FW James, C Jay, D Jenkinson, L Jones, R Laird, HC Lones, G Lyons, MN Mavrogordato, P McCarthy, WG McMinnies, GE Meade, D Morgan, A Moss, S Moss, *Motor Sport,* National Motor Museum, D Prestwich, E Prestwich, S Rhodes, W Rushton, C Shorrock, J Sylvester, D Thirlby, KLM Tidy, G Tottey, AK Tunstill, CJ Turner, J Warnick, CL Whatley, P Willson, E Ventura, and finally our many friends in the Morgan Three-Wheeler Club, with special thanks to L Ayers, C Drinkwater, WD Evans, A Goldsmith, R Richmond, C Wagstaff, W Wallbank, L Weeks, C Wilson and T Wright. For the information on Morgans in Australia we are deeply indebted to the researches of T Wright and members of the VSCCA, especially Mr King and Mr Hedley.

The photographs are credited where this has been possible. However, many have been reproduced from scrap albums and we have not always been able to trace their source. We would like to apologise to anyone who has not been included for that reason.

Foreword

Never before has such a comprehensive and well researched history of the Morgan three-wheeler been attempted, and I would like to thank the authors for the diligence and time they have spent in preparing and writing this historical book. I am sure that those who read it will find the information given of great interest, along with the personal views of the authors as to the various happenings over the years when the car was constructed.

Readers will note the emphasis on reliability trials and racing. In many instances these were the reasons for the modifications made to the cars, but above all, from the very early days, they were vitally important in order to sell the car at all. The competition from other manufacturers of cyclecars was extensive, and in order to ensure production it was absolutely necessary that the vehicle proved itself as a reliable and economical means of transport, able to hold its own when compared to the more expensive four-wheeled motor cars of the day.

The three-wheeler within the cyclecar movement had a definite advantage with regard to road tax, which was the main reason why HFS Morgan did not introduce a four-wheeled car at an earlier time. To the end of his days, I always felt that the three-wheeler was his real love, even though its demise was eventually dictated by business reasons.

This book is a fine tribute to my father, HFS Morgan. Although I consider him to be a great engineer of his time, I know that he himself would not wish to overlook the very large part in the success of the firm played by those who competed in Morgans, and most particularly by those who carried out the racing preparation and tuning of the cars. In many instances, it will be noted that not only were they highly skilled engineers, but also expert drivers, handling their own machines.

Morgan Sweeps the Board

The story brings back proud memories to me, especially when reading about such events as the relay races at Brooklands and the record attempts. It is most gratifying to know that even at the present time, Morgan three-wheeler enthusiasts continue to race and compete in the car, for, as this book confirms, competition must be the true element of the Morgan three-wheeler.

Peter Morgan

Introduction

Books on Morgans have been written before, but we make no apologies for writing a new one. Of no other single vehicle can the saying 'Racing improves the production model' be more apt than of the Morgan three-wheeler. From its inception in 1909 until its demise in 1952 Morgans were actively raced, trialled and used for record breaking, and much knowledge was gained from such competition, some to be used in future production models. The same is true today of the four-wheeler Morgan, but that is a separate story.

In this book we have attempted to follow through the interesting story of the competition Morgan three-wheeler, commenting as appropriate on the various specialized models that were produced through the years, some successful, others less so. We have not just described modifications produced on factory machines, but have included those carried out by the private owner of the day. Many different engines were fitted to Morgans over the years, and we have tried to follow through the thinking of the various engine designers, as the power increased from the modest 10 horse power or so of the first engines to the 100 bhp plus of the final racing designs. We have included some technical information where it appeared relevant because we hope this book will become both a record of the Morgan three-wheelers' achievements and also a reference as to how these achievements were accomplished.

Any vehicle of as sporting a nature as the Morgan is obviously used in almost all levels of competition, from club events up to international. To cover all these would be impossible, so we have concentrated on the most important events of the day, but we have included club events where noteworthy Morgan developments and achievements were involved. We have restricted ourselves to the British-made Morgan, believing the

Morgan Sweeps the Board

French-built Darmont to deserve separate recognition, and have described its competition story in Britain, in the Channel Islands, in various European events and in the USA and Australia.

The task of researching for this book began many years ago, following inspiration from the late Freddie James. It would have been completely impossible without the tremendous help and encouragement we have received from the Morgan Motor Co Ltd and especially its managing director, Peter Morgan. To all who have helped at all we extend a grateful thank you, and especially to our wives Jan and Wendy for their patience and tolerance.

We hope this book will give pleasure to those who remember Morgans in the great days when they would take on and beat in competition vehicles of much greater size and price. Should anyone be able to add anything, no matter how minor, we will be absolutely delighted to hear from them.

J.D. Alderson
D.M. Rushton

March 1978

The Pioneering Days

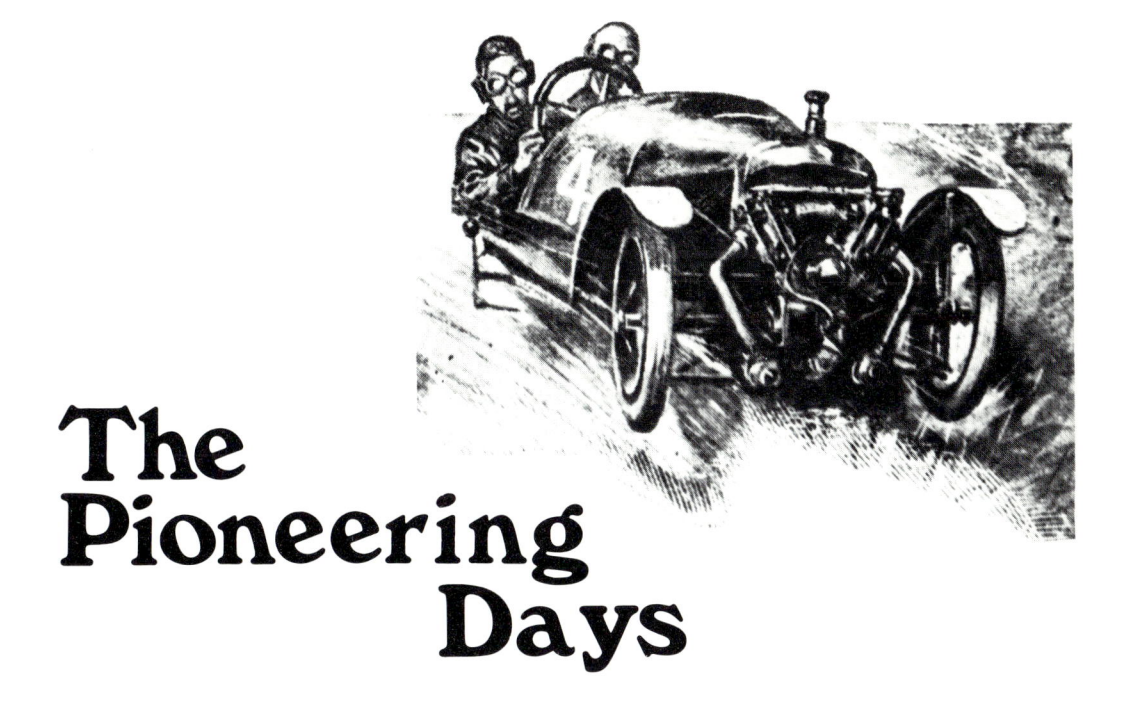

Henry Frederick Stanley Morgan was born on 11th August 1881, at Moreton Jeffries, the son of Prebendary Henry George Morgan, who had succeeded his father as rector of Stoke Lacy in the Diocese of Hereford. Harry Morgan grew up in this small village, with his three younger sisters, Freida, Ethel, and Dorothy.

During schooling at Marlborough, Harry (or HFS as he tended to be called) displayed a natural and consuming interest in mechanical things, and a talent for inventiveness. On leaving school he consequently moved to Crystal Palace Engineering College, where he demonstrated his talents by designing a bicycle on which he proved unbeatable in College races.

HFS's father was not slow to recognize his son's talents and managed to attach him to William Dean, and later GJ Churchward, Locomotive Superintendents of the Great Western Railway at Swindon for further engineering training. He worked here as a draughtsman until 1906.

In 1901 HFS purchased an Eagle Tandem 8 hp three-wheeler, which had a motorcycle type rear end attached to a car type front axle, between the wheels of which sat the passenger in a wicker-work seat. He had previously hired cars from a Mr Marriott of Hereford, once costing his father £28 in repairs when his Benz ran out of control down a steep hill on the Bromyard – Hereford road. The Eagle, besides giving HFS his first summons for exceeding the 12 mph speed limit, was to stimulate his interest in the prospects of three-wheeler design.

For his twenty-first birthday in 1902, HFS's godfather left him £200 which financed the purchase of a 'Star', a more conventional four-wheeled motor car, with a 7 hp 2-cylinder engine. At his coming of age party he promised not to frighten the horses in his

13

Morgan Sweeps the Board

HFS outside Stoke Lacy Rectory on his Eagle Tandem. (Morgan Motor Co)

father's parish on his visits home from Swindon.

In 1906 HFS decided to leave the Great Western Railway and to go into partnership with his close friend Leslie Bacon, opening a garage in Malvern. He still retained his Star for business use. Everything was against him in his new venture, for motorists were universally regarded as nuisances for driving such noisy smelly things, and for a clergyman's son to be selling them seemed to be the limit. Not suprisingly he received many rude letters. These he merely pinned up in the window of his garage, effectively silencing his critics.

As the garage business flourished HFS began to spend more time with Mr W Stephenson-Peach, the engineering master of Malvern College. Another inventive genius, Stephenson-Peach was a descendant of none other than George Stephenson, the locomotive pioneer and designer of the famous 'Rocket'. The object of their association was to bring to fruition HFS's current brainchild: the construction of a motor vehicle that was to be the lightest and simplest it was possible to construct, in

The Pioneering Days

fact a machine midway in concept between a motorcycle and the cars of the day—a cyclecar.

The prototype was a very basic three-wheeled machine, with seating for one and tiller steering, but with one very advanced feature in the form of independent suspension. The main part of the chassis consisted of a single wide bore tube passing from the forward mounted clutch to the bevel box at the rear and containing the propshaft. Bracing tubing passed from the bevel box to the front wheel centre pins. Chain drive to the rear wheel operated via two speeds, which were changed by a simple dog system operated by a lever adjacent to the bevel box. This, incidentally, also served as the seat. The simplicity of its design ensured that it was also very light, and consequently obtained remarkable performance from its twin cylinder Peugeot motorcycle engine.

Initially the car ran without front mudguards and with a simple bucket seat. Later it was made more luxurious with mudguards and modified bodywork giving some leg protection. This prototype carried the famous registration plate CJ 743.

HFS's 'Morgan Runabout' attracted very favourable comments during business trips to and from the garage. This encouraged the two partners to commit themselves to making a few production models, extending their garage and equipping it with machine tools with financial assistance from HFS's ever faithful father. Their experiences with the prototype led them to modify the production vehicles: tie bars were fitted to the crosshead at the front of the chassis in order to stiffen them up, and the silencers were modified into the famous coffee pot design, the lower engine bearing tubes continuing back to the bevel box parallel to the backbone chassis tube and acting as exhaust pipes, ducting the gases away from the front of the machine. They exhibited two models, featuring the two different types of body used on the prototype, and also a chassis, at the Motor Cycle Show at Olympia in November 1910. Both the 8 hp twin cylinder JAP-engined luxurious model, and the 4 hp single cylinder JAP utility model attracted considerable interest, but very few orders. The two men were very disappointed. Leslie Bacon decided that the project was altogether too risky, and quitted the partnership. HFS was very downhearted. 'Perhaps I should be designing aeroplanes,' he said, 'at least if they fail they take their designer quickly with them.'

Luckily, HFS had found one major supporter—Richard Burbridge, the managing director of Harrod's, the famous Knightsbridge store. With his backing, and the guarantee of some sales for the near future, HFS was able to carry on the project single-handed.

He had two immediate objectives. Firstly, he knew that the public would remain unsure of his Runabout until its worth had been demonstrated on the road and in competition against its rivals. Secondly, he had to develop a two-seater, for although the single-seater was eminently suitable for him to run around in on business, it could have only a limited commercial appeal.

At this time, many weird and wonderful types of cyclecar were being constructed throughout the country, by eager enthusiasts in small factories. The challenging concept of a small, usually motorcycle-type engine being used to power a single- or two-seater three- or four-wheeler fired the imagination of many aspiring engineers, and all sorts of spidery contraptions, some practicable, others virtually uncontrollable, were to appear on the scene. One popular marque of three-wheeler was the AC Sociable, a side by side two-seater with a single cylinder engine driving an integral two-speed gearbox and clutch within the rear wheel by chain. Grice, Wood and Keiller were to produce the GWK, a four-wheeler with a vee twin engine driving the differential on the back axle via a four-speed friction drive. Other cyclecars to use friction discs were the Crescent and the Violet-Bogey of French manufacture, whilst flapping belts and various sizes of pulleys provided the transmission on the French tandem-seater Bedelias. M de Peyrecave's Duo went a step further and used both belts and chains. The early GNs produced by Godfrey and Nash used belts but later switched to chains, with a dog clutch gear system not unlike that used on the Morgan.

Compared to the Morgan, many of these cyclecars were simply curiosities, in no way able to provide practical transport. However, the would-be motoring public of the period were not really sufficiently educated in the niceties of motoring design to be able to sort out the effective from the bizarre. They looked to the sporting events to help them in their selection, and the winning awards in both reliability trials and events thus became a crucial aspect of selling a cyclecar.

26th and 27th December 1910 saw HFS driving an 8 hp JAP-engined single-seater with tiller steering in the very first London-Exeter Trial. He won a gold medal, and the motoring press described the Morgan as 'more than holding its own with the motor-bicyclists on the downward journey to Exeter'. British roads were very poorly surfaced in those days, and heavy rain before the trial had made them literally inches deep in mud. Despite this, the motoring press noted that the engine had remained remarkably clean, *Motor Cycling* reporting that 'Contrary to general opinion the mud from the two front wheels does not seem to be thrown on to the cylinder.' The only modifications HFS had made were to fit mushroom-like sparking plug shields and a metal carburettor shield between the two cylinders. He used coil ignition on the JAP.

In May 1911 HFS gained a certificate in the Auto-Cycle Union quarterly trials, but was penalized for not complying with the rules which demanded magneto ignition, not coil and accumulator. Henceforth, magneto ignition became standardized on the Morgan.

The following month he attained further success in a rebodied single-seater, winning a gold medal in the London-Edinburgh Trial—despite the handicap of the front wheels being knocked out of line. On the last bend of Saltburn Bank, he underestimated his speed; the inside front wheel lifted and he crashed into the wall, bending the chassis back several inches. After adjustments he continued and demonstrated once again the soundness of his design by taking every hill in the trial on his top gear of 4 to 1.

In August 1911 the Morgan everyone had been waiting for appeared. A two-seater, it was the result of several experiments with prototypes over the preceding months. Other new features included the use of a steering wheel for the first time, and the famous coal scuttle bonnet that was to become so much a feature of the later Morgans. Its first competitive outing was in the ACU Six Days' Trial. The car didn't live up to its promise, retiring on the second day due to propshaft failure, but HFS was not dismayed. He remarked 'We have gained experience which has enabled us to detect faults and make improvements.'

The Pioneering Days

By now the motoring world was waking up to the Morgan. HFS had triumphantly fulfilled his two objectives and when he exhibited his two-seater at the November Motor Cycle Show in 1911 he was overwhelmed with enquiries. After a year of struggling, orders had at last started to flow in, but he knew that for this success to continue he had to enter the Morgan for all the competitive events he possibly could.

One of the keenest supporters of the Morgan was the Oxford graduate, W Gordon McMinnies. A keen motorcyclist, McMinnies had been the first man to win a motorcycle race on Brooklands track in 1908, and had also ridden in the Isle of Man TT races in 1909 and 1910. He was employed on the editorial staff of *Motor Cycling* when the Morgan had first appeared at the 1910 show. He immediately realized that the machine held certain advantages over a motorcycle because of its stability and the improved protection from road mud afforded by its design. In 1912 he was made responsible for editing a new motoring periodical, *The Cyclecar,* devoted purely to these new machines. As editor he was able to give HFS tremendous support over the next few years.

Meanwhile HFS continued to enter his new two-seater in trials. For the really steep hills, he fitted an air pump to prevent fuel starvation, pressurizing the fuel tank which was under the bonnet. *Motor Cycling* tested this car and wrote, 'Let anyone try the Morgan and I'll warrant that he will forsake the unmechanical sidecar for ever.'

The first race meeting to feature a Morgan was an international cyclecar scratch race held by the British Motor Cycle Racing Club at Brooklands in March 1912. Harry Martin, who had ridden in several motorcycle TTs and now constructed his own motorcycles, entered a Morgan two-seater with wind cutting body, fitted with an ohv

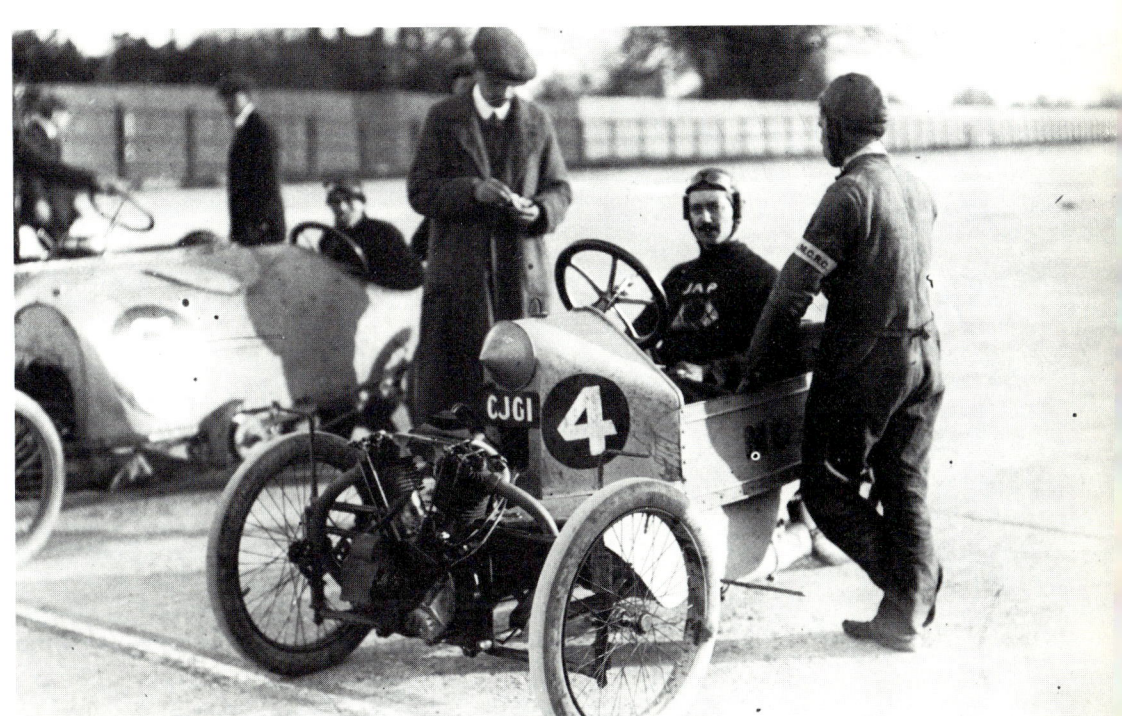

Harry Martin's ohv 90 bore JAP racer competes at the first Brooklands race to feature a Morgan. (Motor Cycle)

Morgan Sweeps the Board

986 cc 90 bore twin JAP engine (90 x 77.5mm). Martin went straight into the lead, followed by a Rollo-JAP. Completing his first standing start lap at 53 mph, he finished his second at just under 60 mph. His passenger was invisible, kneeling on the floor to reduce wind resistance. Such was Martin's speed that he finished the race in 8 minutes 32 seconds, over 2 minutes before the second placed Sabella-JAP. The field had also included two French Bedelias. His win was so convincing that all future cyclecar races were to be handicapped. The magnitude of the success did not go unnoticed by the general public: over 100 orders were placed after the race, forcing HFS to extend his works so that he could turn out 20 cars per week.

In June 1912 HFS Morgan married Hilda Ruth Day, younger daughter of the vicar of Malvern Link, whom he had first met at a dance in Malvern several years previously. Ruth was to give tremendous support to HFS during the following years, frequently accompanying him as passenger in trials and competitions. Amongst their many wedding presents were some brass fire irons, given by HFS's works manager Alfie Hales, and a Worcester china tea service donated by his works employees. They spent their honeymoon touring Wales in an all-white Morgan, and then returned to live in a house owned by HFS next to the Morgan works.

Throughout 1912 cyclecar manufacturers had been competing fiercely for the silver Cyclecar Trophy, which *Motor Cycling* were to award at the end of the year to the person holding the cyclecar hour record. One of the main contestants was the GWK, a 2-cylinder friction drive four-wheeler constructed by three partners, two of whom, J Wood and C Keiller, had like HFS served engineering apprenticeships with the Great Western Railway. By August Wood had achieved 48 miles in the hour.

The BMCRC meeting to be held at Brooklands on Saturday, 9th November was to include the Olympic sidecar and cyclecar races, run concurrently over one hour. Morgan now decided to join the competition for the hour record and duly entered. The opposition of eight cyclecars included Wood.

The race was preceded by time trials. In these A Warren Lambert, the London-based Morgan agent for Surrey and Middlesex, took out a Morgan in high winds to capture the standing start 1 kilometre and 1 mile records at 58.94 and 58.86 mph respectively, using a long stroke 90 bore JAP of 1082cc (85mm stroke). By the end of the year these records had still not been confirmed by the ACU.

For the hour race HFS had constructed a wind-cutting single-seater fitted with an ohv 90 bore JAP, but using the shorter stroke of 77.5mm (986cc). When the flag fell he established an immediate lead although Wood hung on gamely for five laps. However water in the electrics of the GWK then caused Wood so long a delay that Morgan had completed nine laps before he restarted. Many of the other cyclecars fell by the roadside in the fast pace set by Morgan. These included the Morgan driven by Harry Martin, which developed transmission trouble and broke a cylinder. Such was HFS's speed that he completed 55 miles 329 yards in the hour, a full 8 miles more than the second-placed Sabella. Wood managed a creditable third place. In this one race, HFS had gained the cyclecar world record for the hour and also established new records in the process, for the flying start kilometre and mile, and for 50 miles. He was delighted and returned to Malvern a happy man.

By Tuesday evening things were a great deal different. Wood had taken his GWK out

Encouragement for HFS from Ruth before he attempts the hour record. (Radio Times Hulton Picture Library)

at Brooklands again and covered 56 miles 76 yards in the hour. HFS knew that now the challenge was really on, and made immediate preparations to return to Brooklands. An intensely modest man, HFS sincerely doubted his ability as a driver to do credit to his car; on the trip to Brooklands, accompanied by his wife and father for support, he was so tense that the others could almost hear his heart pounding with anxiety.

He took to the track that following Saturday, when all his fears proved to be in vain. His car ran beautifully, covering 59 miles 1123 yards, breaking the 50 mile record at 59.43 mph and achieving a fastest lap of 62 mph. His success was splashed over the pages of *The Cyclecar* by McMinnies and as no more record attempts were made that year, HFS was awarded the Cyclecar Trophy, which he displayed in his Worcester Road showroom during 1913.

HFS rounded off 1912 with a real show of stamina by competing in the Sutton Coldfield AC Trial, the London-Gloucester and the London-Exeter, all within the last week of December. In all three he drove a Morgan fitted with a huge acetylene light mounted centrally on the scuttle. He carried off a silver cup and two gold medals.

All production Morgans prior to 1913 were fitted with air-cooled JAP engines, manufactured at the Tottenham engine factory of his friend, John Alfred Prestwich. However HFS now decided to look at alternatives: the rapid growth of the cyclecar business meant that there there were many suppliers to choose from. One of the problems with the early engines was that they tended to overheat, and this in turn caused failure in the poor quality steels of the exhaust valves. Thus, not only was Morgan looking for alternative makes of engine, he was also to look at water-cooling.

February 1913 saw HFS and Ruth trying out an 8 hp Blumfield engine in the Liverpool AC Trial. It was not an immediate success, as the engine overheated on Bwlch-y-Groes pass, despite Mrs Morgan valiantly holding up the bonnet. One of the exhaust valves stretched, and the tappets had to be adjusted.

In the Colmore Trial that same month HFS was passengered by his youngest sister Dorothy. Rounding a bend, he upturned his Morgan. That evening he insisted on

The Morgan family pose at Stoke Lacy. Left to right: HFS and Ruth Morgan in their famous trials Morgan of late 1912; Geoffrey Day and Dorothy (HFS's sister) in a Standard model; (rear seat) George Hinings and HFS's sisters Freida and Ethel; (front seat) Prebendary and Mrs Morgan (HFS's father and mother).
(Morgan Motor Co)

taking Dorothy to the pictures—purely so that he could see the newsreel of his accident. He was relieved to see that the upsetting was due to freak ground conditions and not to some mechanical fault.

HFS used to carry a suitcase on the tail of his Morgan during trials. The crowd could thus see how useful the Morgan would be for their holidays and so on. Little did they know that the suitcase contained not overnight clothes as they suspected but bricks, increasing the weight on the back wheel and hence the traction.

In December 1912 Gordon McMinnies had acquired a very sparsely bodied single-seater Morgan, fitted with a side valve JAP engine, which he named the 'Jabberwock' after Lewis Carroll's mythical beast. At first he used the car for reporting on trials, but when the *Cyclecar* magazine staged an unofficial hill climb at Alms Hill near Henley and a neck and neck hill climb at Biscombe in January of 1913, McMinnies naturally entered. Later, after several 50 mph laps of Brooklands, his thoughts turned to tuning. He first reduced friction on the transmission by careful preparation. He then modified the engine with larger inlet and exhaust valves and polished ports. He also fitted a large carburettor and an oil lead direct to the nearside cylinder, which he thought was likely to be oil starved. Advanced thinking—but this was not the machine that was to bring him so much glory later.

In January 1913 the authorities announced a Cyclecar Grand Prix to be held in

The Pioneering Days

France in association with the classic French Grand Prix motor race. HFS wished to enter this event but was worried about engine overheating problems under such racing conditions. He therefore decided to investigate the possibilities of the water-cooled system and duly had fitted a 991cc (81.5mm x 95mm) sv Blumfield to the car that NF Holder was to run in the 100 mile BMCRC high speed reliability trial at Brooklands on 29th March. A honeycomb radiator was positioned behind the engine, the coal scuttle bonnet being omitted. Also entered for this event was the air-cooled 90 bore JAP-engined car of Lambert. In the 750cc class an air-cooled side valve 670cc (67mm x 95mm) Blumfield-engined Morgan, which had no bonnet but a torpedo-shaped fuel tank behind the engine, was driven by Vernon Busby, a director of a Birmingham motor accessory company. No leaks were reported from the water-cooled car, and after a delay caused by a broken petrol pipe, Holder finished second to Lambert in the 1100cc class. Busby came first in the 750cc class.

In April 1913 HFS drove a torpedo-fuel-tanked model in both the Birmingham and

Vernon Busby's racer with 670cc Blumfield engine. (Morgan Motor Co).

Morgan Sweeps the Board

Bristol Trials. We suspect that this was one of the new four-speed Morgans specifically developed for trials which called for greater flexibility than two speeds could offer, the four speeds being achieved by an additional two-speed box behind the clutch, although the press did not describe this innovation until May.

On 6th April 1913 HFS's sister Dorothy reached the age of twenty-two, and as a present HFS gave her what we suspect was the ex-Vernon Busby racer. It was fitted with a 750cc racing JAP engine which he wanted her to test for him. As Dorothy was known at the works as Dot, the roundel for the racing number was painted-over by the works manager, Hales, with the letters DOT within it as his contribution.

Dorothy's driving lessons consisted of HFS taking her to Birmingham on business. On the way there he drove though the town and she through the country, and on the way back she drove the whole distance. He took her out again the following day, and that was all the tuition she had. The 750cc JAP was a little horror: it regularly overheated and would not rev slowly.

In May HFS revealed his Grand Prix car, entering it in the London-Edinburgh Trial for evaluation. Basically he had gone for improved stability, lengthening the chassis by 11 inches and thus lowering the seats by moving them from a position on top of the bevel box to one in front of it. The lower chassis tubes were of increased diameter and the steering very raked. An air-cooled sv JAP engine was fitted as the water-cooled unit ordered specially from JAPs was not yet ready, and a simple torpedo tank was fitted behind it. Dorothy passengered him and she recalls it ran so well that they arrived 15

HFS and sister Dorothy north of Carlisle in the rain in the prototype Grand Prix. (Morgan Motor Co)

The Pioneering Days

minutes early at a secret check point just north of Carlisle.

On Thursday, 29th May, HFS took out the torpedo-fuel-tanked four-speed car for the Hereford Trial. Amongst the five other Morgan drivers entered were RD Oliver in an experimental factory water-cooled car, Geoffrey Day (HFS's brother in law and a fellow and tutor of Emmanuel College), and Dorothy Morgan in her new red Morgan, registration number CJ 1348, fitted with a 670cc Blumfield engine. The highlight of the trial was the timed ascent of Birdlip, where the Morgans gained the first four places. The trial finished with HFS Morgan winning the coveted 320 oz silver cup and Dorothy Morgan a gold medal for the best 750cc performance.

Dorothy Morgan was a regular visitor to her brother's works in early 1913. Often she, her brother, her brother-in-law Geoffrey Day (whom she regarded as a rather reckless driver) and factory personnel would take cars out to try them on the local Malvern Hills. She remembers that once they annoyed an old lady as they came down a sheep track. The first few had time to escape while the lady ran back into her house, but poor Alfie Hales at the rear of the expedition received a soaking from her bucket of water.

At weekends HFS used to drive over from Malvern to his father's rectory in Stoke Lacy, to keep him informed of his progress. It was not unusual for the church services to be held up until HFS had fully recounted the story of the previous week's trials. (His parishioners must have been very patient.)

Come June 1913 and HFS's Grand Prix car was now fitted with its special water-cooled ohv 90 bore JAP engine. Designed by Harry Hatch, head of the Tottenham engine firm's experimental department, this engine was of 90 bore by 77.5mm stroke, and featured liberally drilled, dome topped, cast iron pistons, webbed for strength. The

HFS's torpedo tank four-speed Morgan, and RD Oliver's experimental water-cooled model in the Hereford Trial. (D Morgan scrapbooks)

Morgan Sweeps the Board

car had now been rebodied at the front with a honeycomb radiator resembling that of the Vauxhall Prince Henry model, the oil and petrol tanks blending with the radiator into the scuttle.

WD South, the Wolverhampton agent, was the first to use the car, entering it for the Shelsley Walsh Hill Climb. He gained first place in the cyclecar competition despite a boiling radiator blowing steam over the occupants. HFS followed this with another victory, this time in the Porthcawl Sand Speed Trials on 21st June.

Four Morgans were entered for the Cyclecar Grand Prix at Amiens. HFS had entered two, his own as above, and an experimental car equipped with the new 1000cc vee twin Green Precision cyclecar engine, which he hoped would be as successful as their 500cc motorcycle engine was already proving to be. NF Holder was to drive a side valve Blumfield-engined car, and the fourth car, entered by the newly formed Cyclecar Club, was to be driven by Gordon McMinnies. This car also specified the new water-cooled ohv 90 bore JAP and was very similar to HFS's car. The main difference was in the body, McMinnies' car being of one-piece construction, whereas Morgan's own was

NF Holder's Blumfield-engined Grand Prix. (D Morgan scrapbooks)

HFS in suit and WD South in raincoat watch work on HFS's French entry at the Morgan works. (D Morgan scrapbooks)

developed from the London-Edinburgh prototype. Also, whereas Morgan was using separate high level exhaust pipes, McMinnies continued to use the lower chassis tubes as originally designed.

McMinnies tested his car at the South Harting Hill Climb of 28th June. As he roared past the steepest section of the hill the left front tyre left the rim, and the inner tube swelled out like a balloon before bursting with a terrific bang. The machine slithered all over the place before straightening up and continuing up the hill in a cloud of dust to obtain a class win. Fastest time of the day was achieved by Warren Lambert in his 90 bore air-cooled side valve JAP-engined single-seater Morgan. This ascended at terrific speed, throttling back only when the front wheel lifted and when a mudguard came adrift, hitting poor Lambert on the head.

McMinnies and his passenger Frank Thomas worked on their car before the Grand Prix in France, moving the large Amac carburettor to the front of the engine for accessibility and protecting it from direct air pressure by a conical shield. At 55 mph (3000 rpm) the engine was found to vibrate severely, so the top gearing of $4\frac{1}{8}$ to 1 was increased to $3\frac{1}{4}$ to 1 to reduce revs. Examination of the sparking plugs revealed a tendency for the offside cylinder to be excessively oily at the expense of the nearside.

The start at Amiens. McMinnies lines up ahead of HFS, who is alongside no 8, Rex Mundy, with the Green Precision-engined Grand Prix. (McMinnies scrapbooks)

The oil feed was thus re-routed from the crank case to the nearside cylinder, as McMinnies had previously done on his single-seater 'Jabberwock'.

Rex Mundy was chosen to drive the Precision-engined car for HFS. When he arrived at the Cyclecar Club Camp at Boves near the circuit at Amiens, to join the other competitors, it was noted that a huge radiator had been fitted, in place of the specially designed type used by HFS and McMinnies. The engine itself was manufactured by FE Baker, and was of 85mm bore by 85mm stroke with overhead valves. The copper water jackets were as patented by Green, with rubber sealing joints which enabled the jacket to slide over the cylinder on expansion.

Only HFS, McMinnies and Mundy lined up at the start of the Cyclecar Grand Prix on 13th July, as Holder had not put in an appearance. Before the end of the first lap, HFS was out with a broken piston, and Rex Mundy did not get much further: after just one fast lap his left front wheel collapsed. The course was badly rutted and potholed and many a machine was to come to grief.

Despite plug trouble and a puncture which caused a delay early on, McMinnies's green Morgan went on to win the Grand Prix. He had a desperate battle over the last few laps, managing to overtake the second-placed Bedelia only by going off the track onto the grass.

HFS was elated, and naturally McMinnies once again obliged with the full treatment in *The Cyclecar*. He wrote that their victory was due to careful preparation of the car, especially the split pinning and shellacking of every nut and bolt. Interest in the Morgan was at a peak once more, and many enquiries were received from France.

For some reason NF Holder had stayed in England and entered the BMCRC

The Pioneering Days

Brooklands 6-hour scratch race on 16th July—an event HFS described as 'The consolation race for cyclecars that have not been entered in the Grand Prix'. His car went well until the petrol and oil pipes fractured and the engine ran hot through lack of lubrication. It then shed the low gear chain but continued merrily on its way until the clutch pedal disappeared, eventually grinding to a halt after 206 miles.

The Morgan had survived the arduous conditions of Amiens remarkably well, but worse was in store. Later on that same month, the Scottish Six Days' Trial was to present itself as the most severe trial yet encountered by a cyclecar.

Steep hill after steep hill was followed by equally severe descents, combined with an extremely rough and narrow surface. Two Morgans were entered, both four-speed models: one by HFS and the other by J Blackburn, an amateur driver from Sheffield. Both were doing well until the third day, the climb of Applecross in the north-west highlands, a narrow hill with a 2-mile climb of 1 in 6 with four fearful hairpins so tight that many machines had to reverse before they could get round. HFS climbed impeccably, but Blackburn by now had a sick engine, and ended up pushing his car to the top as the starting pin had sheared. This lost him 50 minutes.

On the last day the severity of the route at last told on HFS and he was forced to retire when a wheel-bearing cone split from fatigue. However, Blackburn triumphed with a well deserved silver medal.

McMinnies was driving his Grand Prix victor through the trial to report for *The Cyclecar* when he too suffered the effects of the terrible surface. The Morgan was travelling at about 40 mph when its steering suddenly broke: it ran straight for a telegraph pole which divided it in two, scattering body work for 20 yards or so up the

HFS and Ruth climb Applecross Hill in the Scottish. (Morgan Motor Co)

road, and injuring McMinnies's passenger Johnny Gibson. The remains were loaded onto a passing laundry cart and taken to the Falkirk station for parcelling back to Malvern. McMinnies wrote at the time, 'Poor "Jabberwock de Picardy" will never again take to the roads, its career having been cut short in its infancy.' He spoke too soon!

HFS and Blackburn again entered the English Six Days' Trial, where conditions proved even more farcical than in the Scottish Trial. Blackburn wrecked a cylinder and piston on the third day and was forced to retire. The lessons of the Scottish Six Days' had been learnt by HFS, however, and his machine was now equipped with Hoffmann roller rear wheel bearings, while the steering connections featured an extra bolt. Of the twelve original starters only three finished, and of these HFS won a gold medal. Much good publicity came from the endurance test success.

Meanwhile the Morgan factory had received the remains of McMinnies's Grand Prix car, of which the engine was luckily undamaged. They rebuilt it, but this time as a single-seater. It was to become one of the most potent Morgan racers of the next year.

It made its debut at the Bournemouth MCC Speed Trials held on a drive in Cranford Park in early September. The heats were run with the cars in pairs, with passengers carried. WD South was driving a Green-Precision-engined Grand Prix, almost certainly the same car that Rex Mundy had driven in France. He had trouble pulling up at the finish, skidding the back wheel for 100 yards before the nearside front tyre came off the rim, and the tube burst at the next corner. Rex Mundy himself was McMinnies's passenger. As the new 'Jabberwock' was a single-seater, he had to sit on its tail with his feet inside the body, holding tightly on to McMinnies to prevent himself being thrown off when he changed gear. McMinnies beat all the cyclecars but took second place in the final to George Griffith's Zenith sidecar.

In the September Speed trials at Brighton, McMinnies had a runaway victory in the open class up to 1100cc. At the same meeting RD Oliver was testing another type of radiator behind a water-cooled sv JAP. HFS failed to start, having smashed a big end on the latest JAP engine, a 90mm x 85 mm ohv with the new steel pistons.

Steel was being tried out as a piston material as it was theoretically much stronger than cast iron. Hence the piston could be machined with much thinner walls, for the same strength. This allowed a reduction in reciprocating weight within the engine and as a result higher engine revs became possible, with consequently greater engine efficiency and performance.

On 4th October the Bristol MCC organized the very first speed trials to be held on the sands at Weston-Super-Mare. Torrential rain made conditions extremely difficult, many vehicles sinking through the soft, wet sand. In the first heat of the open cyclecar race McMinnies, with a passenger on the tail, made a bad start but quickly overhauled the field, only to stop some 20 yards from the finish. Failing to restart the Morgan, the two men pushed it over the line, just being beaten into second place. In the next heat the local Bristol Morgan agent, FG Cox, beat HFS in his Grand Prix car. The final went to Cox, with HFS second after McMinnies's car had stopped once more. Perhaps he too was trying the new steel pistons.

Prior to the Motor Cycle Show in November 1913, JAPs announced a modified side valve cyclecar engine, with larger 11 inch internal flywheels, bigger bearings and

The Pioneering Days

McMinnies's rebodied Grand Prix sinks into the sands at Weston-Super-Mare. (McMinnies scrapbooks)

Morgan Sweeps the Board

adjustable tappets for the first time. At the show itself HFS displayed the Grand Prix model, based on the race-winning machine of McMinnies. By the end of the show almost the entire production of 1914 had been spoken for.

Meanwhile George Griffith, the Zenith rider who had beaten McMinnies at Bournemouth the previous September, had taken delivery of a racing 1100cc Morgan. It had a strengthened frame, a horizontal stay rod bracing the bevel box to the front of the chassis, and its body was streamlined with a long pointed tail. Behind the radiator was a vee screen to improve the cooling arrangements.

Another motorcyclist to switch to Morgans was Edward Bradford Ware, an ex-London University lecturer. He had recently joined the JA Prestwich engine concern in the experimental shop, under the direction of the chief designer, Mr Val Page, who replaced Harry Hatch at the end of 1913. Using a 744cc Zenith-JAP, EB Ware had collected thirteen out of the total of fifteen records for motorcycles and sidecars of under 750cc by the end of 1913. In January 1914 he commissioned a special Morgan with a novel streamlined body, in which he was to continue his 750cc record attempts using the very same engine.

In February 1914 the Birmingham MCC re-ran their previously abandoned trial. Although Vernon Busby and RD Oliver both took gold medals, the trial was particularly notable for the appearance of a torpedo-fuel-tanked model, driven by Jack

HFS and Ruth leap away at the restart test on Pebblecombe Hill in the General Efficiency Trial, with an ohv JAP engine shoehorned under the bonnet. (Harry Jones scrapbooks)

The Pioneering Days

Woodhouse and fitted with an air-cooled vee twin Quadrant engine. This engine was presumably the same as that produced by the Birmingham firm of Quadrant for their motorcycle, featuring overhead inlet valves, operated by long push rods, directly over the exhaust valves, and of 1129cc (87mm x 95mm). Unfortunately Woodhouse blew out a plug and was forced to retire on Birdlip Hill.

One month later the Cyclecar Club organized a General Efficiency Trial, with the aim of testing the characteristics that made a good all round cyclecar, as opposed to the sort of trial that merely tested to destruction. For this event HFS drove a green four-speed Sporting model, fitted with a 90mm x 77.5mm ohv water-cooled JAP engine and radiator under the bonnet. Despite lapping Brooklands at a mere 36.24 mph he climbed the test hill at 16.23 mph changing into top gear on the 1 in 5 section. He finished second overall.

A few days later the same machine won HFS a first class certificate in the ACU Spring One-day Open Reliability Trial, and on 4th April he used it to join McMinnies, who had recently trounced the opposition at Kop Hill, for a team relay race at Aston Hill. Four cars for each team were stationed at different points up the hill, a sparking plug being taken from one engine and fitted to the next before its driver could carry on the climb. McMinnies's team proved victorious.

The first Brooklands meeting of 1914 was the BMCRC 100 mile High Speed Trial held on 28th March. In fact, this was something of a misnomer as the winner was the driver whose lap times were most consistent, subject to attaining a minimum speed.

EB Ware was the sole Morgan contestant as Harry Martin failed to start. Ware was using a factory-prepared two-seater car with torpedo fuel tank, to which he had fitted his Zenith's 744cc sv engine of 76mm x 82mm. He had ensured ample provision for oil

McMinnies, with passenger on the tail, battles with RF Messervy's de P in the Relay Race. (McMinnies scrapbooks)

consumption over the long distance by fitting an extra large oil tank at the feet of his passenger, Mr Chater Lea Junior. Setting a very fast pace, Ware immediately demonstrated that records were his aim. After thirteen laps he filled up with spirit and tightened a leaking petrol union, also detaching the low gear chain which had jumped the sprockets. With the help of pushers he got going again, but retired on the twenty-seventh lap when his passenger's scarf caught up in the chain. He had set up a new 750cc hour record of 47 miles 457 yards and a 50 mile record of 1 hour 3 minutes 7.8 seconds.

On 18th April EB Ware appeared at the second BMCRC Brooklands meeting with his specially commissioned single-seater Morgan, powered by his special 744cc ex-Zenith engine. Its highly streamlined body featured a built-in petrol tank high in the short tail, with an external tubular oil tank on the sloping front. Using a hand brake only—no foot brake was fitted—he won the three-lap cyclecar handicap race from the GWK of Keiller at 54.9 mph.

After this preliminary canter Ware set about the more serious business of record breaking. On 2nd May he took the flying start mile and kilometre at 61.02 and 61.95 mph respectively.

McMinnies had been heavily criticized over the past few months for having carried a passenger in a supposedly dangerous manner on the tail of his monocar. At the Wolverhampton MCC open speed hill climb at Style Cop in April, he initially refused to go up with a passenger, but the officials would not let him compete single-handed.

The start at Stile Kop. The hand of McMinnies's infant passenger can just be seen underneath his right hand. (McMinnies scrapbooks)

The Pioneering Days

Without further ado he selected from the spectators a young lad of about three years of age whom he placed between his knees for the climb. As he remarked, 'I had complied with the rules so they couldn't complain.' He finished second to a Buckingham, third place going to the Grand Prix Morgan of Reg Ashton, who had covered the sides under

McMinnies changes his gearing for a hill climb. (McMinnies scrapbooks)

Morgan Sweeps the Board

the fuel tank with louvre panels. The appearance of this feature attracted many favourable comments, and was later to become well known in the Aeros of the 1920s.

The Nottingham Morgan agent at this time was Jack Sylvester, who took on the agency for Bennett's of Nottingham at the 1911 Olympia Show. Incidentally, he never had an official contract for the Morgan agency although he retained it until his retirement some forty years later in 1956. During the winter of 1913/1914 Jack collected a car from Malvern for the music hall artist, Chris Richards of New York. This was no ordinary Morgan, but a special Grand Prix model fitted with a high compression 90 bore ohv water-cooled JAP engine and special high gearing. On the way back from Malvern the fog came down. To add to Jack's troubles, the engine refused to run slowly and stopped time after time. When it became dark he stopped at a cycle shop and bought three cycle lamps, which he tied on with string, covering the rear one with red paper. Setting off again, he kept losing the engine time after time, whenever he slowed to find his way. Finally the starting pin fell out. The prospect of push-starting a high-compression, high-geared Morgan in a fog, jumping in before the engine stopped, and before it ran off the road is a daunting one, but Jack made it back to Nottingham in one piece in the early hours of the morning.

The Morgan was exported to Chris Richards in the USA and entered by Richard Allen, his New York club mate, in the two-day international cyclecar meet on the mile-long dirt track of the Michigan State fairgrounds on 4th and 5th July. It secured easy wins in the 1 mile race and in three 5 mile events, covering one of the latter at an average of 50.03 mph.

Meanwhile, back in England the Bristol MCC once again held their June speed trials on the Weston-Super-Mare sands. The Bristol agent, FG Cox, again distinguished himself by winning the open 1-mile cyclecar race and a closed to club championship race. Cox was driving a water-cooled ohv 90 bore JAP-engined Grand Prix model which featured a one-piece detachable streamlined tail enveloping the rear wheel, similar to the Aero of the 1920s although not quite so upswept.

The Morgan agent for Sheffield was Billie James, one of the pioneer Sheffield motorists. In his very first trial in June 1914 he took a water-cooled side-valve four-speed Morgan through the Scottish Six Days' to win a gold medal.

Trials at this time tended to be exceptionally hard on the machines. However, success was achievable without special four-speed trials devices as McMinnies showed when he entered the 'Jabberwock' in the English Six Days' Trial in July. This trial was very severe indeed: the press called it 'a perfect farce' and HFS Morgan himself walked out in disgust on the fourth day. McMinnies had to drive without regard for his neck, or his machine, to comply with the very tight time schedule, and indeed many tests proved impossible for any of the contestants. In the special speed test on Doncaster race course, McMinnies excelled by beating all the motorcycles to achieve the fastest time of day, recording a fuel consumption of 50 mpg. As the trial was based in Sheffield, Billie James also entered his Scottish Six Days' car, which he ran without the coal scuttle bonnet. James won a bronze medal, while McMinnies gained a gold with the 5 cwt 'Jabberwock'.

There was a great deal of criticism of the trial in the motoring press. Conversely, one of its firmest supporters was none other than Prebendary George Morgan, HFS's

Help for HFS on Grindon Hill in the English Six Days'. (Morgan Motor Co)

father. He believed that there should be at least one trial to destruction in the racing calendar, maintaining that he knew of one firm that would be strengthening certain steering parts as a direct result of this trial.

As a complete contrast the Midland Light Car Club ran a mild open half-day trial from Birmingham on Saturday, 18th July. Dorothy Morgan drove her own car, which had now been painted white and fitted with an 8 hp JAP engine instead of the Blumfield. She gained a gold medal, as did RD Oliver, who was testing a new air-cooled cyclecar engine from the Swiss firm of Motosacoche, which translated literally means 'motor in a tool bag'. Their engine was named the MAG, from the initials of the firm and its address of Acacia, Geneva. It featured overhead inlet valves and side exhaust, with a 45 degree angle between the cylinders (JAP used a 50 degree angle). Bore and stroke were 82mm x 103.5mm giving 1093cc.

On the hill-climbing front, George Griffith's racing Morgan was confidently expected to win the cyclecar class at the South Harting Hill Climb. Just when he was expected to make his climb there was an unexpected pause. The crowd ran down the hill, to find he had blown off a cylinder at the start from his highly tuned ohv 90 bore JAP engine.

EB Ware meanwhile had more success in the 18th July Brooklands three-lap light car handicap of the Motor Cycling Club. Following excellent handicapping, the scratch Singer of Lionel Martin, EB Ware in his 750cc single-seater and a Tweenie (a relatively unsuccessful cyclecar of 902cc, which had been given 2 minutes 39 seconds

Morgan Sweeps the Board

start) dashed across the line with a mere 3 yards between them, EB Ware the victor at 58.8 mph.

A week later EB Ware took his single-seater out at Brooklands again and succeeded in beating his own class J (up to 750cc) record for the flying start kilometre at 65.10 mph and the flying start mile at 63.09 mph. He may have been helped by the south-westerly wind blowing him along the railway straight but nevertheless it was a magnificent performance and the records stood for many years. He was also successful in setting up new class J records for 10 miles at 59.50 mph and flying start 5 miles at 61.22 mph. He achieved this later on the same day when he came second to Lionel Martin's Singer after a fine fight in the 10-mile scratch race. The oil tank had now been moved from the sloping front of the car to the side of the body, within easy reach of the

EB Ware with the streamlined single-seater after breaking records using the 744cc ex-Zenith engine. (Motor Cycle)

36

The Pioneering Days

driver's right hand. Ware might have won the race had he not mistaken the finish, as did Martin, cutting his engine before the finishing line.

If Great Britain had not entered the First World War at the beginning of August, 24th September would have seen an ACU Cyclecar and Lightcar Tourist Trophy Race in the Isle of Man, over the 158-mile motorcycle circuit. HFS produced a very special racer for this event for his intended driver, Vernon Busby, which would doubtless have put up a fine performance. The TT car was built round a long wheel base Grand Prix chassis, with wider rear forks to allow wider band brakes to be fitted to the rear wheel. The engine was a special ohv air-cooled MAG engine of 1078cc (82mm x 102mm) having two inlet and two exhaust valves to each cylinder. The heads were detachable and 30 bhp was claimed. The Amac carburettor received fuel from a 6-gallon tank which formed the rear of the seats and was pressurized by a hand-operated air pump. The wooden body also featured a wedge-shaped tool box behind the engine.

The reliability of the 90 bore racing JAP engine had not previously been an outstanding feature and HFS almost certainly wanted to compare it with the new MAG engine. JAPs had not been complacent however, and a modified water-cooled 90 bore JAP engine of 1082cc (90mm x 85mm) had been developed by Val Page and EB Ware for the forthcoming season. This engine featured a larger crank case than earlier ohv 90 bore engines, incorporating heavy internal flywheels to give better balance. Details included a D-shaped cap to enclose the magneto bevel gears, and a valve lifter mechanism, with double face cam instead of the rack and pinion used earlier. Considerable study had been made of the valves, using various specifications of chrome nickel steel supplied by Kayser, Ellison & Co Ltd of Sheffield. The ports had also been modified and the valve collets lightened. The JAP oil lubrication system was retained but the oil was delivered to the nearside cylinder, as suggested earlier by McMinnies.

EB Ware tested this engine in a four-speed modified Grand Prix model. At the same time, he also tested different makes of the then generally unreliable magnetos, mounting two at the front of the engine with a change-over switch inside the car. During his JAP days, EB Ware also did much useful research on plain and roller big end bearings, including work on what were probably the first roller bearing big ends to feature caged rollers.

Back in America, GF (Richard) Allen took Chris Richards's special Morgan to the light car race meeting on 10th October at Combination Park, Medford, Massachusetts, which was run as a prelude to the Light Car and Cyclecar Show at the Horticultural Hall, Boston. The $\frac{1}{4}$-mile dirt track was difficult to negotiate at speed due to the sharp unbanked corners, but Allen won the $\frac{1}{2}$-mile scratch race.

In England the recruitment drive at the beginning of the First World War had caused 10 per cent of Morgan's employees to enlist. His Wolverhampton agent, WD South, had also joined up, only to find himself, much to his disgust, in charge of a pack of mules.

Brooklands track was now under the control of the military and the Royal Flying Corps lorries were wreaking havoc with the surface. The track authorities were incensed at the damage and insisted that the War Office lived up to its undertakings by making immediate repairs, meanwhile banning the RFC lorries from using it. EB Ware

Morgan Sweeps the Board

visited the track with his magneto-testing Grand Prix model, but was able to make only a sedate tour of it, confirming that no races could be held in the immediate future. In June the War Office sanctioned the repairs and the BMCRC made immediate plans for a Combined Services race for the end of July.

Although repairs to the Railway Straight and Paddock delayed the meeting until 7th August, three light cars and cyclecars took to the track for their race, McMinnies driving the 1914 MAG-engined TT car to win at 45.92 mph although he complained of a slipping clutch. After publication of the times of the sidecar heat, McMinnies, now a CPO in the RNAS, was placed second overall for the meeting.

After the races McMinnies took the TT car onto the track for private trials, touching 75 mph several times and reaching 45 mph on the low gear of $7\frac{1}{4}$ to 1. The tests came to an abrupt end when the 8-valve MAG engine blew off a cylinder head which flew past his head still attached to the carburettor control cables.

This was to be the last race at Brooklands for five years. McMinnies himself sold his single-seater 'Jabberwock' to Mr Goodacre of *The Cyclecar* when he married in 1916, a single-seater being of limited use for two—although he had courted with it, his girlfriends sitting side-saddle on the tail. During the war, he instructed pilots in the RNAS, and later teamed up with AV Roe to continue his new-found love of flying.

Events Galore

On 11th November 1918, the Armistice was signed and the Great War ended. For some time to come petrol was to be limited to use within a 30-mile radius of the licence holder's home. The war had taken a terrible toll in life: amongst those who failed to return was Geoffrey Day, HFS's brother-in-law and his passenger in the 1913 Cyclecar Grand Prix.

The factory itself had not been idle. Cooling the engine under the coal scuttle bonnet had long been a problem, and one that the various holes and louvres that had been cut in its sides had failed to solve satisfactorily. Early in 1917 a small fan was fitted behind the engine, driven off the flywheel by a belt, but later the problem was finally solved by fitting a new wider radiator and combining the oil and fuel tanks to form a D-shaped wind-deflecting tank.

In 1916 water-cooled MAG engines were made available to augment the air-cooled version, claiming 14 bhp at 2700 rpm. Development had also continued of the four-seater 'Family' model. Although the original prototype had been built in 1912, this would not go into production until after the War.

Despite the severe restrictions on competitive motoring, the Middlesex Motor Volunteers had craftily held a trial during the last months of the war, disguising it as a despatch carrying test and hence procuring full army supervision and blessing. Private Sharp's Morgan proved victorious, making light work of carrying the 16 stone of its driver and the 12 of its passenger.

In January 1919 general competitions became possible once more as petrol rationing was relaxed. Brooklands was as yet unusable, following the military presence, but trials were restarted immediately: H Denley secured a silver medal in the Victory Cup Trial, and swept the board in the Midland Cycle and Athletic Club's 200-mile trial with his Grand Prix Morgan.

As the light car was by now tending to displace the cyclecar in popularity, the pre-war Cyclecar Club changed its name to that of the Junior Car Club on 1st April. Cyclecars were accepted for membership, but were to be defined as vehicles having an engine capacity not exceeding 1100cc and an unladen weight of 9cwt. Light car owners were affiliated to the RAC and cyclecar owners to the ACU. Prebendary HG Morgan was quick to point out how useful the JCC would be in allowing comparison between light cars and cyclecars in competition, thus helping public and manufacturers alike.

The first major event organized by the JCC was the South Harting Hill Climb, at the end of June, where the standard class was won by FJ Findon's 8 hp Morgan.

On Wednesday, 23rd July the Essex Motor Club ran speed trials over 1 kilometre on the Westcliffe-on-Sea seafront. A strong south-westerly breeze helped along the competitors but unfortunately also brought rain with it, heavy late on. Amongst the competitors was a new name to Morgans, but by no means a newcomer to racing – William Douglas Hawkes. He had campaigned the DEW (later renamed the Victor) cyclecar before the war for the DEW Engineering Co of Eynsford, Kent, in both trials and races, including the 1913 Cyclecar Grand Prix. EB Ware also entered, driving a brand new experimental Family Morgan fitted with a special 85mm x 95mm (1087cc)

HFS and Ruth in the racer built for the 1914 TT at Stile Kop. (Morgan Motor Co)

Freddie James looking pleased to have won a silver. (F. James scrapbook)

water-cooled sidevalve JAP. This featured an enlarged oil sump and a much cleaner crankcase, as a result of JAP's decision to switch from sand casting to die casting. The inlet manifold was water-heated, a feature Ware had previously used on the ohv 90mm bore engine in his 1915 Grand Prix.

In the closed-to-club class Ware proved victorious at 41.49 mph against Hawkes's 40.68 mph, but Hawkes improved in the open class to beat Ware and claim a silver medal. Eric Longden, another newcomer to Morgans, was third at 39.82 mph.

The first post-war appearance of the 1914 TT car was at the Birmingham MCC's Stile Kop open hill climb, held on a stretch of public road just outside Rugeley, Staffs, in August. The car was now fitted with mudguards front and rear, a short full-width windscreen and different silencers, and carried the famous factory registration plates CJ 743. Driven by HFS and passengered by Ruth, it shot up the 1 in 6 hill to record the fastest time of the day for passenger machines, crossing the line at over 55 mph after several alarming skids.

In September the ACU restarted their annual Six Days' Trials. Seven Morgans entered, including Douglas Hawkes. As the Morgan agents tended to support trials events very strongly, it was no suprise to see Hall of Stevenage entered, as well as Freddie James, son of the Sheffield agent, Billie James. EW Merrill was driving an ancient 1915 Morgan which he had asked the factory to check over prior to the event. When he called in to collect the car he discovered that one of the cylinders of the air-cooled side valve JAP engine had had to be replaced, and so he started with one old cylinder with heavy valves and one new 1919 cylinder with the latest thin valves. The car ran fairly well until the final day when within 30 miles of the finish, he hit a dog and skidded into a bank, twisting the rear forks out of line. After that he struggled on, breaking and mending chains, until he reached Builth. Here the engine 'popped back'

Morgan Sweeps the Board

through the carburettor, igniting the petrol running from the fuel tank which had also been damaged in the collision. After extinguishing the blaze, he managed to battle on, arriving at the finish just one hour late—and too late for a medal.

Of the other entrants, Hawkes had to retire with timing trouble, but HFS went on to win a gold, supported by Hall and James with silvers and Greaves with a bronze in a Precision-engined car.

On the business front, HFS opened his new factory in Pickersleigh Road, Malvern on 16th October—the current home of the Morgan Company—and also made arrangements for Roger Darmont to manufacture Morgans under licence in Paris. This enabled him to avoid the crippling duty previously encountered when exporting cars to France.

On a sadder note, HFS had a serious accident at the factory, whilst in the company of young Freddie James. Slipping on a patch of grease, he threw out his right hand, which caught in a capstan lathe. As a result the third and fourth fingers had to be amputated.

November 1919 saw the first post-war Olympia Show. Morgan introduced two new models, the Family four-seater model, and the Aero, a sporting model, featuring a downward pointing streamlined tail harmonizing with the rest of the body, and with a pair of Auster triplex Aero screens instead of a windscreen. The Aero was fitted with a side-valve JAP engine of 976cc (85.5mm x 85mm), a forerunner of the famous JAP 'KT' engine series. All Morgan models now featured a hinged tail panel for better access to the rear wheel.

Throughout 1919 workmen had been battling to make Brooklands track usable again. By early 1920 the BMCRC and the Essex Motor Club were given the go-ahead for a race meeting on Easter Monday. Unfortunately rain washed out the meeting, which was postponed until Saturday, 10th April. Fortunately this date provided ideal racing conditions and two interesting Morgans were entered.

Douglas Hawkes drove the 1914 8-valve MAG-engined TT car, which he had nicknamed 'Land Crab'. He had modified the car for short-distance track races by removing the large fuel tank behind the seats and fitting a smaller torpedo-shaped combined oil and fuel tank on the scuttle where the tool box used to be.

EB Ware entered his pre-war streamlined single-seater. With his assistant Arthur Church, who had joined JAPs from Vauxhalls during the war, Ware had modified this car considerably. A lengthened, strengthened and slightly wider chassis had been fitted, giving a longer wheelbase so that the tail no longer covered the rear wheel. The radiator was a shortened Grand Prix type, with a tubular fuel tank positioned behind it. The oil tank was still at the driver's right hand, so presumably the old tail-mounted fuel tank was left empty. The hand-brake lever and gear lever were now both on the right-hand side and there was still no foot brake. The engine reflected Ware's decision to concentrate on the development of the water-cooled range: it was a water-cooled, side valve JAP, one of the 976cc KT series.

Hawkes made a fine start from his 42 seconds handicap but slowed towards the finish with lubrication problems, allowing Ware, whose handicap was only 6 seconds, victory by 50 yards. Eric Longden with his short stroke 90 bore JAP-engined Grand Prix model was unplaced.

EB Ware outside his shed in the Brooklands Paddock with the modified pre-war single-seater. (Motor Cycle)

Before the BARC meeting at Brooklands on 20th May, EB Ware had finished the modifications to his single-seater. He had fitted a proper bonnet panel blending in with the radiator and scuttle and the side-mounted oil tank had gone. The KT JAP engine now had a streamlined crankcase cowl, the wheels were fitted with streamlining discs, and the chassis featured much extra bracing from the centre pins to the body. All these modifications brought immediate success, for Ware won the Light Car Long Handicap and finished second to Godfrey's GN in the Cyclecar Short Handicap. Hawkes 'Land Crab' was its usual unreliable self.

Hawkes had better luck the following Saturday at the BMCRC's second meeting, touring home to win the novices' scratch sprint, lapping at 70 mph. Eric Longden again

Ware's racer displaying further modifications at the BARC meeting. (Autocar)

Morgan Sweeps the Board

failed to gain a place. Hawkes's new-found reliability brought him further success the following week at the Thundersley Church hill climb near Southend. He finished third behind Frazer-Nash's GN and Malcolm Cambell's Talbot 'Blue Bird'. He would probably have done even better had he been carrying a passenger, as the 'Land Crab' had trouble gripping the loose surface.

Jack Sylvester of Nottingham, accompanied as always by his sister Margaret, drove to one of his greatest trials successes on the Ilkley LC and MCC open trial in June. Their MAG-engined De Luxe model, which had a very low bottom gear, was the only passenger machine to finish the trial, failing to climb Park Rash, the dreaded trials hill in North Yorkshire, by only a few feet. Their achievement was all the more remarkable when one realizes that the throttle cable broke only 10 miles into the trial, forcing Jack to continue to the end of the trial with the end of the wire attached to a file. He thus had only his left hand available to steer with, as he had to use his right to operate his makeshift throttle, which had naturally lost all sensitivity after the repair. During their many years of working together Jack and Margaret had Morgan trialling techniques off to a fine art. The secret of reliability trials lay in maintaining a constant road speed, and Jack found that the best method was to try to keep to a constant engine speed in top gear, no matter what the road surface. Naturally a good ear for the engine note was essential for this. To assist them, Jack carried a Kew 'A' certificate watch for master timing, hung a smaller watch around his neck for quick reference, and also consulted the clock on the Morgan dash. All these were extra to the watches Margaret herself carried.

Morgans at this time were prone to a steering shimmy at certain speeds, which produced a vibration so severe that it seemed as though the machine would disintegrate. Jack's answer to this was to lean hard against the steering wheel, having

Jack and Margaret Sylvester climb the 1 in 4 of Harden Bank during the Ilkley Trial. (Sylvester collection)

Events Galore

first smeared the front of his leather coat with castor oil.

Many Morgan agents were entering the now flourishing speed trials, held on public roads throughout the country under the supervision of the police. These trials were interrupted by numerous intermissions to allow routine traffic to get through, and of course the police had to turn a blind eye to the frequent violations of the nationwide 20 mph speed restriction. As mudguards were not compulsory many racers could be driven to and from the venues. Amongst the Morgan agents doing well in these events were Horrocks of Bolton in Lancashire, Hall of Stevenage in Luton, and Freddie James in Yorkshire, using his Grand Prix model which he called 'Kango'.

Whilst Ware was winning on 24th July on Westcliffe Promenade, Hawkes had taken the 'Land Crab' to the JCC South Harting Hill Climb, gaining a walkover victory in the three-wheeled cyclecar class. In the class for 1100cc racing cars, however, he faced stiff opposition in the shape of the formidable Archie Frazer-Nash, who had entered his famous racing GN 'Kim'. Hawkes made a tremendous start and drove all out, powering the 'Crab' round the bends in a series of beautifully controlled slides. But once again the gremlins struck and he blew off the nearside cylinder, luckily bringing the machine to a halt without injury to its occupants. Whilst Douglas was expressing his astonishment at finding no trace of his piston, the gleeful crowd were making off with the shed pushrods and other souvenirs.

Douglas Hawkes stirs up the dust at the South Harting hill climb.(Motor Cycle)

Morgan Sweeps the Board

One week later, on 2nd August, Hawkes had the repaired 'Land Crab' running in the BARC Brooklands August Bank Holiday Meeting, where he joined battle with Ware once more. It was EB Ware, however, who came away with the honours, winning the second event, the Third Light Car Short Handicap, in his 976cc single-seater. Hawkes's MAG engine had lived up to its normal reputation and conked out, while Archie Frazer-Nash's formidable 'Kim' demolished itself upon spinning backwards through the trackside fence. Ware also went on to win the seventh event, the Second Light Car Long Handicap, after the early leader Hawkes had been eliminated by engine trouble caused by his new cylinder, and had retired in a cloud of smoke.

Ware was having problems of his own with his slim single-seater, however, and the little three-wheeler was bouncing about in an alarming fashion on the damp track. When it began to rain again, before the ninth event, the Second Cyclecar Short Handicap, he contented himself with his two previous wins and only really opened up on the Railway Straight, cutting out for the banking and allowing Hawkes's 'Land Crab', misfiring as usual, victory from Godfrey's GN.

EB Ware was now busy preparing a special narrow-bodied two-seater Morgan at JAPs to use in the forthcoming Grand Prix Cyclecar Race, scheduled for 29th August. Because of the appalling condition of the roads in Amiens, the scene of McMinnies's triumph in the 1913 Cyclecar Grand Prix, the venue had now been moved to Le Mans.

Arthur Church with Ware's racer, now with braced rear forks, outside their Brooklands shed. (Church scrapbooks)

Events Galore

Morgans had supplied Ware with a modified Grand Prix chassis strengthened with double lower chassis tubes joined together by lugs, one above the other on each side. The radiator was a shortened Grand Prix type, and the body, constructed at JAPs, was made very low and narrow, with hinged flaps on either side of the tail to allow access to the rear wheel and transmission. To differentiate the new red car from his red single-seater Ware named it JAP II, although the competition life of his single-seater was by now virtually over anyway.

For the ACU Six Days' Trial later in August, HFS, Frank Boddington—the Worcester agent, and Freddie James entered four-speed models, whilst Freddie's brother Billie James Jnr drove a Grand Prix, all using Parson's chains on the back wheels. Park Rash was included in the first day. This was considered to be unclimbable by a three-wheeler, despite Jack Sylvester's near success in June, but Hall, the Stevenage agent, astounded everyone with a brilliant climb, both fast and sure. The other Morgans were not so successful, despite vigorous bouncing for grip, and all succumbed. In spite of this the Morgan team of HFS, Hall and Freddie James all took gold medals.

Fred James needs assistance on Park Rash despite four speeds. (James scrapbooks)

HFS gets higher up Park Rash than Billie James. (James scrapbooks)

Meanwhile EB Ware's hopes for the French Cyclecar Grand Prix had met a setback. JAP II was not completed in time, and so he had to transfer the long stroke 90 bore ohv JAP (1082cc) into the Morgan factory's own entry—a Grand Prix with a narrower tail than standard. All seemed well as he arrived at the docks with his suitcase strapped to the bonnet side, and two spare disc wheels strapped on the tail. But when the Morgan was being lifted onto the ship, it was dropped onto its nose with disastrous results to the rocker gear and other frail parts. Ware had to dash back to JAPs to make repairs. Cross, tired and minus skin on most of his knuckles, he was eventually able to set off again, but he arrived at Le Mans too late to practise or to get to know the circuit.

Steadily improving his lap times as his knowledge of the circuit increased, Ware had climbed from last place at the start to lead the field by the fourth lap, but just when all seemed rosy, the jinx struck for the final time. His engine overheated at approx. 75 mph and developed a misfire. Closer examination revealed that water was coming out of one exhaust pipe due to a cracked cylinder, presumably caused by topping up the radiator with cold water. Ware decided to continue on one cylinder, covering a further ten laps at about 40 mph but failing to finish within the time limit.

Douglas Hawkes was also entered, driving a standard touring GN. The car lacked speed, however, and he also failed to finish within the time limit.

On his return from Le Mans, Ware set to to get JAP II completed. He entered the narrow two-seater for the BARC Autumn Brooklands meeting on 25th September complete with the ohv 90 bore JAP engine. Alas, its debut was completely overshadowed by 'Land Crab', now going better than ever. In the first race of the day,

EB Ware and Arthur Church test 'JAP II' at Brooklands using the ohv 90 bore JAP engine. (Motor Cycle)

the Fourth Light Car Short Handicap, Hawkes was given 6 seconds over Ware in JAP II and 26 seconds over Archie Frazer-Nash's new racer 'Mowgli', fitted with a very special 1¼ litre ohc engine featuring four-valve twin-plug alumin-bronze heads. The Crouch on 56 seconds maintained an early lead, but Hawkes gave his all entering the finishing straight, overhauling the field to win at 72mph.

Hawkes's engine reliability continued with the Autumn Junior Spring Handicap over 2 miles, in which 'Land Crab' just held off Godfrey's GN to win at 71¼ mph despite a broken steering arm.

Ware was obviously finding his narrow Morgan body a bit too cramped, as he quickly shortened the steering column to give himself more room, cutting away the lower part of the steering wheel rim for extra leg clearance. Ware raced with disc wheels, and obviously still pinned his faith on a single hand brake as no foot brake was fitted.

At the 1920 Motor Cycle Show in November, HFS introduced modified rear fork ends, allowing detachable rear wheels, and standardized the lengths of the two chains. The Aero model now featured a vee-shaped wind deflector behind the radiator, as used on George Griffith's racer before the war. Tapering hubs with large bearings were now standardized for the front wheels.

The London-Exeter Trial classically brought the 1920 trials year to a close, with awards for Harold Holmes, who was soon to team up with Stanley McCarthy to form 'Homacs'—a new London distributor, and for Billie Elce, another London Morgan agent. The 1921 trials year proper was opened with the Essex Motor Club Trial in

Morgan Sweeps the Board

February, which was held in Epping Forest. EB Ware and Arthur Church drove what appeared to be their Le Mans Car, now fitted with a water-cooled KT JAP to a walkover in the three-wheeler class.

Although Ware had entered his 90 bore engined JAP II in the Easter Monday BARC Brooklands meeting, he failed to appear, allowing Eric Longden to uphold Morgan prestige with a second place to Cushman's GN in the Easter Cyclecar Handicap, driving his own 90 bore JAP-engined Morgan. When JAP II did reappear, at the Essex Motor Club's Kop Hill Climb, it was equipped with a very highly modified side-valve JAP engine. Ware was now to concentrate on racing this engine. After victory in one cyclecar class and a second to Godfrey's GN in another, Ware took his Morgan home on the back of his Renault lorry.

By the BMCRC meeting at Brooklands on 16th April, Ware had really got his new engine sorted out. In the speed trials held before the races, he attained 70.34 mph for the flying kilometre compared with Longden's 43.63 mph. With such a marked difference in speed it was obvious who would win their three-lap race but Ware endeavoured to play up to the crowd by dropping right behind, only really opening the throttle on the last lap. Naturally he won quite comfortably. Ware's engine had a capacity of 1088cc, attained by lengthening the stroke of the basic KT unit.

The ACU introduced a new type of trial on 27th April designed to test absolutely standard production machines, rather than modified trials models. ACU officials selected three Morgans at random from various showrooms and sealed them against interference from their drivers, HFS, Stanley McCarthy and Billie Elce. All three triumphed in the trial to gain certificates, easily completing the required twelve laps of Brooklands at 35 mph before the finish.

At the joint BMCRC and Essex MC Brooklands meeting on 7th May, Longden and Ware met again in the Sidecar and Cyclecar Open Handicap. At the beginning Ware relieved the boredom in the paddock by shearing JAP II's starting pin. With the aid of the two assistants he had to push start the car. It gave one tremendous leap on firing and very nearly left them all behind, but Ware and his passenger clung on and eventually gained control. Although the Morgans couldn't catch the sidecars they were well handicapped in that Ware on scratch had almost caught Longden on 1 minute 18 seconds after racing over 8¼ miles.

Up on Southport sands there was a large crowd to watch the sand racing held on 21st May, so large in fact that it disrupted the timing wires. Over the years Southport was to prove extremely popular with Morgans: on this occasion alone Horrocks, Jones, Ecroyd and Killery all tasted success, and there was at least one special-bodied Morgan amongst them. Southport always acted as a stimulus to the amateur engineer and many specials were produced over the years to compete at these friendly events.

In the Scottish Six Days' Trial HFS had his usual taste of Scottish luck when he was forced to retire his four-speeder with a sheared flywheel key. Hall did little better when he overturned his two-speed model but did gain a silver medal as did Boddington, despite getting lost.

ERC (Tiny) Scholefield was a relative newcomer to Morgans. Even so, he very nearly made a clean sweep of the prizes at the JCC Dean Hill Climb on 6th August. He spoilt his record in the final class of the day, however, when he tried too hard to

Events Galore

improve on his own fastest time of day and rammed the bank at the hairpin, turning over, though luckily without serious damage. Tiny used a forward pointing cone to ram air into the carburettor of his Grand Prix.

For the Six Days' Trial at the end of August the ACU had tried to produce an event on the lines of the JCC General Efficiency Trial, with tests for reliability, hill climbing, silencers, brakes, fuel consumption, speed over 25 laps of Brooklands and finally an assault of Brooklands test hill. Each member of the Morgan team of HFS, Boddington and Elce won a gold medal, and HFS astounded them all by recording 67.1 mpg with his JAP side-valve engined. Standard.

Towards the end of August the Worcester and District Motoring Club combined to hold the first of their annual speed trials over a timed $\frac{1}{4}$ mile (in later years a flying kilometre), on the estate of the Earl of Beauchamp at Madresfield. Only a mile or so from Malvern, the Madresfield Speed Trials became the place for the fastest Morgan drivers to gather and do battle, thereby hoping to impress HFS himself, who also patronized the events. At this opening meeting it was HFS who gained the honours, winnning the passenger class up to 1200cc, but failing to beat an HE car for fastest passenger time of the day.

Undaunted by the previous year's disaster, EB Ware had again entered the French Cyclecar Grand Prix, which was to be held at Le Mans on 17th September. He was to drive the works car he had used the previous year, now fitted with a new tail, similar to that on his own JAP II, and a side-valve engine. He was supported by four French-built Darmont Morgans driven by Stoffel, Desvaux, Baudeloque and Vuilliamy. Ware's Le Mans gremlin from the previous year had not deserted him, however. On the night before the event, whilst practising on the circuit, he hit and killed a dog, badly bending the Morgan after running on two wheels for some way at speed. Ware worked all night straightening out his machine and was tired and rather shaken by the time the event started.

Fastest on the initial lap was Vuilliamy's French Morgan but Ware also started well, holding third place for some considerable time before his luck faded once more. He found himself unable to engage top gear, completing a lap in bottom and over revving his engine and breaking a tappet rod in the process. After repairs he set off again, but ran into tyre problems, the left front tyre puncturing three times before leaving the rim at speed. The wheel then collapsed and Ware was out of the race. He was not disgraced however: Stoffel's was the only Morgan to finish, in fifth place, and a total of fifteen of the twenty starters failed to complete the race.

As the 'Land Crab' had been in Douglas Hawkes's hands for some time now, it was hardly suprising that the works turned out a new racing Morgan for the flourishing speed trials. It used a standard long wheelbase chassis, fitted with an aluminium 'tear drop' body, rounded at the front behind the engine and terminating in a long vertical point at the rear. William Carr, the Post Office manager at Furnhill Heath near Worcester, campaigned the car with an 8-valve MAG engine—possibly out of the 'Land Crab' itself which was fairly inactive at this time, due to Hawkes's other racing activities.

Early in the year the JCC had captured the imagination of the motoring world by announcing a long distance race to be held on 22nd October over 200 miles at

Morgan Sweeps the Board

Brooklands, at a time when a race of 20 miles was thought excessive. Despite the obvious prestige such an event was to hold, the only Morgan entered was Ware's JAP II. Outwardly little modified, it was fitted with a tuned side-valve JAP engine featuring an aluminium fir cone valve cap over the exhaust valve to help dissipate heat (he had suffered exhaust valve failure at the BARC Whit Monday meeting), and a similar fir cone as a core plug in the cylinder water jacket. To improve the driver's comfort an aluminium blister had been inserted in the side of the body, over the site of his thigh. The car carried its racing number 6 mounted on a vertical plate on the tail, as demanded by the regulations.

Ware made a very good start and led the 1100cc class for nineteen laps, reaching fourth position overall, including the 1500cc competitors, before transmission trouble set in and forced his retirement. Although he had covered less than a third of the distance, Ware's amazingly consistent lap speeds impressed everyone, and it was no surprise to learn that he had captured the 50 mile class K record at a speed of 75.55 mph.

Before Brooklands closed for repairs in December, Ware went out again with JAP II to take the 5 mile flying start, the 10 mile standing start and the flying start kilometre records, at 79.30 mph, 75.92 mph and 86.04 mph respectively.

It was obvious that tremendous development had gone into the JAP engine over the last year. Part of this development could be explained by the introduction of aluminium pistons. Themselves a development from the aero engines of the First World War, they possessed the great advantage of low weight and greater heat dissipation, thus allowing higher engine revs and increased compressions to be used. Roller bearing big-end bearings were introduced concurrently following much pioneer work by Ware himself. Perhaps the most significant development at the JAP factory, however, was the result of a disagreement between designer Val Page and his boss John Prestwich. In 1906, before he joined JAPs, Val had been apprenticed to the Clement Talbot factory and had seen for himself the importance of large valves for engine efficiency, from the results of their own racing programme. JA Prestwich insisted that valve size was of no importance, but eventually he allowed Val to go ahead and modify a 250cc side-valve engine accordingly. EB Ware tested this engine, which immediately reached the amazing figure of 8000 rpm, later hitting 10,000 rpm. The point had been proved and a new breed of JAP engines was developed around this principal.

At the Olympia Motor Cycle Show in late 1921 JAPs announced the first such engine, their 'Sports' unit—a new air-cooled twin guaranteed to propel a car at 80 mph. It was of standard KT bore and stroke but featured all the above JAP developments, the large exhaust valves necessitating $1\frac{3}{4}$ inch exhaust pipes. To differentiate this engine from the standard KT unit it was named the KTC, but it still retained a single two-lobed camshaft operating all four valves. Externally the engine could be recognized by its fir cone valve cap coolers.

On the last day of 1921 a new name appeared in the list of London-Gloucester Trial drivers—Harold Beart, who went on to win a silver cup for his performance with his MAG-engined Grand Prix. A Norfolk farmer's son, Harold Beart was at that time serving an engineering apprenticeship in Croydon. Whilst he got considerable enjoyment from trials he never took them very seriously and was to achieve much greater fame in racing later on.

Events Galore

In the Colmore Cup Trial held in March 1922 another hitherto unknown driver joined HFS and Bill Carr—George Norman Norris, a Vickers aircraft inspector. Like Beart, Norris was to achieve greater success in racing.

Although JAP were riding the crest of a wave as the most successful proprietary cyclecar engine manufacturer, they could not afford to be complacent. In nearby Willesden, the Belgian Hubert Hagens, a director of the British subsidiary of the French Anzani engine company since 1916, had been developing a series of engines from a French 500cc single. A standard cyclecar engine (type CC) was announced in March 1922 and featured a bore of 85mm and stroke of 95mm, giving 1078cc, with the ohv cylinders at the unusual angle of 57 degrees to each other. Naturally it had the latest innovations, featuring roller bearing big ends and aluminium alloy pistons, and claimed 26 bhp in both air- and water-cooled forms.

For the 1922 JCC General Efficiency Trial in March EB Ware entered a Standard model, fitted with the new KTC engine. Naturally he set up the fastest time of the day in the Brooklands Test Hill ascent test, and recorded $63\frac{1}{4}$ mpg over the road route, showing the great efficiency of the new engine. The absence of front wheel brakes cost him marks in the braking test, as his rear wheel locked and slid on the slippery surface, allowing Godfrey's GN to claim overall victory and take the prized Westall Cup.

As the 1921 Stock Machine Trial for production machines had been so successful, the ACU decided to make it an annual event. For the 1922 trial, also held in March, six production Morgans were entered, all gaining special certificates of merit. All were reported to enjoy the final test of speed at Brooklands. Driving one of the Morgans was George Goodall, service manager for Fryers of Hereford, the local Morgan agents. Goodall was a true Morgan enthusiast, having owned nothing else since 1912, and he had been trials driving with them from 1913 onwards.

EB Ware's highly modified side-valve engine in JAP II had been stretched to 1098cc (85.7 x 95mm) for the April BMCRC Brooklands meeting. In the 600cc-1100cc passenger handicap he had an exciting tussle with Claude Temple's Harley-Davidson side car, and with his new compatriot at JAPs, Herbert le Vack, on a Zenith sidecar fitted with the KTC engine, development of which was to be taken over by le Vack. Ware finished third, beating le Vack into fourth place.

During April Freddie James went to the Morgan factory to borrow the works racer, as previously used by Carr except that the tail was now more upswept at the lower edge. The engine was still the 8-valve MAG and Freddie remembers that as he was about to set off with the car, HFS rushed out with a box of a dozen or so sparking plugs. 'What will I need all these for?' Freddie asked. 'You'll soon see,' HFS replied, and sure enough Freddie spent the journey home changing plugs every few miles as they were fouled by the tuned engine. Freddie took the car to the Sutton Bank Hill Climb, only to find that it had been postponed for a week owing to the bad weather.

On 30th April he set off for the hill climb once more, but he never made the course as the timing gear sheared on the way. He and his passenger pushed the car for over a mile to the nearest village, where Freddie rang his father in Sheffield. Billie James immediately stripped an MAG engine from a standard Morgan in the showroom and set off with the appropriate part. Unfortunately, the racing MAG type was completely different.

'JAP II' after its record-breaking runs at the JCC meeting. (Wilson collection)

Meanwhile Ware had taken JAP II with the 1098cc engine to Brooklands, for the JCC Spring Meeting. In event four, Ware romped home an easy winner, lapping at between 80 and 90 mph, and in the 10-lap handicap he broke the flying 5 mile record and the standing 10 mile record at 83.26 mph and 79.60 mph respectively, although he was unplaced. Naturally he was rehandicapped for the final event of the day, finishing fifth behind Frazer-Nash's GN.

At the British Anzani factory in Scrubs Lane, Willesden, Hubert Hagens had now introduced a modified ohv air-cooled Anzani engine, fitted with special heads incorporating four valves per cylinder, especially for racing. Harry Martin, making a return to Morgan racing, borrowed the works racer which had now been fitted with one of these new 8-valve Anzani engines, and entered it in the ACU South Midland Centre Brooklands Meeting. He finished third in the 1100cc passenger machine event, behind Godfrey's winning GN and de Lissa's fast MAG sidecar outfit.

Martin took out the same machine at the BMCRC third Brooklands meeting in June, gaining a second in the two-lap passenger handicap, and winning the five-lap passenger handicap from le Vack's KTC-engined Zenith after scratch man Ware had suffered propshaft failure on the first lap. Hubert Hagens himself was in attendance, no doubt keeping an eye on Martin and also on the Anzani-engined Trump motorcycle entered by Trump director Col. RN Stewart. Whereas the 8-valve Anzani engine as used by Martin was of standard Anzani cyclecar dimensions—1078cc with a bore and stroke of 85mm x 95mm, the Trump was equipped with an 8-valve engine of 83mm x 92mm, giving 994cc.

Because of police restrictions, the Sutton Coldfield and North Birmingham Automobile Club travelled to Angel Bank, near Cleobury Mortimer, for their speed

Events Galore

Harry Martin in the 8-valve Anzani-engined factory car at the BMCRC meeting, with Hubert Hagens standing alongside. (Motor Cycle)

hill climb on 1st July. Despite frequent interruptions to allow the routine traffic to pass, and heavy rain, HFS comfortably won the 1100cc car class from Norman Norris, both using 976cc JAP Morgans.

Martin took out his Morgan again for the fourth BMCRC meeting in mid-July. One of the novelties of the event was a 100-mile handicap, for which Martin fitted an extra fuel tank low down on the nearside of the body. Ware retired after four laps with tyre trouble in JAP II, now of 1090cc. Martin struggled on, misfiring badly, but failed to gain a place.

Douglas Hawkes had seen relatively little Morgan racing since 1920 although he had finished third with 'Land Crab' at the JCC Brooklands meeting in May. During this period, Hawkes had been successfully campaigning the 1912, 15-litre Lorraine Detriech 'Vieux Charles Trois' and latterly a Horstman. He had not given up Morgans, however, and visitors to the works in mid-1921 had noted his new racer under construction. On 29th July Hawkes made his debut with the new car at the Ealing and District Brooklands meeting.

Morgan Sweeps the Board

Called 'Flying Spider', this was a very special single-seater Morgan. Behind the engine, its unique long wheelbase chassis relied only on the beefed-up backbone tube to the bevel box, the two lower chassis members having been dispensed with. The body was, of necessity, very narrow and indeed very few people other than Douglas could get into it. Even he had to remove part of the offside body panel to do so.

Fitted with an 8-valve MAG engine—presumably that used in 'Land Crab', Hawkes drove the car to second place in the 1500cc three-lap handicap. One week later, at the BARC Brooklands Bank Holiday meeting, he tasted victory, beating ABC's Crouches, Aston Martins, and Joyce's single-seater AC at 74.5 mph in the Light Car and Cyclecar Handicap.

This year the JCC 200-mile race on 19th August was to be run as two events: one for 1100cc cars in the morning, and one for 1500cc cars in the afternoon. Three Morgans were entered. EB Ware was again driving JAP II, but he now had extra tanks fitted, one in the scuttle, and another, a torpedo-shaped tank slung on the nearside of the body. Harry Martin had entered what we presume was his Anzani-engined racer, as used in the BMCRC 100-mile race. Douglas Hawkes, however, had an entirely new car. The chassis was a wide track Aero chassis, featuring a Hartford shock absorber attached to a loop over the rear wheel as indeed did the other Morgans. The body was a prototype flat-sided Aero, as was to be announced at the October show, but the whole bonnet was replaced by a pointed fuel tank, and the oil tank was positioned across the flat tail, behind the seats. The hand brake and gear selector levers were external, and Hawkes used a piece of spring steel behind the gear lever to keep the dogs engaged.

Hawkes's engine was also very special. In March 1922 Hubert Hagens of Anzani had revealed an 8-valve air-cooled racing motorcycle engine with valves operated by overhead camshafts, designed for attacking the American-held high speed records. Whether this same 994cc engine (83mm x 92mm) was enlarged to 1078cc (85mm x 95mm) for Douglas Hawkes to use, or whether Douglas used a sister unit is uncertain, but the resemblance was very strong. The overhead camshafts (one to each cylinder, each with two cams, and each operating a pair of valves) were carried in oil-tight heavily ribbed aluminium cam boxes on top of the cylinders, and operated by vertical drive shafts with spherical ends and floating driving pegs. The nearside camshaft also drove a Best and Lloyd oil pump supplying oil to the cam boxes and the bases of both cylinders. The flat bottomed crankcase differed considerably from the production pushrod 8-valve Anzani type, and also had a large timing chest for the bevels involved in the camshaft drive system. Twin carburettors were fitted, and each 4-valve cylinder

The start of the 200-mile race, with Ware changing gear alongside Pressland's Crouch. (Radio Times Hulton Picture Library)

Events Galore

head carried twin plugs fired by two chain-driven magnetos mounted on either side of the crankcase. The pistons were of slipper type with one gas ring and three oil grooves in the skirt. Altogether the engine looked very impressive.

Hagens spent a great deal of time helping Hawkes test the engine at Brooklands, where it was noted to be very fast but somewhat erratic.

The start of the race caught the competitors by surprise, as they had thought there was a minute in hand. Ware was quickly away, reaching second position after the first lap, but Martin had been caught on the hop and it was a few minutes before he got going. Poor Douglas Hawkes had real problems, however, requiring a plug change before he could fire his engine, and forced to wait nearly a quarter of an hour at the start.

Once going Hawkes's luck didn't improve; a steering pin broke on his first lap and he had to come into the pits for repairs with the nearside wheel wobbling alarmingly. To join him in his misfortune came Ware with a fountain of water streaming from his nearside cylinder. Ware caulked the damaged water jacket and returned to the fray, but soon his radiator was boiling once more.

When Hawkes got going for the second time he certainly was fast, but he was running very erratically. The need for further plug changes lost him yet more time, and it was rumoured that his propeller shaft was also overheating. Finally he punctured his offside front tyre. After a long pit stop he really motored, lapping at 88 mph before his engine cried 'enough' and blew up in a big way, losing a cylinder on the twenty-second lap.

Hawkes at the pit counter, his 200-mile car having steering problems. Note the special air-cooled ohc Anzani engine. (National Motor Museum)

EB Ware about to pass Eric Longden's 'Chunky Chunky' following repairs to the water jackets of Ware's engine. (Autocar)

EB Ware was doing little better, for the crack in the water jacket was extending. He gave up the unequal struggle a mere four laps later. His had been the last Morgan in the race: as early on as the tenth lap, Martin's engine had developed a misfire and refused to restart once stopped. Thus all the Morgans were out of the race before even the half-way mark had been reached. One wonders what the Morgan pit staff thought of the sign pinned on the pit noticeboard: 'Is racing worth while?'.

For the annual ACU Six Days' Trial HFS took the opportunity to compare engines in his team of four-speeders. HFS had the side-valve JAP engine, Hall the MAG and Carr an Anzani which impressed all with its speed and quietness. All, however, took gold medals so there could be little in it.

Back at Brooklands in one of the more friendly and personal smaller race meetings, run by the Surbiton MC on 2nd September, Hawkes's 'Flying Spider' with an 8-valve MAG won the Surrey Sprint Handicap at 73.56 mph.

The following Saturday, Hawkes was back in his old 'Land Crab' for what was probably its final event—the JCC South Harting Hill Climb. With the 8-valve MAG engine once again in place, Hawkes made a really fine ascent, showing perfect judgement and cool driving as the fragile-looking vehicle hurled around the corners, failing by only $\frac{1}{4}$ second to beat Frazer-Nash's GN (Kim 2) in the class for 1100cc racing cars.

Hawkes was also entered in his 8 hp Talbot, in which he came second on formula in the standard two-seater class up to 1100cc. The fastest on time was Holmes's Anzani-Morgan, followed by Parsley's JAP Morgan. In the ladies' class Mrs Hawkes drove her husband's Talbot to another second place, but at least had the satisfaction of beating Mrs Frazer-Nash into third.

Towards the end of September Norman Norris borrowed the 200-mile race car that Hawkes had raced and took it to the Sutton Coldfield AC's hill climb at Angel Bank. Now fitted with an ordinary pushrod 8-valve Anzani engine, the Morgan proved unbeatable in Norris's capable hands, gaining victory in the light car classes.

HFS and Ruth enjoy a joke in the English Six Days'. (Sylvester collection)

For the following weekend Hawkes repossessed his 200-mile car and refitted the special ohc 8-valve Anzani engine, now repaired from the 200-mile race damage, for the Essex Motor Club Brooklands Speed Championships. In the 1100cc class Hawkes won his heat against Hawkins's GN and Peaty's ohv Blackburne-engined Bleriot-Whippet, but he had bad luck in the final, falling back after a good start to allow Frazer-Nash in his rebodied GN 'Mowgli' to secure the championship.

On 29th September, as part of the Morecambe Carnival, the newly built Lancaster-Morecambe road provided an excellent venue for speed trials. Horrocks, the Bolton agent, wanted to do well in this event and asked his assistant Chris Shorrock, later to achieve fame with superchargers, to help him. Chris built up a Morgan chassis for him, soldering instead of brazing the lugs for added strength, as is the practice in aeroplane construction. Horrocks had written to MAG who allowed him an 8-valve MAG engine on one month's loan. Chris Shorrock travelled to London to collect the engine. He stripped it down to check it over and then tuned it and fitted it to the new chassis. A simple aluminium body was constructed for the racer, which henceforth was known affectionately as 'The Kettle'. Come the day and Horrocks's efforts proved worthwhile. He clocked 33 seconds to gain an easy victory in the 1100cc light car class over the Morgans of ER Barker and HV Hughes, the latter being a regular Southport competitor with a water-cooled sv JAP-engined special.

In November Messrs Burney and Blackburne, engine manufacturers of Bookham in Surrey, announced their KM series, designed by Harry Hatch, late of JAPs. These were water-cooled 60 degree ohv engines of 1090cc later enlarged to 1098cc (85mm x 96.8mm), featuring roller bearing big ends and aluminium pistons, and claiming 32

The specially prepared flat-sided Aero displayed at the Olympia Show. (Morgan Motor Co)

bhp. During tests in a stripped Morgan, 85 mph had been obtained with minimal tuning, and 75 mph was thought within reach of standard touring Morgans. Facilities were made available for fitting twin plugs to each cylinder head by removing the compression taps. Initially only three studs held down the cylinders to the crankcase, although this was soon changed to four for the production KMA engines.

At the 1922 Olympia Motor Cycle Show Morgan introduced a new model, based on the body design of Hawkes's 200-mile racer. This new Aero featured flat body sides and a flat top to the tail. It was exhibited clad in shining polished aluminium and nickel plate, with black wings. In later years this type of Aero tended to be known as the 'Flat Sided Aero' or '200 Mile Aero' and it was to be very popular with the speedmen, having an outside gear lever. A water-cooled Anzani 'CC' engine was fitted, but Morgans also offered side-valve and overhead valve Blackburne engines as well as the trusty JAP sidevalves.

Just before Brooklands closed for winter repairs, Douglas Hawkes attacked short-distance records with his 8-valve ohc Anzani-engined 200-mile car. Although his tyres were initially found to contravene the FICM regulations, necessitating further runs, he took the H2 records for 5 miles, 10 miles, flying $\frac{1}{2}$ mile and flying kilometre at 85.14 mph, 81.7 mph, 87.89 mph and 86.94 mph respectively. Doubtless HFS was well

Events Galore

pleased with the timing of the runs to coincide with the show.

The seventh London-Exeter Trial brought the year to a close with golds for Sawtell, Broom and Holmes of Homac whose partner McCarthy joined Smith in winning silvers. Morgans had entered every London-Exeter Trial since the year in which the marque began, attaining nineteen golds and ten silvers from thirty-three entries. No other light car or cyclecar had been able to approach this kind of performance.

March 1923 saw the return of the annual JCC General Efficiency Trial. EB Ware and HFS had obviously learnt from their experience of the previous year, and EB Ware's KTC-engined Standard had now been fitted with internally expanding front wheel brakes. The Morgan's weakness overcome, Ware walked away with the Westall Cup, making best performance in most of the tests imposed. Morgan immediately announced front wheel brakes as options for all new models.

March was one of the busiest months on the racing calendar. In the annual ACU Stock Machine Trial, HFS drove a JAP-engined Grand Prix, accompanied by Bennett in an Anzani Grand Prix and Norman Norris with an MAG-engined De Luxe. In the Victory Trial, Norris used an 8-valve Anzani engine which proved remarkably fast on the hills, although he failed to feature in the results. The Morgan team of HFS with his

Norman Norris ascends Portway hill, followed by the Morgans of HFS and Bennett, and also a TB (Goodall scrapbook)

61

Morgan Sweeps the Board

JAP, Carr's Anzani and George Goodall of Hereford with his usual MAG-engined Trials Standard won the Watsonian team prize and a gold medal apiece. Chippendale, a mechanic with the Colmore Depot, gained a silver.

No less than seventeen Morgans entered the London-Land's End Trial at the end of the month, including Beart, Norris, Maskell, Holmes, McCarthy and the Reading Morgan agent, Julian. Seven golds were won, and three bronzes. One unfortunate Morgan entrant, FW Dame, overturned on the second bend of Porlock. The St Albans agent, Hall, won one of the golds despite the fact that he had not had time to run in his engine—a brand-new Anzani.

April saw the season of speed trials well underway with the Chatcombe Pitch Hill Climb on the 7th. Goodall entered his MAG-engined trials car NP 636, prepared by fellow Fryers employee, salesman Cecil Jay. The competition was very strong in that several 8-valve Anzani-engined Morgans were also present. Charles Whatley had one fitted on his new yellow Grand Prix: he clocked 34.3 seconds. But the Morgan stars were to be HFS and Norman Norris, both with 8-valve Anzani-engined wide-track flat-sided Aeros. We suspect that Norris's Morgan was Hawkes's 200-mile car, as the special oil tank was still visible on the tail, although a conventional bonnet and dummy radiator had been fitted and also a massive steering wheel. His time of 33.4 seconds was fast, but not fast enough to catch HFS who clocked 32.3 seconds to win the RAC plaque. HFS's car was basically similar to Norris's but with both fuel and oil tanks in the bonnet as in normal Aero practice. Against these wide-track specials poor Goodall never stood a chance although his time of 36.4 seconds was very creditable.

Goodall soon tasted success, however, winning his class at the Avonmouth Speed Trials held one week later. It may be that he had persuaded HFS to lend him the factory 8-valve Anzani wide-track flat-sided Aero. This was definitely the case for the Angel Bank hill climb on 21st April. On this occasion even Norris couldn't come near him with his own 8-valve Anzani racer. Goodall convincingly won the 1100cc class and was fourth fastest overall behind Raymond Mays's Bugatti.

Norman Norris was a personal friend of Cecil Burney, one of the Blackburne directors and doubtless he had persuaded him to make a special engine available for him. He returned his ex-Hawkes car to Morgans for modification to take this new engine. When the newly equipped car appeared at the JCC Spring Meeting at Brooklands on 28th April, it tasted immediate success by beating Du Cane's Bugatti to win the Junior Short Handicap at 76 mph. Norris was passengered by his brother-in-law Carol Holbeche, and his car was noted to have a straight-sided rim on the rear wheel, the split rim helping to prevent the tendency of the tyres to leave the rim at speed, a problem prevalent with the beaded-edge type.

The 1923 Scottish Six Days' Trial spared HFS his usual bad luck in this event and he triumphed to win a silver cup. The other Morgans didn't do so well, however. Boddington failed to start because of rheumatism, Wickham's Grand Prix suffered broken rear forks, and Bill Carr was eliminated after a brilliant display with engine failure of his Anzani CC.

On Saturday, 12th May snow fell at Brooklands during the Ealing MC meeting. Arthur Maskell, a newcomer to racing though not to trials, who later became yet another London Morgan agent, drove an Anzani CC-engined Grand Prix to victory in

A Blackburne engine, victorious in its first race at Brooklands, fitted to Norris's racer. (Mrs Dawes collection)

the three-lap novices' handicap. Douglas Hawkes with 'Flying Spider' joined Maskell in the three-lap three-wheeler handicap, but neither was successful. The air-cooled ohc 8-valve Anzani engine used by Hawkes in 1922 had proved very temperamental due to overheating problems, and so Hawkes had persuaded Anzani to make a water-cooled version. Incidentally, another overhead camshaft Anzani vee-twin engine had made its debut in a motorcycle at the BMCRC meeting on 5th May. It was a two-valve-per-cylinder air-cooled engine of 996cc (78mm x 104mm), designed by the autocratic Belgian Hagens for record attempts by Claude Temple. The overhead camshaft conversion was very similar to that on Hawkes's engine, and probably derived from it.

On 21st May, a young student named Eric Fernihough stripped his air-cooled side-valve JAP-engined De Luxe Morgan of mudguards and other non-essentials for the Spread Eagle Hill Climb at Shaftesbury. His future promise became evident when he took home six cups and made fastest time in the car classes with his humble entry.

The BMCRC Brooklands meeting on 26th May saw Norris just fail to catch Hatton's Douglas sidecar in the 1100cc Passenger Handicap with his Blackburne-engined racer. EB Ware was also present at the track with a Morgan equipped with a new experimental air-cooled 90 degree JAP engine. Trials showed this engine to have excellent performance and flexibility and the 90 degree angle much reduced engine vibration. Val Page believes that this engine could have been JAP's best ever, but times were unsettled, and the project was delayed and finally abandoned.

The Essex MC Brooklands meeting on Saturday, 2nd June featured Norris and Douglas Hawkes both on scratch in the first event, the Essex Junior Short Handicap. At the other end of the field, the 'limit' car awarded the most favourable handicap was an Amilcar. Hawkes in 'Flying Spider' and Norris with his Blackburne both went well, threading their ways through the field but just failing to catch the Amilcar. Norris

Morgan Sweeps the Board

finished second and Hawkes third. Norris also drove into second places in the 8¼-mile Junior Long Handicap and the three-lap Passenger Handicap.

From 31st May until 2nd June Skegness ran three days of speed trials on the sands. In the car events held over the first two days CH Pettit's two-year-old Grand Prix with a new Anzani CC engine won the 1100cc touring car class. Two days later, stripped of wings and windscreen it won a heat in the 1100cc sidecar class but failed to catch Winn's Douglas sidecar in the final. The sand was very wet, and boards had to be placed under the wheels at the start, to prevent the competitors sinking and to give them some grip for the vital first few yards.

Two ACU events were held on 1st July. At the Western Centre ACU Speed Trials at Chatcombe Pitch, Charles L Whatley, passengered by K Goddard as usual, drove his yellow 8-valve Anzani-engined Grand Prix. Morgans had supplied the car with this engine from new, with a neat dummy radiator fitted in behind.

The ACU Surbiton meeting at Brooklands on the same date saw Norris continue his run of success and reliability. He entered four events on the programme, gaining one third place, and two fourths after some good handicapping, lapping at 85 mph with the Blackburne. This engine was proving an extremely reliable and versatile unit. It was at

Charles Whatley awaits the start at Madresfield. (C Whatley)

Events Galore

home both on the track and on the road, for Norris always drove it to and from speed events from his lock-up garage near his home in Kenilworth.

The annual Madresfield Speed Trials were held this year on Thursday, 12th July and heralded a new name amongst the great Morgan drivers, that of H Clive Lones, a power-station engineer from the Midlands. Clive had recently purchased a side-valve Blackburne-engined Grand Prix, not the most sporting proposition, but with the help of a tuning book by George Newman of Ivy-Precision, he reworked the inlet ports and raised the compression to such effect that he clocked 46.6 seconds—sufficient to beat many of the favourites including Whatley's 8-valve Anzani. HFS was driving an 8-valve Anzani-engined wide-track Aero, with which he took the general class at 42.4 seconds, despite a delay caused by a thunderstorm.

Two days later HFS took the Anzani-engined wide-track flat-sided Aero to Angel Bank, where he convincingly won the 1100cc Light Car Class. The car was noted to have a radiator installed behind the 8-valve air-cooled Anzani engine. In fact, although these engines were fast, they were proving unreliable, being prone to valve failure and collapse of the weak valve operating system, as well as having a tendency to overheat. As the radiator showed, their days on the racing Morgan were numbered.

On the same day the Colwyn Bay Speed Trials were held. In these, local George Cowley easily won the 1100cc class with his 10 hp Morgan, from Basil Davenport's GN. Fine weather produced many thousands of spectators who lined the course along the promenade.

July also saw George Goodall enter the second factory 8-valve Anzani-powered wide-track flat-sided Aero in the Hereford Speed Trials at Rotherwas. Despite breaking a valve 250 yards from the finish, his time over the ¼-mile course proved unbeatable in the open class. Goodall had also taken along his MAG-engined trials car.

Goodall's two Morgans, the MAG trials car, and the Anzani widetrack racer. (Goodall scrapbooks)

Despite breaking its dynamo chain, it still won two classes for touring cyclecars. As usual both vehicles were prepared for Goodall by young Cecil Jay.

Meanwhile Harold Beart at Croydon had decided to enter the racing scene. He traded in his MAG Grand Prix at Homacs for a new Aero, which was fitted with one of the latest ohv Blackburne engines. This he proceeded to tune, and entered it for the MCC Brooklands meeting also held on 14th July. His future racing promise was evident in the 1500cc three-lap handicap when he streaked home in second place at a speed of 78 mph, just failing to catch the winning Palladium with its much better handicap.

Four Morgans contested the three-lap handicap at a wet BMCRC meeting at Brooklands on 18th August. George Cowley appeared in a very neat racing Morgan, with Anzani engine, possibly Horrocks's 'Kettle'. He started as the favourite, but failed to respond to the flag, loosing several seconds in getting underway. Beart and Norris with their Blackburnes soon showed their usual high speed, threading their ways through the field despite being baulked by slower sidecars, but they were unable to catch the speedy sidecars of Greening, Sinnett and Baragwaneth, and finished sixth and seventh respectively.

Horrocks's 'Kettle' had been fitted with an 8-valve Anzani engine in early 1923, with only a foot band brake for retardation. In view of its success Horrocks was eventually persuaded to produce two replicas, both fitted with air-cooled side-valve JAP engines, which were sold through the Atherton garage of John Miles Bullough. Bullough retained one for himself, which possibly made its debut at Southport Sands as early as 1st September. Here Bullough won the novices' classes for sidecars and cars up to 1500cc, but gave second best overall to local HV Hughes, driving a water-cooled sv JAP-engined aluminium-bodied special Morgan. Hughes won the other four small car events, including the 10-mile race. Long-distance events on the sands were made possible by fixing posts at either end of the 1-mile straight used for the sprint races, which thus formed turning points.

On Tuesday, 11th September, Douglas Hawkes took 'Flying Spider' onto Brooklands for record breaking. The car now sported Hartford shock absorbers on the front wheels, cunningly arranged to turn with the steering, and was powered by a water-cooled ohc 8-valve Anzani engine. Outwardly this engine differed little from the air-cooled version except that a water pump was driven off the front of the timing cover, twin Zenith triple diffuser carburettors were fitted, and the magnetos had been replaced by CAV coil ignition. After establishing Class H 1 records for the flying kilometre and mile at 92.17 mph, Hawkes then adjourned until 13th September, when he made further attempts at short-distance records. Once again he was successful, establishing standing start records for the kilo, mile and 10 miles at 65.18 mph, 73.21 mph and 86.52 mph, and also the flying 5 miles at 88.99 mph. Obviously happier with the water-cooled engine, Hawkes then started to prepare for the JCC 200-mile race in October.

September also saw Norris at Kop Hill where he won the Essex MC three-wheeler class with his virtually unbeatable Blackburne racer. He was nearly twice as fast as Julian's Morgan and achieved fastest time in the class for cars up to 1500cc. On 17th September George Cowley's 988cc Morgan beat Bullough's KT JAP-engined Morgan

Horrocks's 'Kettle' in March. (Morgan Motor Co)

by 2 seconds to win the 1100cc class during the Morecombe Carnival meeting on the Morecombe-Lancaster New Road.

The Bexhill Speed Trials were held on 22nd September and once again Norris was virtually invincible, beating Ivy Cummings's GN to win the racing car classes of up to 1100cc and even up to 1500cc with a time of 29 seconds. Ivy Cummings could gain revenge only in the unlimited racing class with her other entry, the Bugatti, whilst S Constable completed the Morgan success by taking the 1100cc class for standard sports two-seaters with his MAG-engined Grand Prix with a time of 40 seconds.

It was obvious that Harry Hatch had designed a very good engine in the ohv Blackburne, and Norris and Beart especially were proving its paces. Very few production engines had been fitted to Morgans so far, although HFS was obviously impressed with its capabilities, for even standard KMA engines now claimed 35 bhp at 4000 rpm.

Only two Morgans took part in the 1923 ACU Six Days' Trial, both being Trials Standard models. Hall drove his MAG to a gold medal, but Carr's water-cooled

Hall leads Carr during the ACU Six Days', with Spouse's TB following. (James scrapbooks)

Morgan Sweeps the Board

Anzani was forced to retire during the final test, the high speed test on Brooklands, with a blown head gasket. The TB of Frank Spouse was also notable, winning the Hopwood Cup for the best individual performance in the trial.

For the JCC 200-mile race on 13th October HFS entered a team of three, Beart, Norris and Hawkes, the former two being powered by Blackburnes and the latter by an Anzani. Both Beart's and Norris's cars were returned to the factory for modification. As Norris's was a previous 200-mile veteran it needed little work, although the tail-mounted oil tank was reduced in size. Beart's car was fitted with a similar tail-mounted oil tank, leaving the bonnet space free for fuel. We believe that separate 5-gallon fuel tanks were also fitted beneath the chassis backbone tubes on both cars, to the design of HFS.

Douglas Hawkes's car was a modified wide-track flat-sided Aero, with its radiator moved back 8 inches to allow for the two Zenith carburettors on the ohc water-cooled 8-valve Anzani engine now transferred from 'Flying Spider'. This engine appears to have been uneconomical on oil and petrol, as the normal fuel tank was used for carrying its oil supply, and a special 14-gallon tank was fitted below the chassis backbone. Hartford shock absorbers were fitted to the front wheels as used on 'Flying Spider'.

All three cars were fitted with the latest straight-sided Dunlop rear wheel to counter any chance of tyre problems.

There were two private Morgan entries. EB Ware had entered the veteran JAP II fitted with a stretched (85.5 x 95mm, 1090cc) tuned KT water-cooled side-valve engine, with an additional fuel tank slung from the left side of the body. After many years of Morgan racing, Ware was at last using a footbrake, operating the usual band to the side of the rear wheel.

As Horrocks, the other private entrant, failed to turn up, only the four Morgans practised for the race. Ware was noted to be very fast and surprisingly quiet, a result of the silencer regulations enforced for the event after pressure from the local residents.

Harold Beart was using one of the latest developmental racing Blackburne engines, and Norris probably was as well. These were the KMB prototypes with larger crankpins and gudgeon pins than the side-valve-based KMAs. Unfortunately as practice progressed the big-end of Beart's engine began to fail, and as it was such a special engine he was unable to obtain a replacement being able to change only the rollers. As he drove from the paddock to the starting line on the day of the race itself, Beart felt the engine give out and thus had to withdraw.

As in 1922 the race was divided into two classes, with the 1100cc class starting first at 10 am. When the flag fell the Morgans all made good starts. As they came round for the first time, Norris and Hawkes were fourth and fifth to the three Salmsons. Ware was first into the pits with a puncture in the offside front wheel; indeed he was the only pits visitor during the first 50 miles. He had to return again later on to replace a steering connection which had been left off when he changed the wheel.

Norris meanwhile was really hounding the Salmsons. His was the only British car to get near them, impressing everyone with its speed and stability by lapping consistently at 84 mph. After forty laps, however, Norris began to drop back and was finally forced to retire on the forty-fifth lap with stripped timing gears.

The start of the 200-mile race, Hawkes leading the Morgans of Norris and Ware, with Heaton's Derby laying a smokescreen. (Autocar)

Hawkes who had been a distant fifth at the 50-mile mark, behind Norris and the Salmsons, was the first Morgan driver to leave the race. He developed engine trouble and after only thirty-one laps was forced to retire when a valve collar broke up.

Ware was way down the field, but running well after his early stops. He continued circling the track steadily until the finish, coming in seventh having covered sixty-nine laps.

The 1500cc class was run in the afternoon. Douglas Hawkes went out again, driving Mr Boston's Horstman to fifth place. Obviously he was a man of stamina even to contemplate 400 miles of bumpy Brooklands in one day, or perhaps he had known that his Morgan was unlikely to last the distance.

At the 1923 Olympia Motor Cycle Show the flat-sided Aero was replaced by a rounded-tail version. The flat-sided version could still be made to special order as the '200-mile Aero'. Also exhibited was a Blackburne-engined single-seater having a streamlined cowl over the crankcase and disc wheels.

During 1922 Val Page had designed a new racing 996cc (80mm x 99mm) side-valve JAP engine with twin camshafts, each having two cams. On Friday, 27th October 1922 this engine, when fitted in a Zenith motorcycle, had become the first to lap Brooklands at over 100 mph. When JAPs announced their models for 1924 this prototype became the basis for the KTR twin camshaft 976cc (85.5mm x 85mm) engine.

On 20th October the BMCRC ran a championship meeting. Event 9 was a five-lap scratch race for 1100cc three-wheeled cyclecars, the first ever three-wheeler championship. Six Morgans entered, Norris, Beart, and Ware from the 200-mile race, accompanied by Cowley, R Barker, and AB Johnson. From the outset no-one could doubt the supremacy of Norris who stormed to victory, setting up new records for the 10-mile standing start and 5-mile flying start in the process at 85.78 mph and 89.36 mph respectively, and finishing at an average speed of 86.77 mph. Only Beart, now with his KMB repaired once more, challenged Norris, but he fell out with tyre trouble as did Cowley. EB Ware brought 'JAP II' into a poor second place, but it was obvious that the side-valve engine was no match for the ohv Blackburne.

At the same meeting Bert le Vack had had an easy win in the sidecar championship using a new ohv 996cc JAP engine, again designed by Val Page. This was the prototype JTOR engine, having a bore and stroke of 80mm x 99mm. The bottom end assembly was based on the 4-cam KTR side-valve unit. Ball bearings were employed for the valve rockers, and ball and roller bearings were used throughout the engine. The cylinder heads were detachable, and contained hemispherical combustion chambers with large valves. Lubrication was via the new JAP oil pump, driven off one of the cam wheels through a worm reduction gear, and giving one stroke of the pump plunger for every forty engine revolutions. In tests on JAPs' Heenan and Froude dynamometer, the engine easily provided 31 bhp. As JAPs had no silencing or exhaust scavenging equipment in their test house in the early days, this must have been quite something to witness.

On 6th November Norris was back at Brooklands for the traditional Show time attempts at records. He was predictably successful, gaining the world's flying start mile and kilometer at 89.82 mph and 90.86 mph. Over the flying kilometer he maintained a one-way speed of 91.94 mph, a British record for any 1100cc cyclecar. Drawing attention to these recent achievements HFS commented: 'I venture to think that this is proof positive that the three-wheeler can hold the track at high speeds—a point which some critics have questioned.'

Once again the London-Exeter brought the racing year to a close with entries from Sawtell, Maskell, Beart, McCarthy, Holmes and Jacobs. Four or five Morgans followed one another down a wrong turning in Andover during a snow blizzard, causing quite a stir further along the route, but Sawtell, Maskell and Jacobs won gold medals.

Down at Fryers Garage in Hereford, a shy young man with a stammer was completing his apprenticeship. Born into a wealthy family involved in breweries, he had been given a 1912 Morgan by his mother at the age of thirteen in 1920. Named Ronald Tooms Horton, this young enthusiast had acquired one of the new style Aeros, complete with biplane mascot on the ohv Blackburne's radiator and immediately entered it in trials.

The first open trial of 1924 was held on 23rd February for the Colmore Cup. Horton entered his new Aero, registration number CJ 6343, in company with George Goodall, HFS, Chippendale, Norris, Weston and Bill Carr. This, the ninth Colmore Trial, was thought to be the severest so far organized, but Ronnie Horton completed it successfully to win a gold medal, as did Carr and HFS. Chippendale gained a silver and Goodall, who had problems with his chains jumping the sprockets, gained a bronze. Norris unfortunately was forced to retire with tyre trouble.

15th March saw Horton competing as one of the Morgan entries in the Victory Cup Trial with his new Aero, and also marked the date of the seventh General Efficiency Trial of the JCC. Two Morgans were entered, and both proved highly successful. EB Ware was the outright winner for the second successive year driving his KTC-engined Standard model Morgan, whilst Norman Norris driving one of the new type Aeros, carrying factory registration AB 16 and fitted with ohv Blackburne and front wheel brakes, came third. Between them the two Morgans were first in seven of the nine tests.

The same two drivers came away with the honours at the Essex MC Kop Hill Climb on 29th March, Norris taking his Blackburne racer to victory in the 'Sports' and 'Racing' classes for three-wheeled cyclecars, whilst EB Ware took his Standard model to victory in the touring class.

Ron Horton ploughs up Mill Lane in the Victor Cup Trial. (Autocar)

One week later the Western Centre of the ACU held the first open hill climb of 1924 at Chatcombe Pitch. Passengered as usual by Ruth, HFS drove AB 16, one of the new Aeros with front wheel brakes and ohv Blackburne engine, to tie for first place with George Goodall, who was driving the wide-track flat-sided Aero he had been borrowing from the factory in 1923. They achieved this double victory despite delays caused by smoke crossing the course from a nearby bush fire. Clive Lones was the other Morgan entrant to record over 50 mph up the 1 in 10 to 1 in 20 hill, his Morgan now having the correct engine for speed, the ohv Blackburne.

Having comfortably won the Easter BMCRC five-lap 1100cc passenger handicap, Norris returned to Brooklands for the JCC meeting on 3rd May. Although he was heavily fancied to win the 1100cc handicap from scratch position, it was soon apparent that Harold Beart's was actually the faster Morgan. Beart, on 14 seconds, finished a very close second to Hall's Frazer-Nash which started on 42 seconds. When the Grand ten-lap Handicap was run off, Norris found some extra speed for some very quick laps but sadly retired on the third.

Beart had by now finished his engineering apprenticeship and had rented a couple of lock-up garages in Croydon from a Mrs Stacey. Here he spent his time preparing his Morgan for racing. Often he would visit his friend Harry Hatch, at the house he shared with his two brothers and his father in the Blackburne factory grounds in Surrey. Naturally Beart thus gained access to the latest Blackburne developments and this co-operation was now obviously paying dividends. Beart's 200-mile Aero was running

Morgan Sweeps the Board

with neat wind scallops on the scuttle in an attempt to improve streamlining.

The London-Land's End Trial on Good Friday featured no less than thirteen Morgans, including the immaculate Mr and Mrs Morgan dressed in snow-white overalls, but only four gained golds.

Easter continued with the Easter Monday hill climb of the Chester and District MC and LCC at Llinegar Hill near Mostyn. In the 1100cc class Bullough's JAP-engined Morgan came third, victory going to Basil Davenport's GN and second place to Wilson's Anzani-Morgan.

The ACU Stock Machine Trial this year was a family affair. HFS and Ruth drove a side-valve JAP-powered Aero, Mr and Mrs Goodall an MAG-engined Grand Prix, and Mr and Mrs Carr a side-valve Blackburne engined Standard model, all the engines being water-cooled. All the Morgans used gears of 5 to 1 and 10.75 to 1, and were fitted with front wheel brakes. Each husband and wife team gained a gold medal, and the three pairs together won the team prize. Carr's side-valve Blackburne made a particularly favourable impression.

Goodall had had enough of the unreliable 8-valve racing Anzani. Consequently, the wide-track flat-sided Aero he borrowed from the factory was accordingly converted to take the ohv Blackburne. It was also strengthened across the front frame with bracing tubes from the front crosshead to the lower chassis tubes behind the engine. Goodall named the car 'Jim' after the nickname 'Sonny Jim' given to his son. On 10th May he took the car to the SUNBAC Angel Bank hill climb, using the registration NP 4061 from the car he had recently driven in the ACU Stock Machine Trial. Heavy rain delayed the proceedings but HFS's Blackburne Aero proved the fastest of the cyclecars, winning the 1100cc class in $30\frac{3}{5}$ seconds, over 3 seconds ahead of Goodall. Bob Blake, son of a Nottingham stockbroker, Sir Arthur Blake, and a very close friend of Morgan's Nottingham agent, Jack Sylvester, tied with Goodall for second place with his Blackburne-engined flat-sided Aero and won the 1100cc handicap event.

The same day saw a remarkable occurrence at Brooklands when all the competitors at the BMCRC meeting refused to race, in protest against noise restrictions which were preventing certain cars from going onto the track. These restrictions were the result of complaints from the local residents, who took strong exception to the noise generated

HFS and Ruth in the Stock Machine Trial. (Morgan Motor Co)

Events Galore

Bob Blake at Clipstone Drive. (Sylvester collection)

by Brooklands. They naturally placed the track authorities responsible in an extremely delicate position. The 'strike' committee viewed the restrictions with grave apprehension and urged the sport's governing bodies to take action to restore their previous freedom. Amongst the entrants for this meeting had been Harold Beart, Norman Norris and EB Ware.

Another popular course for speed trials in the 1920s was a private drive on the estate of the Duke of Portland at Clipstone near Mansfield. This was home ground for Nottingham Morgan agent Jack Sylvester, who had entered earlier events with Velocette motorcycles. For the event on 17th May he entered a KMA Blackburne-engined Aero, carrying the factory registration AB 16. Bob Blake also entered a flat-sided Aero with KMA engine and aluminium bonnet panel. Both cars ran without front wheel brakes. Bob won the 1100cc passenger machine general class, $\frac{3}{4}$ seconds faster than Jack and much faster than his 1923 attempt with a standard Anzani CC-engined Aero. For these events, Bob and Jack passengered one another, but when the Mansfield Club Championship was run later in the evening Jack ran solo. He clocked $21\frac{3}{5}$ seconds, knocking 2 seconds off his previous time but could only finish in third place, at a speed of 83.33 mph

On 31st May the Wye Valley MC and LC and Midland Car Clubs co-promoted speed trials along a road within the Shell-filling factory complex at Rotherwas near

Morgan Sweeps the Board

Hereford. The course was hardly ideal. The road was badly rutted and steeply cambered, and a thunderstorm in the late afternoon made it positively dangerous; in fact, the meeting had to be abandoned later on after a couple of bad motorcycle spills. Each competitor was allowed two runs over the flying-$\frac{1}{2}$ mile. On the first run, Goodall in the red Morgan 'Jim' beat HFS driving a Blackburne-engine Aero with new enlarged front wheel brakes. The second run reversed the positions when HFS, in spite of some wild skids, made fastest time of the day in 25.6 seconds, over 1 second faster than Captain Harvey's racing Alvis. As usual, Goodall had also entered his MAG-engined trials car. This cleaned up the classes for touring cars with a time of 33 seconds, whereas Harvey's touring Alvis could only manage 34.6 seconds.

On 7th June Brooklands saw Beart once again in winning form. He won the three-lap private owners' handicap for any class of motorcycle, after starting on scratch and running right though the field to win by 50 yards, at a speed of 84.70 mph, from Michael McEvoy on one of his own make of Anzani-powered motorcycles.

Thursday 10th July brought the annual Madresfield Speed Trials. As expected Harold Beart won the experts' and general classes up to 1100cc, with a time over the standing start kilometre of $41\frac{3}{5}$ seconds. The surprise of the day was the time of Clive Lones who clocked $38\frac{3}{5}$ seconds in the members only 1100cc class, easily beating Lewis's Frazer-Nash and Horton's Aero. Clive, passengered as usual by his wife Nel, was running his stripped ohv Blackburne Aero, registration number NP 4200.

Also amongst the award winners was a new name to Morgans – that of Robert Rainsforth (Robin) Jackson. Robin's father had been connected with the introduction of gas-welding techniques to the Clyde shipyards, but since his death Robin and his mother had lived in Malvern. Robin's first Morgan had been a pre-war side-valve JAP-engined De Luxe model, purchased second-hand from Boddington of Worcester circa 1922, and later fitted with an MAG engine. He had now acquired a new Aero, registration number NP 3394, with which he clocked 49 1/5 seconds.

Two days later Beart was at Brooklands for the BMCRC races, renewing his battle with Norris. Two 50-mile races were on the card, with a three-lap private owners'

Norris (1) and Beart (2) get away in the 50-mile handicap (Mrs Dawes collection)

Events Galore

handicap sandwiched between them. The two Morgan Blackburnes were entered in the final 50-mile event, and both started on scratch. By half-distance Beart had drawn out a useful half-lap lead from his sister three-wheeler, but as he roared past the Vicker's sheds on his eleventh lap his engine developed a nasty misfire. He stopped on the railway straight, to pull out with plug trouble. Norris meanwhile continued to circulate rapidly but was unable to catch Vic Horsmann's winning Triumph outfit, although he had averaged 84.23 mph. Beart had been passengered by Joe Stacey, son of the friendly Mrs Stacey from whom he rented his lock-ups. He had slightly modified his Aero for Brooklands by fitting a stronger chassis tie bar, but he was still unhappy with the strength and quality of the engineering on the production Morgan. To the accompaniment of tea and cakes from Mrs Stacey, he had been spending many hours formulating ideas on how to improve the design of racing Morgans. Amongst those he was regularly tapping for inspiration was the Blackburne designer, Harry Hatch.

Three Morgans entered the Scottish Six Days' Trial which started on Monday, 21st July. HFS and Ruth, attired in spotless white, reported in a very smart blue Trials Standard model with a KT JAP engine, while Bill Carr drove his usual NP65, now with a side-valve Blackburne engine under the Standard model's bonnet. Frank Spouse had switched allegiance from the TB three-wheeler to become the Scottish Morgan agent and he drove a KMA Blackburne-engined Aero. HFS drove impeccably as always to win a silver cup. Spouse failed on the Inverfarigaig and Loch Losgoinn observed

An immaculate HFS and Ruth with their blue Morgan on Diabaig in the Scottish Trial. (Motor Cycle)

Morgan Sweeps the Board

sections, gaining a silver medal. Poor Bill Carr crashed into the wall on Tornapress on the third day, bending back the front crosshead which forced his retirement. Carr was not immobilized however: two brawny Highland spectators spent several hours straightening things out with rocks, enabling him to return slowly to Inverness under his own power.

Both Jack Sylvester and Bob Blake travelled up to Sheffield with Jack's aluminium-bonneted KMA Aero for the Sheffield and Hallamshire MCC's flying ½-mile Ringinglowe Road Speed hill climb. The short rolling start took advantage of a dip in the road, enabling the participants to put on speed before crossing the start and entering the 1 in 20 rise. Freddie James, the Sheffield Morgan agent, had been entering these annual events for the past couple of years but his local knowledge failed to prevent Jack and Bob driving Jack's Aero to win a class each. Jack remembers that after his run Freddie James and supporters were a little disturbed at the weird smell of his exhaust, believing him to be using an illegal fuel. In fact, Jack was using newly made exhaust pipes and the smell was merely that of some resin remaining inside the pipes from when he had been bending them into shape.

On the same day, Goodall in 'Jim' and Jackson driving his ohv Blackburne-engined

Jack Sylvester and Bob Blake get under way with a push start at Ringinglowe Road. (Sylvester collection)

Events Galore

Aero NP 3394 were competing at the ACU Wessex Centre event on Kingsdown Hill, near Bath. Despite intermittent rain, and a crowd that kept encroaching dangerously onto the narrow road, Goodall's racer gained second place in 24 seconds in the 1000cc sidecar and 1100cc three-wheeler class; Jackson, some 4⅘ seconds slower, achieved third.

At Southport on 23rd August both the Horrocks replicas made an appearance. John Miles Bullough's car, which he had named 'Creeping Jane', proved the most successful, gaining four firsts and two thirds. Bullough was a real character on the sand, always wearing a battered bowler hat, held on with a rubber band and pulled well over his ears. 'Creeping Jane' seems to have relied only on a foot brake for stopping: there would be less drag with just one band brake, an advantage in straight line sprinting.

The other Horrocks replica had been purchased from Bullough's garage by Albert Moss. He could only finish second to Bullough on this occasion, his car having the normal hand and foot band brakes on the rear wheel.

In August 1924 JAPs made a new vee twin engine available. The JTOR prototype used by le Vack during the current season was the basis for the new engine. In order to allow it to be fitted within standard size motorcycle frames, it was necessary to reduce the overall height of the cylinders. Consequently, the bore and stroke of the KT series was adopted, giving 976cc. This new engine, the KTOR, featured a patented automatic lubrication system using a new mechanically timed rotary sleeve valve to regulate crank case breathing. This had entailed some modifications to the crankcase. JAP took this opportunity to introduce the same crankcases on their future 4-cam side-valve engine (KTR). The big end contained four rows of rollers held in place by washers at the sides. Plain domed aluminium pistons with buffed heads were fitted featuring fully floating gudgeon pins with aluminium end caps.

For the JCC 200-mile race on 20th September, HFS entered Norris and Beart, and as usual recalled their Morgans to the factory for overhaul. EB Ware entered privately once more, but pensioned off 'JAP II', commissioning Morgan to build him a wide-track flat-sided Aero similar to that of Norris. All three cars used the additional 5-gallon fuel tanks fitted under the chassis backbone tubes and had small oil tanks on the tails.

Although JAPs had been concentrating on side-valve engines for Morgans, the recent successes of the ohv Blackburne coupled with the success of the new JTOR engine in le Vack's motorcycle had made them reconsider. For this 200-mile race EB Ware was to run a prototype ohv water-cooled unit of 1090cc (85.5 x 95mm), incorporating many of the features of le Vack's engine. Although based on the old '90 bore' used after the war, Val Page's new design featured transverse rocker arms running in single row ball and needle roller bearings, spaced at 3⅜ inch centres, housed in lugs cast integrally with the now detachable cylinder heads. Because of the resemblance of these lugs to part of a certain animal's anatomy, this and the later production engines became known as 'dog ear' JAPs. The hemispherical cylinder heads contained two valves at 45 degrees to each other. The bottom end of the engine was based on the new KTOR JAP, featuring the 4-cam layout and rotary valve oiling system. Oil was still introduced to the passenger-side cylinder. The water passage from head to barrel did not rely on coring passages, but on hollow bosses cast on the sides of

Morgan Sweeps the Board

the water jackets of both parts, which were united when the head was in place and made water-tight by suitable washers, whilst the main head gasket was of plain annealed copper.

During practice all the Morgans had problems. Ware's engine was blowing gaskets and he was troubled with driving chains. For practice he was passengered by a young apprentice from JAPs named Harold Christmas, but Prestwich wanted someone of experience for the race itself, picking TR Allchin, a noteworthy motorcycle racer. Arthur Church, Ware's regular passenger, was to be pit attendant following his wife's refusal to let him race after she had a premonition of an accident.

Both Beart and Norris were working on their Morgans up to the last minute. Norris was trying twin ML magnetos, placed one above the other, and he at least was definitely using straight-sided wheels and tyres all round (we suspect that the others were as well). The bonnet louvres of Norris's car were cut away leaving rectangular holes beneath the bonnet fuel tank.

The JCC decided to run all three classes (1500cc, 1100cc and the new 750cc class) together, lining the cars up at the start in three rows according to class. Once again the Salmsons were 1100cc class favourites, driven by Wilson-Jones, Count Zborowski and ex-Morgan racer Douglas Hawkes. True to form, Wilson-Jones streaked into an early lead, followed by Hawkes and then Norris on the first Morgan. EB Ware was in trouble right away, his engine refusing to pick up, and he brought up the rear. Norris soon settled down to a ding-dong battle with Zborowski's Salmson, but Ware's bad luck continued as he pulled into the pits with a broken top gear dog.

It was not long before all three Morgans hit trouble: Ware pushed his machine into the pits for further adjustment, Beart came in with a flat rear tyre, and Norris free-wheeled in with a broken top gear chain. After a long pit stop Beart eventually succeeded in fitting a new rear tyre, but the Blackburne engine now refused to fire despite vigorous attempts at push starting and needed further attention.

Once he had rejoined the race, Ware settled down to lap at around 90 mph, until his rear wheel suddenly began to wobble. Ware himself looked anxiously behind, but carried on until the thirty-fifth lap when the car swerved across the track opposite the fork and collided with the iron fencing opposite the pits. It spun round several times and threw out the occupants before turning over. Ware landed on the grass, unconscious, while Allchin was flung onto the concrete, splitting his crash helmet almost in two. Allchin got up and staggered towards the track side but then collapsed to be carried off semi-conscious. Both men required hospitalization.

Meanwhile the race went on. Beart's engine had fired and he was back in the race, but after two laps he returned to the pits to attack the rear bodywork with a hacksaw, to provide more clearance for the rear wheel. Norris, the only real opposition to the Salmsons, was also forced to call at the pits towards the end of the race. Although he was back circling the track at the end, he had no chance of finishing the distance in time. The class had been won so easily by Wilson-Jones's Salmson, followed at some distance by Ringwood's Frazer Nash.

The cause of Ware's crash provoked much speculation at the time. In fact, the tread on the rear tyre had stripped off and become caught in one of the driving chains, locking the rear wheel solid. Following a two year stay in Weybridge Cottage Hospital

EB Ware at the pits before his accident. (Autocar)

recovering from the crash Ware claimed that his racing was an extension of his duties at JAPs, and therefore that he was entitled to compensation from his employers. This claim was refuted as he had entered privately. After this episode, JA Prestwich drew up contracts of employment indemnifying the company, which all employees were obliged to sign. Ware himself never raced again but retained close links with the sport, finally becoming a stipendiary steward to the Speedway Control Board.

Ware's crash had far-reaching consequences for the three-wheeler movement, as the JCC immediately barred them from future events. Protests were made to the RAC but fell on stony ground since they reminded everyone that three-wheelers came under the jurisdiction of the ACU and really shouldn't have been racing against four-wheelers in the first place.

Just one week later over 10,000 people lined the course on the sands at Birkdale for the Southport sand races. In the 1-mile sprints, Albert Moss with his sv JAP-engined Horrocks replica proved most successful, winning the 1100cc general and novices' events, whilst Bullough in his similar machine, wearing his famous bowler hat pulled down over his ears, won the 1500cc general class and came second in the 2000cc class.

On Saturday, 11th October the BMCRC ran their second annual track championship meeting. Rain disrupted the event before the 1100cc scratch three-wheeler championship, which was consequently run off the following Wednesday. Beart and Norris were the two Morgan contestants with their 200-mile Blackburnes, still carrying their team numbers on the tails. Norris gained a very slight lead in the first lap which he held for the next three. On the last lap, Beart gave it everything, passing Norris on the members' banking to win by 30 yards at 83.99 mph.

Beart's car had shown itself at last to be the fastest of the two Blackburnes, and it was he who returned to Brooklands for the Showtime record spree. Only two days later he took the two-seater 1100cc records for the flying start 5 miles and standing start 10 miles at 94.33 mph and 89.88 mph respectively. Three days later and he was out again, this time taking the British flying start kilometre and mile at 94.74 mph and 93.11 mph. On 6th November he drove without a passenger to claim the world's flying mile for 1100cc single-seaters at 94.21 mph.

Blackburnes had built probably only three special KMB racing engines, which were unique in having steel internal flywheels. Obviously Beart and Norris had one a piece, and we suspect that HFS at this time had the third. These three engines incorporated all the latest thinking from Harry Hatch and were to prove formidable for many years to come.

The London-Exeter Trial held on 26th December was blessed by howling gales and torrential rain, but few of the Morgans used their relatively inefficient hoods. Amongst the failures was a young batchelor in the jewellery trade named Geoff Harris, having his first taste of Morgan competition. Although retiring on this occasion Geoff Harris was to become a trials driver to be reckoned with in later years.

1924 was to be the last year of Morgan racing for Norman Norris, as he was offered a drive for Lea Francis in a factory-prepared racer for 1925. Consequently the famous flat-sided Aero passed to his brother Bernard's garage in Birmingham, the local Rhode agency.

Robin Jackson was now at Cambridge University reading engineering, where he

Some of the wet London-Exeter competitors at Staines. 232 – BBF Russell; 233 – AC Maskell; 236 – MJP McMahon. (Motor Cycling)

naturally supported its motor club. On 28th February he drove for the Cambridge University AC team against Oxford in the Intervarsity speed hill climb at Aston Clinton near Tring. Robin was driving a new Morgan, a Blackburne-engined flat-sided Aero, registration number NP 5504, fitted with wind scallops rather like those on Beart's Aero, and the latest flared Aero wings. One of his fellow team members was Keith Prowse, driving another Blackburne Aero featuring disc wheels and a streamlined cone in front of the crankcase. Both appeared very fast, Jackson eventually proving to be 1¼ seconds faster than Prowse but 5 seconds slower than one of their rivals, Arnott in a Brough Superior. The Oxford team won the unlimited class although Cambridge turned out to be victorious overall.

That Jackson's car had similarities to Beart's was not surprising, as Jackson had been helping Beart at his Croydon premises near the railway station. During 1924 Beart had started to organize his ideas as to what constituted the ultimate in racing

Keith Prowse on Aston Clinton hill. (Jackson collection)

A different cornering technique for Robin Jackson. (Jackson collection)

Morgans, and had now begun construction of his brainchild. He had located an old cycle maker living locally who provided invaluable help with the project. Beart basically thought the standard Morgan too crudely engineered and too flimsy for racing. His plans were for a much stronger version incorporating the latest engineering principals.

Three sets of chassis lugs were cast from patterns produced by his cycle maker, and one set was machined up by this same individual who expertly brazed the widened chassis together using heavier gauge tubing. The bevel box was redesigned, being wider and stronger than the current production version and featuring adjustable ball races allowing the bevels to be accurately meshed together. As Beart recently commented, 'the factory bash with the hammer wasn't quite good enough for me.' The rear forks were sprung on 7-leaf quarter-elliptic springs and a Hartford shock absorber was attached to a hoop over the rear wheel for damping. At the front special steel sliding axles were cast and machined to allow Hartford shock absorbers to be fitted, a feature similar to that used by Hawkes in 1923, and the normal tubular centre pins were replaced by hardened and ground Ubas steel pins screwed in position and arranged for pressure-gun grease lubrication.

The classical Morgan twisted strip steel steering link was replaced by tubing and the steering connections by spring-loaded ball joints. A Ford Model 'T' epicyclic steering reduction box was fitted into the steering column, a system that had been developed to overcome the heaviness of the direct Morgan method. Such a system was not new: it had been used by Bernard Whomes, an electrical salesman of Bexley Heath, in his Anzani-racing Morgan in 1923, finding favour both on the road and at Brooklands.

To avoid the inevitable friction, band brakes were dispensed with completely, and non-Morgan internally expanding brakes were fitted to the front wheels, operated by an outside hand brake. Mounted with the hand brake was the gear lever, spring loaded to prevent jumping out of gear, and to the top of it was fitted a magneto cut-out button to facilitate fast gear changes without declutching or closing the foot-operated throttle.

There were two fuel tanks: the HFS-designed 5-gallon tank from Beart's old 200-mile Aero was fitted under the frame backbone tube, and this was to be supplemented by a separate 9-gallon tank in the body for long distances.

Oil was supplied to the racing KMB engine, also out of Beart's Aero, through two drip feed lubricators, adjustable by the passenger, from a large tank behind the driver. It was supplied to the transmission chains by copper pipes from a drip feed fed by a separate pressurized tank. For Brooklands, gears of 3.33 to 1 and 5.95 to 1 were chosen.

The 1924 KMB engine was fed by a Brown and Barlow 'Prayerbook' carburettor which had the advantage of operating like a perfect venturi when on full throttle. Air was given a slight boost by forward facing air rams leading to a metal bowl set on edge behind the carburettor.

Beart had the body designed by a member of the local RAF station and streamlined according to aeroplane practice. It could be quickly removed from the chassis for maintenance.

A lot of time had been spent on designing and constructing the car. Indeed, probably the only true Morgan parts on it were the front springs. Even the wheels were modified, having taper roller bearings fitted to them as well as the latest Dunlop well base rims for

One of the Morgans squeezes by an obstructing car in the Colmore at the foot of Bushcombe hill. (Autocar)

the Dunlop racing tyres (26 x 3.75 inches at the front and 27 x 4.20 inches at the rear). Doubtless Mrs Stacey had supplied Beart and his happy band of workers with many cups of tea and biscuits over the year.

In the Victory Cup Trial in March 1925 HFS won a gold medal, as did Bernard Norris, Norman's brother, with a Rhode. A silver was won by George Goodall but poor Chippendale locked his wheels and turned over during the braking test. Goodall, passengered as usual by Cecil Jay, was using NP 636 but had replaced the MAG engine with a water-cooled Anzani. As the bonnet no longer fitted over this wider engine they competed without it.

Back on Southport sands bowler-hatted Bullough beat Moss's similar Horrocks replica for the 1100cc general class on 21st March, although Moss himself won the novices' class. Bullough also won the 2000cc class from Basil Davenport's GN 'Spider'. Like Moss's similar car, Bullough's 'Creeping Jane' was fitted with the popular Ford

George Goodall and Cecil Jay in the Victory Cup Trial. (Goodall scrapbooks)

Model T epicyclic steering box conversion.

It was not always easy to persuade the police authorities to close certain stretches of public road just for the purposes of speed trials. If inconvenience to the public was thought likely to be minimal, the chief constable would usually give his consent and despatch constables to attend in order to control spectators. The whole position was very odd, as these constables were then expected to ignore the competitors' repeated breaking of the nationwide 20 mph speed limit.

Towards the end of 1924, Mr Justice McCardie in a case heard by him in the Kings Bench Division pronounced such speed events illegal; as the police had no right to restrict access to a public right of way. The counties of Warwick, Worcester and Stafford immediately complied with this ruling, banning future events in their territories.

What finally sealed the fate of speed trials was an unfortunate accident at the Essex MC Kop event on 28th March. Francis Giveen driving an ex-Raymond Mays Bugatti

Morgan Sweeps the Board

Goodall in 'Jim' at the Whitecross Road speed trials. (Goodall scrapbooks)

hit a spectator and broke his leg, causing the RAC to stop the meeting. As a result committees of the RAC and the ACU met and decided to withhold further permits for such events. However, further meetings featuring Morgans were to be held before the enforcement of the ban took effect.

On Saturday, 4th April the Western Centre of the ACU held flying ½-mile speed trials on the Whitecross Road leading towards Hay-on-Wye from Hereford. George Goodall in his Blackburne racer 'Jim' proved unbeatable, winning the RAC plaque for the fastest 1100cc cyclecar with a time of 24⅕ seconds. Robin Jackson had enlisted Beart's help in getting to the meeting, transporting his Aero on Beart's old Cleveland lorry. Unfortunately this blew the head gasket near Cirencester, so poor Jackson had to drive the Morgan the rest of the way. The journey was worth it, however, as he came second to Goodall with a time of 25⅖ seconds, which gave him victory in the closed to club 1100cc competition, just beating Clive Lones. Other Morgans were driven by

Events Galore

HFS, who could only record 26⅔ seconds and Bob Blake. Naturally, all were powered by ohv Blackburnes.

On the same day the West of England flying ¼-mile speed trials were held on Brentor Straight near Tavistock. Local amateur H Dobbs did very well with his Blackburne Morgan, winning the 1100cc open class and coming joint second with Walsgrove's Riley to Joyce's flying AC in the 1500cc class. In the unlimited open class Dobbs was timed at 81 mph to come third behind winner Joyce's AC and Walters's 10½ litre Peugeot in second place.

Thus the era of public road speed trials closed on a high note for Morgans. From now on they were to be severely restricted in their ability to compete against their four-wheeled 1100cc cousins, although some events did continue in private grounds. At Brooklands, the JCC ban restricted Morgans to motorcycle events. The motoring press carried a great deal of comment on the JCC's desertion of the three-wheeled cyclecar, as the club had, after all, been formed from the Cyclecar Club. Luckily sand racing at Southport was to continue, unaffected by the ACU and RAC bans.

Still Faster

When Ronald Horton's parents died he moved to live with his uncle in Birmingham. Here he purchased Norman Norris's racing Aero from the garage of Bernard Norris. He registered the car as OM 4000 on 8th April 1925. It was fitted with a KMB Blackburne engine and reputedly weighed only 5 cwt. Now that three-wheeler racing on Brooklands was severely restricted, Horton was to become a regular and noteworthy racer on Southport sands. He began this new career on 18th April. Racing his recent acquisition without the new regulation Brooklands silencers fitted by Norris towards the latter half of 1924, Horton made a clean sweep of the 1100cc awards, beating Bullough and Moss in the general class as well as winning the novices' award. That was not all, for only Joyce's amazing AC stopped him from winning the 1500cc and 2000cc classes outright. He was again the fastest novice in both of these classes and the 3000cc. Horton also won the 10-mile sidecar race, although in the 10-mile car race he had to give first place to Walker's large Peugeot after Joyce retired. Local Southport exponent Bullough, now with one of the new KTOR engines in 'Creeping Jane', won the 2000cc class for single-seater racing cars, and gained a class win, one second and three thirds.

Compared with Brooklands, Southport was the venue of the true amateur. There were no pits here for expensive equipment, just individual piles of spanners and fuel tins left on the sands. Even the course was unknown until just before the start, when tests were carried out to find the hardest parts of the foreshore. Ronnie Horton, although now wealthy, was always kept short of ready cash, often setting off for the sands from Birmingham at 4 am with only 10 shillings in his pocket. Wins became essential in order for him to convince the Castrol man that he was worthy of some free

Morgan Sweeps the Board

Castrol R racing oil; this he would promptly sell for money to buy petrol to return home.

The restrictions on speed trials had not affected long-distance trials, which continued normally. In the London-Land's End in April, excess speed proved the downfall of several Morgans. On Porlock hill Collier's Anzani Aero turned over, and Russell's Blackburne Morgan fell on its side; at South Molton, 'Jumbo' Goddard hit a bank with his Anzani Morgan, badly damaging the front crosshead and wheels and requiring medical attention, while at Blue Hills Mine SG Smith crashed into a wall injuring the foot of a spectator. The experienced Holmes, McCarthy, Maskell and Hall all drove safely however, to win gold medals.

In the 1000-mile ACU Stock Machine Trial Morgans were represented by George Goodall and Cecil Jay in an Anzani CC-engined Aero, registration number AB 16, and by Bill Carr driving a side-valve JAP Morgan De Luxe. Both Goodall and Carr arrived in style for the start on 27th April at the Birmingham BSA factory, chauffered by HFS in his 1922 Silver Ghost Rolls-Royce. Goodall drove for two days without rocker covers and suffered plug troubles, but both Morgans showed up well and won gold medals.

The sand racing season continued at Southport on 16th May with six Morgans entered. Ronnie Horton once again took the 1100cc general class from Moss in his Horrocks replica, now fitted with a 4-cam side-valve JAP (KTR). However, Moss did win the 1100cc novices' class from newcomer Syd Keay of Prescott, who was driving a Blackburne-engined Aero. Ron Horton had now replaced the brakeless straight-sided front wheels used by Norris with some beaded edged wheels fitted with brakes, presumably to help him in the corners in the 10-mile race. After lying third at one stage, he finished unplaced.

In addition to sand racing, speed trials were now being held in all sorts of odd places to overcome the ban on public roads. Way back on 13th April the Mansfield and

On Southport Sands for the May meeting are the Morgans of Bullough (with bowler hat), Moss, Horton, and, in the distance, Orford. (Warnick collection)

Still Faster

Keith Prowse stirs up the dust. (Jackson collection)

District MC and LCC had borrowed a road in Rufford Colliery grounds, by kind permission of the Bolsover Colliery Company. Jack Sylvester proved faster than clubmate Bob Blake, both Blackburne-powered, to win the 1500cc light car class.

On 16th May the North London MCC wouldn't even disclose to outsiders the Hertfordshire venue of their speed trials. Keith Prowse's Aero Blackburne came second to Baragwaneth's Brough Superior in the unlimited sidecar class.

The London-Edinburgh Trial had ceased to become a test of hill climbing: indeed, for 1925 there wasn't a single observed hill. Hall decided he would attempt this trial with a 1912 Morgan, purchased a few days beforehand for £12. He succeeded, but failed to gain an award.

A two-day sand meeting was held on Skegness foreshore on 8th and 9th June, tempting Ronnie Horton and Jack Sylvester into entering. Jack was using his usual

Morgan Sweeps the Board

Jack Sylvester on Skegness sands, with his rear wheel on 'Jack's Plank'. (Sylvester collection)

aluminium bonneted flat-sided Blackburne Aero, with rear shock absorber. He started with his rear wheel on 'Jacks plank', a plank of wood under the back wheel for initial grip. Only three entries were received for the class for 1100cc sports models, but the scrutineers deemed that Horton's racer and Croft's Austin Seven contravened the regulations, allowing Jack a walkover victory. The second day's racing saw Horton successfully winning both his heat and the final in the unlimited capacity handicap, still using the beaded-edge front wheels.

The Madresfield Speed Trials were of course held on the private drive of the Earl of Beauchamp's estate. The 1925 meeting, held on 11th July, turned out to be a bit of a disaster for the Morgan drivers. Of the seven making runs, five either failed to finish or passed the timekeeper misfiring badly. The bright star in the Morgan firmament was HC Lones who with a time of $38\frac{3}{5}$ seconds won the cup for the fastest amateur driver of a car or three-wheeler up to 1500cc, presented by Robin Jackson and his mother Mrs Valentine Jackson, as well as winning HFS's cup for the fastest Morgan. Lones was using his Blackburne Aero, registration number NP 4200 as in the previous year, but

Still Faster

stripped of mudguards and windscreens. He finished over 10 seconds ahead of Broughton Eyre's Morgan. The failures were Goodall, Jackson, Ridley, Beart and Horton.

Beart, finding little opportunity for entering races at Brooklands with his new racer, was busy preparing to attack records. He had rented one of the sheds inside the track adjacent to the Blackburne shed, making tuning very easy. On Tuesday, 21st July, he went out and took the standing 10 kilometres at 88.78 mph, and the flying 5 miles and 5 kilometres at 99.10 mph and 99.62mph respectively. There last figures were so close to the magic 100 mph that Beart returned the following Saturday. For the flying 5 miles he just failed in his ambition, although beating his previous time, recording 99.67 mph. But for the flying 5 kilometres he recorded 100.40 mph, the very first time the 100 mph barrier had been broken during any cyclecar record attempt. Beart was obviously now the king of the Morgan. Many Morgan speedmen were to visit him for help and advice at his Croydon premises, including Ron Horton with his ex-Norris racer.

On 1st August Rufford Colliery was once again the unlikely venue of speed trials, using the smooth tarmacked 1 in 20 hill which stretched through wild moorland towards the grim pithead and large slagheap. Three Morgans entered, those of Horton, Jackson and Bob Blake, all being Blackburne-powered as usual. Although the programme had Jack Sylvester down to drive Blake's Aero, in order to avoid the displeasure of the Blake family, Bob did in fact drive it in the trial, coming third at 66.1 mph to Horton's 70.2 mph and Jackson's 66.5 mph.

Only one Morgan apiece entered the two six-day events, both winning gold medals—Frank Spouse in the Scottish Six Days', and Bill Carr in the International Six Days'. Bill Carr drove a water-cooled Anzani-engined Trials Standard, NP 65, and helped his East Midland Centre team to win the British Motor Cycling Championship with a brilliant display, losing only one time mark.

Speed trials continued in profusion at private venues. At Gopsall Park on the estate of Lord Waring, Jack Sylvester took home two firsts, and then bettered this at Stalybridge on the Carrbrook private road with no less than six. At this same meeting, local driver John Bullough was rather upset to be beaten by Ron Horton in the racing classes.

Fine weather greeted the competitors at Southport sands on 15th August. Horton had to accept second-best to Basil Davenport's GN in the 1500cc class, but otherwise excelled, gaining six of the eight Morgan victories. Syd Keay, passengered by the acrobatic Alf Slinger, won the 1100cc novices' class in his Blackburne Aero from Albert Moss, and John Miles Bullough took the unlimited three-wheeler novices' class (a driver ceased to be a novice after three wins). Three of Horton's class wins were gained in one event, the 10-mile car race around the posts at either end of the mile straight. Things might have been a great deal different if the straight eight Miller of Higgins, the early leader, hadn't burst into flames after five laps.

On 19th August Beart took his streamliner onto Brooklands again to pulverize the previous world-class H2 records for the flying mile and kilometre, recording 102.65 mph and 103.37 mph respectively as the average speed over each. One run of the flying kilometre was covered at 104.68 mph making Beart's Morgan the fastest unsupercharged car in the world under 1500cc—an achievement HFS was delighted to

Morgan Sweeps the Board

publicize on his show stand later in the year.

Robin Jackson took his Blackburne Aero up to Colwyn Bay for the 5th September meeting, when he won the unlimited sidecar general class on the wet promenade, although Hudson's 1000cc Tornado Anzani won the experts' class. Two weeks later Hudson was battling against other Morgans on the other side of the Pennines in the Doncaster Petrol St Leger Speed Trials, the oldest speed event in the north. Together with the Broughs of Patchett (winner) and Baragwaneth he beat the Blackburne Morgans of Freddie James and Bob Blake into fourth and fifth place in the unlimited sidecar class for experts, although Bob did take home a bronze medal for the general section.

The 12th September Southport sands meeting saw Clive Lones join in the action with his Blackburne Aero. He immediately tasted success, beating Ron Horton in the flying kilometre 1100cc class, although Horton gained revenge in the similar event over 1 mile from a standing start. Syd Keay with the acrobatic Slinger gained two novices' wins with his Blackburne Aero. Lones's victory had shown that Horton was not the invincible driver he had appeared to be earlier in the season.

The end-of-the-year record-breaking stint continued with Beart taking H2 records up to 100 miles on 18th September. He covered 100 miles effortlessly at 91.54 mph, breaking the 50 kilo, 50 mile, 100 kilo and 1 hour records in the process. On 7th October Robin Jackson took his stripped Blackburne Aero onto Brooklands. Driving without a passenger he established class H1 records for the standing start kilo and mile at 64.30 and 69.70 mph respectively, and then driving with passenger the class H2 records for the standing start kilometre and mile at 64.04 and 71.03 mph.

Three days later Harold Beart pushed his record-breaker onto Brooklands to defend the BMCRC three-wheeler 1100cc championship he had won the previous year. As both Jackson and Lones failed to appear, Beart's only opponent was Ronnie Horton, now with the brakeless straight-sided front wheels back in place and Brooklands silencers, mandatory since March. Beart made a slow start, allowing Horton a commanding lead at the end of the first lap but obviously gaining quickly all the time. As they entered the last lap, he slipped past Horton, coming off the home banking to win by 6 yards at 83 mph.

Beart and Horton at the start of the three-wheeler championship. (Motor Cycle)

Still Faster

The JAP production year ran from 1st September to 31st August. For the forthcoming 1926 season the Tottenham concern at last announced the LTOW engine, the production version of the ohv water-cooled engine used by Ware in the 1924 200-mile race. In standard form the new 1096cc engine with 5¼ to 1 compression produced 32 bhp at 3000 rpm, but with dome top pistons over 50 bhp was anticipated. JAPs also redesigned the water-cooled KT engine to incorporate the large valves and ports of the single camshaft KTC engine and gave it a larger water jacket. The air-cooled KT engine was now also modified and made virtually identical to the old single camshaft KTC engine. As JAPs were now concentrating on ohv engines for racing, these being less prone to hot spots than the side-valve versions, the 4-cam twin camshaft KTR engine was demoted to produce the KTCY, the 8/30 engine with semi-racing timing.

Another seafront promenade, this time Blackpool's, was closed for speed trials on 17th October when Syd Keay convincingly won the 1100cc three-wheeler class from the Morgans of AL Jackson and RJ Haslam, another Southport sand racer. Spectators and dogs crossing the course made the driving hazardous.

On the same day the Motor Cycling Club satisfied the ambitions of its sporting fraternity by running a one-hour high-speed trial around Brooklands track. Nine Morgans joined in the fun, eight gaining gold medals for averaging over 41mph, including Maskell's Aero, HFS's 'next year's' De Luxe (a redesigned model which was officially announced at that year's Motor Cycle Show) and CJ Turner's Blackburne Aero. HFS achieved his gold despite a broken lower windscreen, which cut him on his finger and Ruth on her face. Joe Turner, who worked for Fitt's Motors in Whitstable, suffered from the effects of bumpy Brooklands, losing a headlight onto the track. Ron Horton drove with an Anzani engine on his Morgan, which successfully took him to a gold. Although all the cars were road-going models, they had first to be fitted with Brooklands silencers and fish tails, which were measured by the scrutineers, before they were allowed onto the track.

Thirteen Morgans rounded off the year by taking part in the London-Exeter Trial, including Joe Turner and Harold Beart in Blackburne Aeros. HFS had rewarded Beart for his tremendous record achievements by helping to set him up as a Morgan agent in premises at Kingston-on-Thames.

Ron Horton was anxious to remain competitive for the forthcoming season and on the advice of Vivian Prestwich – one of John Alfred Prestwich's five sons – he had become one of the first customers for the new 'dog ear' JAP engine. Clive Lones was another such customer, finding the KMB Blackburne to be unreliable in his hands and heavy on his pocket as Blackburnes didn't give him any help. Lones had approached JAPs for assistance and been offered free access to all their second-hand racing parts, so naturally he was keen to swap engines. He was too canny to give up the Blackburne entirely, however, until he was sure the JAP was faster, which wasn't for some time to come.

The Southport sand races of 1926 began earlier in the season than usual, with a meeting on 9th January. Bowler-hatted Bullough with his KTOR-engined 'Creeping Jane' took the 1100cc general class but came second to Basil Davenport's GN 'Spider' in the 1500cc class. Newcomer F Ivan Carr drove a Blackburne-engined Aero to third place in the 1100cc novices' class. None of the other Morgan Southport regulars entered for this meeting.

To help select the Cambridge team for the forthcoming intervarsity speed trials against Oxford, the Cambridge UMCC decided to organize a speed trial. Held on 13th February on the drive of Wimpole Hall, these races were notable for the outstanding performance of Eric Fernihough's 494cc Morgan, which easily won the 600cc sidecar and unlimited sidecar classes by over 6 seconds, in a time of 28.7 seconds. As the Morgan ran bodiless, Fernihough predictably had difficulty finding a passenger who was prepared to hang on, a problem compounded by his habit of driving around corners with his inside front wheel well in the air.

Fernihough shared rooms at Cambridge with Robin Jackson. Fortunately, Professor Dykes, their director of engineering studies, was happy for them to pursue their motoring projects, providing their studying didn't suffer. In December 1925 Eric had taken delivery of a racing chassis from Morgans, incorporating a few of his own

January 15th 1926. 'Ferni' and Robin Jackson after towing the Morgan to test spring rate etc. The rear number is that of the towing vehicle, Robin Jackson's Frazer Nash. (GE Meade)

special suggestions, and since then he had been rapidly building up his racing Morgan. Obviously he worked with his room-mate, Jackson, and as Jackson had worked for Beart some of his ideas also filtered in. To reduce friction the rear band brake was dispensed with and a Hartford shock absorber was fitted over the rear wheel. The track rod was fashioned with Ubas steel and, in common with the drag link, fitted with spring loaded ball joints reducing back lash to a minimum. A 2¼-gallon fuel tank was slung beneath the frame, feeding a twin float chamber carburettor via an aeroplane pressure pump and filter. The bevel box and chains were both lubricated by dripfeed.

For the engine 'Ferni' selected a 1925 single port ohv JAP of 494cc (85.7mm x 85mm). This was modified to fit the Morgan by fitting a special rear bearing to take the thrust of the Morgan clutch and also a special drive for the magneto.

Construction progressed ominously quickly until, on test driving, they made the rather alarming discovery that the machine steered in the opposite direction to the steering wheel. An over-enthusiastic attempt to lower the centre of gravity had resulted in the steering column coming below instead of above the link arm. All-night work generated enough additional ironmongery to set matters right, and the next day the 500cc Morgan JAP special completed a trial run of 200 miles of snow-covered roads without trouble. No body was fitted: one plank of wood served as a seat, another as a foot rest and a third as a backrest, and as such the complete machine weighed a mere 615 lb. Thus the machine was completed in time for the Cambridge team elimination

'Ferni' races in the snow. (Mavrogordato collection)

trial. 'Ferni' was a perfectionist, going so far as to polish bearing surfaces. He took very great care and set high standards of cleanliness in assembly.

On the same day that 'Ferni' excelled at Wimpole Hall, the eleventh Colmore Cup Trial was taking place. Buckland Hill was in such bad condition that several three-wheelers withdrew rather than face its 18 inch deep rutted surface. Goodall's Anzani-engined trials car was the first to drive, plunging through the worst of it in fine style until a stone lodged in the front wheel speedometer drive, locking the wheel. The Morgan skidded and dropped into a rut, tipping up and ejecting its occupants onto the bank. Little damage was done and Goodall made an excellent restart to complete the hill in style. Ron Horton was running with a large sheet of lead behind his rear number plate, for extra grip, and he also climbed well.

Gypsy Lane proved the undoing of Chippendale's Anzani-engined Standard Morgan. It ran for 10 yards with the offside front wheel 2 feet in the air, before eventually turning over. He righted the Morgan to complete the climb. Horton retired at the foot of the hill with tyre trouble and the other two also failed to complete the course, although an Omega three-wheeler did get through.

For the Victory Cup Trial in March, Ronnie Horton was to try out a prototype ohv Anzani engine, on which the rocker mechanism operated beneath the valve springs, which stood proud. On his way to the start, when he was having a 'blast' along a clear road, one spring decided to leave the engine, shooting off into the air and through a bedroom window. Poor Ron thus had to withdraw. Of the surviving Morgans, HFS took a gold medal, Goodall a silver and Carr finished but failed to gain an award. All were using the Anzani CC engine which was very popular for trials.

On 6th March the intervarsity speed trials were held on the 1 in 14 hill at Henley Park. The Morgans were untouchable in the sidecar classes, Jackson's usual Blackburne Aero NP 5504 taking the unlimited class from Fernihough's 494cc special which was now partially bodied. Fernihough had entered with a 596cc engine, but as this gave trouble he was forced to spend most of the Friday night getting the 494cc engine ready. His second place to Jackson was followed by an easy win in the under 600cc class, helping Cambridge to gain a comfortable overall victory.

Amongst Fernihough's and Jackson's many Cambridge friends were GE (Ted) Meade and David Scott-Moncrieff. Meade would often ride with 'Ferni', holding the stopwatch for flying quarter mile trials on the road near Cadnam, whilst Scott-Moncrieff often passengered both men, although the fine art of cornering on two wheels frightened him so much that he refused anything on three wheels for almost half a century. Fernihough's fiancée, Kathleen Butler, helped him tremendously with his special Morgan which was now prepared for records on Brooklands. On 31st March, with Miss Butler as passenger, 'Ferni' took Class I cyclecar records from 5 to 10 miles, the flying start 5 miles at 73.12 mph, and standing start 10 miles at 69.65 mph, as well as similar records for the 5 and 10 kilometres. The Morgan had been fitted with a Ford Model 'T' reduction steering box for easier control over bumpy Brooklands, and the neat aluminium body was finally finished, although it was detached for record breaking. 'Ferni' used a maximum engine speed of 5700 rpm. Passengering for 'Ferni' was not an easy task because, while the driver simply drove, the passenger had to hold on and at

The novices' 1100cc event, with Moss, no 108, and Carr, no 36, in the distance. (Autocar)

times hold the driver on, pump petrol from the pressure tank, pump oil, count laps, look for pit signals and keep an eye on the gauges.

At Southport on 20th March a bitterly cold wind blew across the course. Bullough's KTOR engine at last beat Ron Horton in the 1100cc class, and Albert Moss took the novices' section with Ivan Carr third. In the 1500cc classes Bullough couldn't beat Basil Davenport's 'Spider' and Syd Keay came third with his Blackburne Aero. Bullough completed his success by gaining a second in the unlimited sidecar class; his KTOR engine was now really on song. Ron Horton was using his new LTOW engine on his racer for this meeting, but it was proving unreliable. In the 20-mile sidecar class, Baragwanath's Brough Superior led Horton on the first lap around the posts, but Horton had a clear lead over the field by the second. Unfortunately, he was forced to retire on the fourth lap, and scratched from the last race. Obviously all was not well with the new engine.

John Bullough's winning ways continued at the 17th April Southport meeting. He had now modified his KTOR engine to obtain 1096cc and he clocked 83.47 mph over the flying kilometre, to win the 1100cc class from Mucklow's Frazer-Nash. Several Morgans failed to start, hardly surprising in view of the appalling weather, but a notable first appearance was made by Eric Fernihough whose 494cc special clocked

The 1500cc event, with Moss, second from left, and Carr, second from right, battling into the distance. (Autocar)

72.62 mph over the same distance. Many times were unpublished as the timing apparatus broke down completely.

One week later SH Constable's old 1100cc MAG-engined Grand Prix proved that it was still a force to be reckoned with in the south-east. It won the 1100cc standard and supersports class of the Kent and Sussex LCC Lewes Speed Trials, although against only the one competitor, JD Barron's Anzani Morgan. That same day, 'Ferni' was contesting the North London MCC Speed Trials on a private road near Hatfield, convincingly winning the class for sidecars up to 500cc.

Towards the end of March, Arthur Maskell, a London Morgan agent, had taken delivery of a special bodied ohv Blackburne-engined Morgan. Built with a four-seater Family back end grafted onto an Aero front, the new Family Aero was immediately entered in trials complete with three passengers. In the London-Land's End Trial in April Maskell won a silver medal; he failed to finish in the London-Holyhead but won a gold in the London-Edinburgh in May. Also entered in the London-Edinburgh was Stanley McCarthy with one of the new LTOW JAP-engined Aeros, and RD Smith

Maskell's Family Aero in the London-Holyhead. (Morgan Motor Co)

with one of the special Anzani engines. The former took a gold – as usual.

1926 was the year of the great General Strike, and motor competition was not unaffected. The Madresfield Speed Trials were cancelled, along with the ACU Stock Machine Trial, for which Goodall, Carr and HFS had entered.

Speed trials returned to Southport on 22nd May, although less competitors than usual took part because of the strike. Only three Morgans turned out for the three-wheeler class, in which Keay proved to be untouchable, easily beating Bullough's enlarged KTOR 'Creeping Jane' and Ivan Carr's Blackburne Aero. Keay's Morgan now had crude streamlining for the front crosshead. Keay was the only Morgan driver in the 10-mile race for sidecars and three-wheelers. Showers of sand repeatedly penetrated the carburettors, causing the engine to misfire after every corner and finally to stop on the fourth lap, but despite this handicap he finished third. Sand was the big problem for sand racers: it got absolutely everywhere and consequently reduced the life expectancy of the mechanical components. To avoid this problem for the future Syd Keay tried tying a tarpaulin over the engine: after this had blown back over his eyes when he was on his way home one time, causing him to crash into a ditch, he decided not to continue with it.

During this period, the relationship between the British Vulpine engine company, makers of Anzani engines, and the Morgan company was steadily deteriorating. The problem was that an increasing number of engines were breaking off the heads of exhaust valves whilst still under guarantee. When the engines were returned, Charles Fox, the current owner of Vulpine, merely had the valves replaced. Several Morgan agents refused to take any more new Morgans fitted with Anzani engines, as their reputations were suffering. Finally HFS decided to cancel his contract with Fox. He thereupon took Morgan to court, but lost the case. This helped bankrupt the company, which went into liquidation in June.

Speed trials were being held at Lewes on Race Hill at regular intervals. On 29th May a Morgan enthusiast by the name of F. Arnold Boggis drove his ohv Blackburne-engined Aero, 'Semiopit', to make fastest time of the day. In June, Robin Jackson took the honours with his 'Morgan Special', whilst Constable's five-year-old MAG Morgan once again proved invincible in the standard sports class.

Robin Jackson's visits to Harold Beart's Croydon workshop in 1924 had stimulated his own ideas as to what constituted the ultimate racing Morgan. At his workshop in Malvern he had been building a special: he had taken around three years to complete it since he had to fit its construction in with his university studies. For chassis lugs Jackson had asked Beart for one of the sets of castings left over from the construction of his record breaker. Beart could sell him only an incomplete set, as he had used the last remaining complete set in constructing a replica of his record breaker, which had been commissioned by Ferdinand Tonquist. This incomplete set lacked the sliding axle castings, and these Jackson had cast in steel to his own design by Lake and Elliot of Braintree.

Assisting Jackson at Malvern was Frank Loxley, and also Mr Mann who had worked for Boddington and hence knew all about Morgans. Machining the lugs took many months, but at last the chassis could be put together. Unlike Beart who cheerfully brazed his chassis together, Jackson was worried that the brazing process might weaken the joint, and so he used best-quality Chater Lea solder to sweat the tubes into position. The front crosshead was widened, and inside the crosshead tubes were pinned special tapering steel sleeves, machined with a .001" per inch outward taper. The idea of the sleeves was to give stiffness at the point of maximum stress, without actually touching anywhere else.

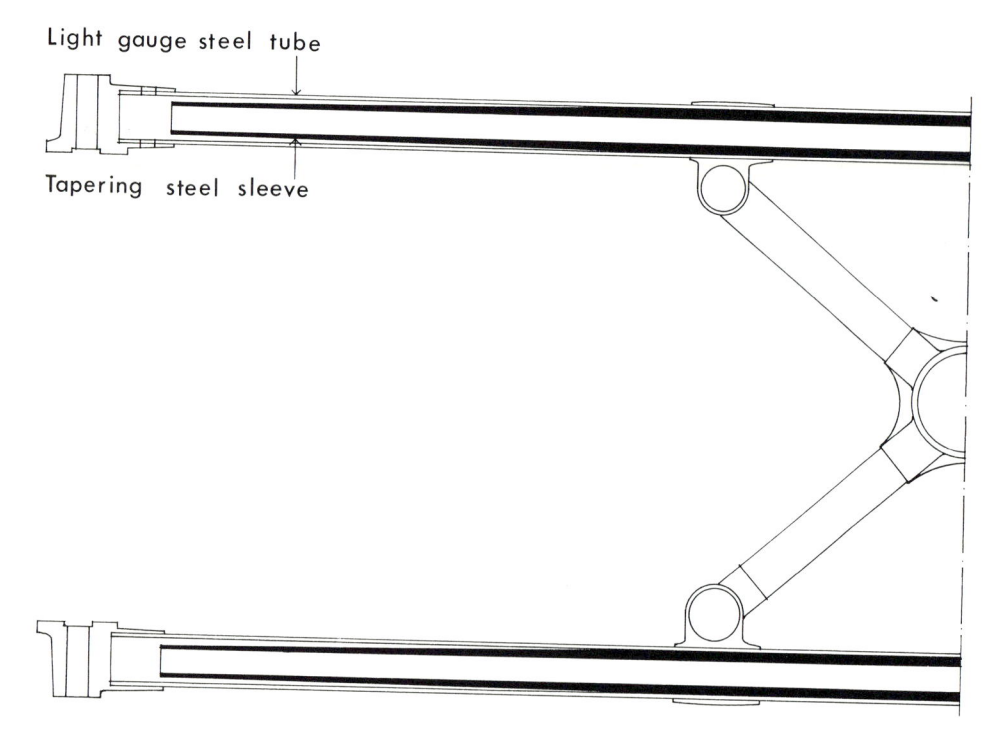

Light gauge steel tube

Tapering steel sleeve

Robin Jackson's arrangement of tapering steel sleeves.

Besides the sliding axles Jackson also designed his own bevel box, rear fork assembly, rear wheel, and shock absorber mounting. The bevel box was fabricated from sheet steel, fitted with machined housings for the bearings. A Timken taper roller bearing was fitted behind the propshaft pinion, and the countershaft had a similar Timken taper bearing behind the crownwheel, with a leak-proof ball bearing on the other side of the counter shaft. Both crownwheel and pinion were manufactured by Alfred Herbert Ltd of Coventry, and were much stronger than standard, although the standard ratio of 2¼ to 1 was retained. Bevel box lubrication was by high pressure lubricating oil, instead of the production Morgans' sticky grease.

A standard one-piece propshaft was made out of Accles and Pollock tubing of uniform thickness. Jackson overcame the racing Morgans' propensity for propshaft whip, whereby the propshaft tended to hit the sides of the backbone chassis tube at high revolutions, simply by inserting a turned piece of ash inside the propshaft tube before the front end was soldered into position.

Like Beart, Jackson also used a Model 'T' Ford steering reduction box, just behind the steering wheel. When finished the complete bodiless special was quite heavy, although very strong: it was destined for use with the large-capacity Blackburne vee-twins.

Whilst the above special was undergoing completion at Malvern, Jackson built another special. This was much simpler in construction. Jackson merely removed the body from his 200-mile-Aero, NP 5504—selling the body to local enthusiast, Lionel Creed—and replaced it with a very light low aluminium body to his own design. As the Morgan chassis on this car had been little modified, apart from a rear shock absorber being fitted, it was quite a lightweight special.

Contemporary reports merely refer to the 'Jackson Special' without specifying which of the two was in use. Certainly by early 1927 the low aluminium-bodied one was used, with only small Blackburne engines, assisting identification.

Meanwhile 'Ferni' had returned to Brooklands for record breaking on 30th June with his 494cc Morgan special. Here he took the records for Class I three-wheeled cyclecars for the flying kilometre and flying mile at 71.81 mph and 71.71 mph respectively, passengered by his fiancée Kathleen Butler. The beaded edged rear tyre was replaced by a straight sided tyre for safety, and narrow section Avon tyres were used all round.

On 3rd July Clive Lones, accompanied by his usual mechanic and passenger, his wife Nel, reappeared at Southport with his Morgan, which now sported the LTOW JAP engine. Syd Keay beat him in the 1500cc class, but Lones did come third in the unlimited sidecar novices' class.

This year Lones was the only Morgan entrant at the Stalybridge Speed Trials on 31st July. He successfully won the 1100cc racing classes and came second in the sidecar classes.

On 30th July it was Kathleen Butler's turn to do the record breaking. Passengered by 'Ferni', she took 50 kilometre, 50 mile and 1 hour records at 58.56 mph, 57.97 mph and 58.40 mph respectively. The following day they swapped places and 'Ferni' took the 100 kilometre, 2 hours and 3 hours at 56.97 mph, 56.53 mph and 57.68 mph.

On 28th June the Scottish Six Days' Trial started from Edinburgh. Frank Spouse gave his customary brilliant display, gaining a silver cup with his ohv JAP-engined Aero, but both HFS and Bill Carr retired, the former with leaking engine coolant, and the latter after damaging his chassis once more. Carr was driving an Aero fitted with one of the new ohv JAP engines and carrying his usual registration, NP 65. He entered the same vehicle for the International Six Days' in August in company with Ron Horton and George Goodall. All were using the new JAP engines, Horton driving his old 1924 Aero CJ 6343, now re-engined. All these proved successful, losing only 20 marks between them compared with the 310 of the sole surviving sidecar team. Each car had been fitted with slotted links in the steering arm to provide adjustment for the increased lock necessary for the hairpin bends, while Parson's chains were used on the rear wheels, helping to prolong tyre life by preventing wheel spin, or so Carr believed.

On 31st August 'Ferni' and Miss Butler returned to Brooklands for long distance

Ron Horton storms Jenkin's Chapel. (Horton collection)

Bill Carr in the International; note modified tie bar. (Radio Times Hulton Picture Library)

records, taking 2-hour stints at driving, and passengering each other. They took records up to 6 hours with the 494cc engine at 49.51 mph. Then, when 'Ferni' was driving, the rear tyre suddenly burst and the Morgan shot high into the air catapulting Miss Butler on to the banking before turning over with 'Ferni' still in it pinned by the huge steering wheel. Miss Butler landed on her head and shoulder and slid along the concrete until the steepness of the banking set her rolling down it. Her crash helmet was worn down to the last shreds of material; wrists, knees, elbows, ankles were rubbed bare and her shoulder blade and pelvis were fractured. 'Ferni' received facial wounds that left him scarred for life and had one hand and foot put out of action. A spectator, Anthony Hamilton, took them to hospital where they spent such an uncomfortable night that they discharged themselves and, between them, drove their tow car the $97\frac{1}{2}$ miles home. The following day, GE Tottey drove an Omega JAP to recapture several of 'Ferni's' records. This leap-frogging approach to record-breaking was strictly by arrangement. The idea was to capture and recapture records with the minimum speed possible, thus ensuring that none of the bonus money available for record breaking was lost by wasting any speed in hand.

Another Morgan driver returning to record breaking was Harold Beart. He took his

Freddie James takes W 113 through a Sheffield to Holyhead trial. (James scrapbooks)

racer to Brooklands in September for trials with a JAP engine. JAPs, keen for success, were offering better bonus money than Blackburnes, and so Beart's famous KMB engine had been returned to its owners. Initial trials with the tuned ohv 1096cc water-cooled JAP were very promising, Beart easily reaching 100 mph.

Ron Horton reappeared on the racing scene at Colwyn Bay on 11th September. The only opposition turned out to be Syd Keay, as both Jackson and Lones failed to appear. One of Syd Keay's friends was Ken Green, who lived in Colwyn. When Syd told him that Ron was looking for a passenger he quickly volunteered, being rewarded by victory when Ron won from Syd at 60.79 mph.

On the same day, Sheffield agent Freddie James was driving his new Morgan, one of the new Family Aeros, fitted with an LTOW JAP engine, for the Sheffield and Hallamshire MC & LCC in the MCC Inter Team Trial. Freddie had been regularly entering trials for the local S & H club for some years, latterly with an ohv Blackburne-

Horton's JAP-engined racer on Southport Sands. (B Davenport collection)

engined Grand Prix. His Morgans always had distinctive registration numbers, the Grand Prix carrying W 113, and the new Family Aero W 157. One of Freddie's favourite trials tricks was to travel with a 2-gallon petrol can strapped on the tail, or so it seemed. In fact, it needed two people to position it, being full of lead.

Whilst Constable was once again proving victorious at Lewes Hill on 18th September, the local sand racers at Southport were engaged in battle. Ken Green was passengering Ron Horton in his JAP-engined racer, winning the 1100cc mile race from Mucklow's Frazer Nash and Keay's Morgan Blackburne. One of the pressmen asked Ron how he judged when to change gear, expecting an answer involving engine revs. Horton's answer, given with his usual stutter, was 'W-when I-i've p-passed everyone!'

By the first corner of the 10-mile car race, Horton already had a large lead and seemed set for an easy victory. But when he reached out for the hand brake, he unfortunately locked the front wheels. The Morgan skidded over the marker flags and then turned over. Ken called out anxiously 'Are you alright, Ron?'. He was met by complete silence and presumed the worse. Happily, however, when the Morgan was turned upright Horton was quickly on his feet, having been winded by the steering wheel. Ken needed minor hospital attention for a head injury.

At this meeting the Southport Motor Club had devised a 'Grand Prix' type course, with more corners than the usual two. Syd Keay entered for this novel 50-mile event. His tremendous acceleration, helped by the antics of his acrobatic passenger Alf Slinger, soon put him over two laps ahead of the field. He was even able to stop to shore up a trailing exhaust pipe, whilst still coming home the victor.

Racing on the sands at Southport stimulated the development of special techniques for that extra bit of speed needed for victory. A good start was essential, helped by

Morgan Sweeps the Board

watching the starter's shoulder which moved fractionally earlier than the flag. The passenger was a vital member of the team, leaning out over the tail on the bends and bouncing violently for grip. Ron Horton had rigged up a magneto cut-out switch on the steering wheel, made from an old hacksaw blade, which facilitated fast gear changes, as did filing the gear dogs to give lightning selection.

Two erstwhile regulars on the Morgan scene at Southport were notable by their absence at this meeting. Albert Moss had retired, selling his Horrocks replica to RJ Haslam, a garage salesman of Leigh, Lancs. And poor John Miles Bullough, who had been experimenting with methanol as a fuel for 'Creeping Jane', brazing together two single float carburettor chambers to cope with the increased fuel flow, had sadly became seriously ill. He died without ever trying out his system in a race.

In September, Robin Jackson took his 1096cc Blackburne-engined special to Syston Park for the Grantham and District MC's road races. He finished second in the 1100cc passenger novices' class, successfully outbraking Crichton-Maitland's Brough Superior for the corners, but unable to match his acceleration on the straights. Jackson came to love the Syston circuit, with its long uphill straight leading via a sweeping right-hand bend to a farmyard complete with chickens. It continued through a narrow gate to a right-hand hairpin bend, and then back onto the straight once more.

At the Olympia show in October, HFS added the Family Aero to the range of Morgans, and also showed a special Aero, built to order, which had a streamlined body, giving the appearance that all the panelwork had been made in one piece with the bonnet. All models now sported wider bevel boxes ('wide B'), rear forks and rear

Jackson at an early Syston—more haste, less speed. Later the body was sold to Lionel Creed, and the chassis formed a special. (Mavrogordato collection)

wheels, and all models except the Standard had their chassis lengthened and widened by 3 inches.

For the show Burney and Blackburne announced an improved ohv engine for the Morgan, the KMC, claiming over 40 bhp at 4000 rpm with a compression ratio of 5¼ to 1. Developed from the racing KMB, the new engine had strengthened conrods, larger crankpin and driving side bearing, and a new oiling system and modified valve gear.

JAPs' new ohv engine was now available in three forms, known as LTOW standard, LTOWC sports and LTOWR racing. The cylinder bores of these and the KT series were now standardized at 85.7mm. All JAP engines were now fitted with an oil pump, mounted on the timing cover, force-feeding oil direct to the big-end bearing in the case of the twin cam engine, and to the cylinder wall in the single cam side-valve engine. Stanley Greening had become JAP's chief designer, having replaced Val Page who had moved to Ariel Motorcycles in Birmingham.

On 23rd October, Harold Beart took his JAP-engined streamlined racer onto Brooklands and succeeded in capturing the 2-hour record at 63.63 mph. Four days later he was back once more, taking one time and four long distance records. Sadly for Beart the same month saw the death of his great rival and friend, Norman Norris, who was killed when his Lea Francis overturned at speed on Magilligan Strand in Ireland.

Beart had not been the only Morgan record breaker at Brooklands in October, for Fernihough had attempted Class J records with his large engine (599cc), taking records up to one hour. Sure enough, GE Tottey promptly beat them with his Omega.

Before the MCC Brooklands High Speed Trial that year, Joe Turner returned his Blackburne engine to its makers, where it was stripped and rebuilt by Ted Baldwin, their engine overhaul mechanic. The effort proved worthwhile for Turner's Aero covered 67.8 miles in the hour after a battle with a massive Hispano-Suiza. He was followed home by Maskell with 64 miles, Ron Horton in his JAP-engined Aero CJ 6343 with 62 miles, and Goddard with 61 miles—an impressive speed demonstration of production Morgans, which HFS was delighted to publicize.

RD (Dick) Caesar, another Cambridge undergraduate, had persuaded his parents to buy him a new dark green Blackburne Aero for his twenty-first birthday. Robin Jackson had tipped him off that Morgans would supply a better than average KMC engine if he told them that the car was for competition. Thus equipped, Dick entered his Morgan as a member of the Cambridge team for the Intervarsity Trial. Then his thoughts turned to modification, and especially to lowering the centre of gravity for racing. This was to become the first Caesar special, of which more later.

The competition year of 1926 was characteristically brought to its close by the London-Exeter Trial. Earlier in the year the MCC had decided to ban trade members from future trials, and this was the first event to be affected by the ruling. Despite this it remained as popular as ever, with Morgans gaining eleven golds, three silvers and one bronze. Amongst the gold medal winners were Eric Fernihough driving a works trials Morgan and Geoff Harris in a new ohv JAP Aero with the registration ML 1142. Another JAP Aero was driven to a silver by HR Taylor and featured high-level exhaust pipes and rather nice helmet front mudguards. Many Morgans lost their dynamo belts connecting the front mounted dynamos to the engine flywheel. HW Baker still gained a gold, despite his passenger leaning out with a pocket torch to light the way.

Morgan Sweeps the Board

Once again the Southport season started early. On January 8th 1927 and in dismal weather CW Orford's Blackburne Aero comfortably won the 1100cc general class.

The classic factory trials Morgans of the last few years had been the short-chassis Trials Standard models, a blend of the front half of a De Luxe and the wrap round tail of the Standard model, but now the ohv JAP Aeros were proving popular. In the Colmore trial in February, however, it was the private JAP Aero of Ronnie Horton that showed the way, gaining a gold and the cup for the best passenger machine performance. HFS and Chippendale took silvers and Goodall a bronze. He had now joined the Morgan Motor Co as works manager, in place of Alfie Hales, who was seriously ill.

Before the Intervarsity Speed Trials, the Cambridge University AC once more held selection trials. Jackson's aluminium-bodied special made a spectacular run, ensuring his selection for the Cambridge team. This special was now fitted with a 497cc air-cooled vee-twin Blackburne engine (60mm x 80mm), similar to that used by Walter Handley to gain second place in the 1926 Senior TT race in his Rex-Acme. Small pipes were run off the main exhaust pipes to warm the inlet manifold. When the actual event was held in March, Oxford proved victorious, although Jackson's Frazer Nash did win the 1100cc class.

Four Morgans entered the Victory Cup Trial. HFS and George Goodall were both

HFS and Ruth in the Victory Trial. (Harry Jones scrapbooks)

Still Faster

in factory JAP Aeros, the former carrying AB 16 and the latter NP 636. Goodall, passengered by his young son, drove without windscreen or mudguards and gained a bronze. HFS, Horton and Chippendale also completed the course successfully.

The Spring Southport Meeting was held on 12th March. In the 1100cc general class, Syd Keay proved faster than the Lones family, Clive being passengered by his wife Nel. Lones took two other second places, in the 1500cc general class to Basil Davenport's 'Spider' and also in the unlimited sidecar class.

The next Southport meeting was held on 9th April, when a newcomer to the Morgan ranks caused considerable interest. Following the Intervarsity Trial the previous autumn, Dick Caesar had been working on his Morgan. The front track was widened and the tail lowered by repositioning the rear spring hangers beneath the rear wheel spindle instead of above. This lowered the tail by around 6 inches but necessitated cutting a hole in the top of the tail panel to allow the rear wheel to protrude, a special cowl being prefabricated to cover this. The KMC engine did not escape Dick's attention. The valve gear was lightened, the compression raised to $6\frac{1}{4}$ to 1, and the valve guides shortened considerably. This, with polishing of the ports, made 6000 rpm possible, consistent with 90 mph in theory. Fuel was fed from a lightly pressurized fuel tank via a hand pump.

When he had completed these modifications, Dick offered the car to his friend Steward Brownbill, a poultry farmer living near Liverpool who fancied racing it at Southport and paid him £75.00 for it. Just before the event, Dick travelled up to Liverpool from Bristol to help tune the car. As he had built it, he was duly offered the first drive, with Brownbill passengering. After the 1-mile races were run, with Ivan Carr's Blackburne Aero winning the 1100cc class from Mucklow's Frazer Nash and Lones's JAP Aero, they went out on a warming-up lap for the 10-mile sidecar race. Southport was notorious for its gullies, and they hit one of the worst at high speed. Stewart was thrown forward into the air, giving him an excellent view of the engine. Luckily he caught the edge of the skuttle which prevented his eviction and landed him back on board. On their return to the 'pits', the third member of the party, Geoffrey Armitage, asked if all had gone well, whereupon Stewart told him that he was just about all in, and asked him to take his place. Thus Stewart Brownbill ended up a spectator, watching his own car's easy victory in the 10-mile sidecar race.

The success of the widened and lowered Morgan had not gone unnoticed, and it was not long before the reasons for this success were incorporated into the racers of other Morgan sportsmen. One of the drivers thus intrigued had been Syd Keay, who went on to win second place in the 10-mile car race.

Robin Jackson got to know Harry Hatch at Blackburnes very well, gaining access to engine spares without having to put any money down beforehand. On 3rd May Robin took his 497cc Blackburne vee-twin engined lightweight special onto Brooklands, and collected Fernihough's 50-kilometre Class 1 record at 65.83 mph.

After Horton's Southport accident in 1926, the factory had seized the opportunity to rebuild the car for him, incorporating all the latest thinking on racing design. Basically it was a new car that he collected in May. It now had a beefed-up wide 'B' type chassis, which had been widened and then lowered by cranking the top tube of the crosshead and inverting the lugs of the lower one. Onto this chassis was fitted a slim streamlined

Horton in his new racer outside the Morgan factory. (Harry Jones scrapbooks)

body, which fully enclosed the rear wheel for the first time on a Morgan, having a hinged top panel to allow access to the transmission and the oil tank, now fitted behind the rear seat. The old floor mounted 200-mile Aero fuel tank installation had been retained. The new racer had a new engine as well, the ex-Harold Beart KMB Blackburne, obtained from Burney and Blackburne.

Trials successes continued. BBF Russell drove a 'Newt', a saloon-bodied Aero Morgan that he had produced in London, to win a bronze medal in the London-Land's End, one of thirteen Morgan medal winners (six gold, three silver and four bronze). In the ACU Six Days' Stock Machine Trial, two LTOW JAP Aeros were entered, driven by Bill Carr, and Freddie James. Carr experienced tyre trouble and failed to get an award, but Freddie won a gold, no doubt helped by the fact that the Peak District was home ground to him.

The first time test of Horton's new racer was at the Coventry Ace Club's event, held on 9th July on Shackerstone Drive, on Lord Waring's estate near Atherstone. He beat the Lones family's Blackburne Aero to make fastest time in the three-wheeler class.

Clive Lones had been one of the few Morgan drivers to take part in races at Brooklands since the JCC ban in 1924. Things had not always gone well, on one occasion he lost a tyre, and on another blew up a Blackburne engine on NP 4200. During a longer race in 1927, possibly the 50-mile race at the BMCRC meeting on 23rd July, the crosshead tie bar broke on his Aero, allowing both the front chassis tubes to bend. Rather than retiring Lones continued, to find that the more the chassis bent the easier his car was to handle. He communicated this information to HFS and a week or so later accepted an invitation from HFS to come to the factory. On the jigs he found a chassis with cranked tubes incorporated into it. 'No doubt the bend won't be enough

Carr (45) and James (31) replenish their Morgans in the Stock Trial. (James scrapbooks)

Harold Beart helps Clive Lones (standing) repair his Blackburne engine at Brooklands (Lones collection)

Morgan Sweeps the Board

for you', HFS commented, but Clive had the new chassis built into an Aero, registered NP 6876.

For some time there had been concern amongst the sporting Morgan drivers about the lack of opportunity to race against cars of similar engine size at Brooklands. By mid-1927 they decided that if no-one else would do anything about it, they would have to do it themselves. As a result, on 4th August the previously predominantly social Morgan Club changed its constitution to allow membership to any ACU-defined cyclecar (ie under 8 cwt and under 1100cc, either three or four wheelers). To foster the new image the club changed its name first to the Cyclecar Club and then, following an objection from the JCC which itself had previously been called the Cyclecar Club, to the New Cyclecar Club. A racing committee was drawn up, including Beart, JJ Hall and EB Ware, who was now recovering from his accident, to plan the first Brooklands meeting for mid-1928.

JC Chippendale achieved notable success in the Midland C & AC 24-hour trial when he won the Jordison trophy for the best performance of a passenger machine over 500cc, as well as a gold medal. He was driving CJ 743, now a short chassis Trials Standard which was fitted with a water-cooled Anzani engine and had a special bonnet finishing behind it as the production bonnet wouldn't fit over the ohv engine. HFS drove AB 16, a JAP Aero, to win a silver medal as did Goodall, also in a factory car.

Clive Lones also took part in a few trials. As he did not have a suitable car himself, he borrowed the short-bonneted Anzani-engined Trials Standard car from the factory, as used by Chippendale. In the Inter Team Trial in June he joined Ron Horton's Morgan in the Worcestershire Club team, and both were noted to be very fast. Horton's car leapt high in the air when he hit a bump avoiding a stranded motorcyclist.

Four Morgans were entered for the Scottish Six Days' Trial, the star performance being that of Geoff Harris in his JAP Aero ML 1142 with which he lost no marks at all, despite turning over when avoiding another car. Frank Spouse, also JAP Aero-mounted, took a silver medal after losing marks when he fitted a replacement chassis tie bar. Vidler lost a front wheel on the second day when a stub axle broke, forcing his retirement, and Watson withdrew on the fourth with a broken bevel box.

The International Six Days' Trial held in August saw Bill Carr competing in his JAP Aero NP 65, and Ron Horton in his JAP Aero CJ 6343. Despite finishing, neither won an award as they both lost time as a result of chain trouble.

The Southport sand races held on 20th August saw only one Morgan entered, that of a newcomer to Morgan racing—Tommy Rhodes of the Portus and Rhodes garage of Liverpool. Tommy had purchased a new metallic grey Aero with red upholstery and tuned its Blackburne KMC engine. He lowered the rear of the Morgan, probably by the simple method of repositioning the rear springs on top of the bevel box angle irons rather than below, as supplied, and he made a neat cover for the rear wheel which consequently protruded through the tail. His success was immediate: he had a walk-over victory in the cyclecar general and novices' class, as well as winning the novices' class in the sidecar and three-wheeler event.

Ronnie Horton had now got his new racer really competitive. At Shackerstone on 27th August he had the crowd fleeing in panic to the shelter of the trees lining the narrow straight road, as he slid on the rough surface. He won the unlimited sidecar

Tom Rhodes's lowered Aero on Southport Sands. (Syd Rhodes collection)

class by 1 second from Slater's Norton.

On week later Horton was at Madresfield for the speed trials, now being held once more after a year's absence. He proved the fastest of the ten Morgans, tying for the 1100cc three-wheeler and sidecar class with Greenwood's Brough Superior. In the run-off Horton went first, flashing by, sometimes sideways on as his rear wheel swung from side to side in the loose gravel, aiming for the seemingly very narrow gate at the end of the drive. Greenwood proved that decisive bit faster to take the class, while Horton took the Morgan and Jackson cups with his time of $33\frac{2}{5}$ seconds.

The fastest amateur was Clive Lones with a time of $34\frac{2}{5}$ seconds, and the Morgan 'A' cup, for the fastest Morgan Runabout driven and owned by an amateur who had never won a first-class award in any open speed trial or hill climb, went to R Griffin. Amongst the other entries were George Goodall with his Blackburne-engined 'Jim', Robin Jackson with his racing KMB-engined Beart-inspired special, which he ran as a bare chassis with two bucket seats bolted on, and Jack Sylvester of Nottingham. Jack had obtained an 8-valve Anzani engine for the meeting. On the way to Madresfield, on the Burton-Lichfield road, he and his passenger, Reg Baker, were well pleased with its performance. Unfortunately, as they warmed up before going to the start the internal flywheels shifted, seizing the engine. In considerable embarrassment, they pushed the Morgan behind a hedge and spent the next two hours or so plying Alfie Hales with alcohol until he agreed to lend them a Morgan to get home in.

Two weeks later the Southport sands saw Horton continue his demonstration of superiority, when he recorded a shattering 93.21 mph over the flying kilometre, beating the fastest sidecar by 7 mph and Basil Davenport's 1500cc GN 'Spider' by 5 mph. Tommy Rhodes with his lowered Blackburne Aero clocked 78.76 mph and CN Taylor, a Cambridge undergraduate driving a Blackburne Aero, 73.58 mph. In the 1-mile standing start races Horton was once again invincible, averaging 75 mph to beat Tommy Rhodes and Syd Keay. Tommy won the novices' section with a time of 68.81 mph.

The last motorcycle event of the day was the 10-mile race. Horton and Keay were

Morgan Sweeps the Board

Brownbill's ex-Caesar Aero on Southport sands. (Brownbill collection)

joined by Stewart Brownbill with his ex-Caesar lowered Aero, now painted turquoise blue with cream wheels. As usual Stewart towed his car to the meeting behind his 1925 12 hp Darracq, helped by Geoffrey Armitage.

It was Horton who took the lead from the flag, only to have it taken from him at the first corner by Edwards's Brough Superior. Once on the straight again he quickly retook it to race away in the lead for three laps. Then engine trouble developed and Horton fell back, his radiator boiling furiously. Syd Keay worked his way up to second place by the fifth lap but then he too dropped back, finishing fourth behind Horton in third place.

For some time JAPs had been working on the JTOR engine, first raced by le Vack in 1923. Indeed, Joe Wright had raced one in 1926 in his Zenith motorcycle. For the 1928 JAP production year, which began in September 1927, the JTOR was added to the catalogue. Together with the latest KTOR engines, it could be obtained with D-shaped aluminium rocker boxes and push rod tubes for better lubrication of the valve-operating mechanism. The KTOR produced 45 bhp while the JTOR with only a marginal increase in capacity (981 to 996cc), claimed 55 bhp and was to be developed into a remarkable racing engine. JAPs also announced a modified lubrication system for their KT engines, the oil now entering the oil box direct from the crankcase, and not through the timing case as in the past.

Still Faster

Another special vee-twin JAP engine achieving considerable success was the ohv 731cc (74mm x 85mm) unit which GE Tottey had been using for record-breaking in an Omega three-wheeler in late 1926. Tottey had built this unit himself at the JAP factory during the winter of 1924 from no less than five different engines. It seems to have impressed JAPs themselves for we believe that several copies were produced including a water-cooled version. This was specially tuned by le Vack and later fitted to the four-wheeler Avon-JAP built by JAPs for Kaye Don in 1926, of which more later.

One of these engines was used by Jim Hall, a competitor who was trying to make a living from record-breaking. His initial attempts were on two wheels but he then switched to three, first with a 1096cc Omega-JAP, then with a 350cc twin port JAP-engined HP. His next three-wheeler was a Morgan, prepared by Beart, to which Teddy Prestwich of JAPs fitted one of the special 731cc engines. On 20th September he attempted long-distance records at Brooklands, successfully taking Class J records up to 200 miles from Tottey. As he continued with his long-distance record attempt, one of his mechanics noted a tyre beginning to strip and warned him to come into the pits. Unfortunately, he instead decided to keep going, and the mechanic's fears were confirmed when the back tyre burst at around 80 mph. The car somersaulted several times along the Railway Straight, throwing Hall out. Both he and his passenger, Vic Derrington, a maker of Brooklands silencers, were taken to Weybridge Cottage Hospital with head injuries.

That the JAP was not the only type of engine suitable for record-breaking was demonstrated by Robin Jackson, when he captured three Class I records for 50 miles, 100 kilometres and 1 hour from Eric Fernihough at 66 mph, with his 497cc Blackburne vee-twin aluminium-bodied special. Fernihough himself took to the track the very next day and took longer distance Class I records from 100 miles to 3 hours at around 62 mph.

The Annual MCC high speed 'hour blind' was held on Brooklands in heavy rain on 22nd October. The Morgans were required to cover twenty laps of the outer circuit for a gold medal, although 1100cc cars and sidecars had to cover only nineteen. HR Taylor, a one-legged Morgan enthusiast who enjoyed using his JAP Aero in club competitions, showed that he was in no mood for dawdling. Soon he and Kipling in a Bugatti were well in the lead. Geoff Harris made a slow start with his JAP Aero, and Ron Horton in CJ 6343 developed clutch trouble after two laps, which delayed him somewhat. At the finish Taylor had covered twenty-five laps, in the rain, averaging 70.5 mph to win a gold; this speed was faster than that of the best solo motorcycle, and was only improved upon by the unlimited class of cars. Macaskie also did very well to win a gold, as his JAP engine was only the side-valve KT type. It is interesting that he had fitted a proprietary Hambling three-speed gearbox instead of the usual two-speed arrangement. Harris took a silver medal, and Horton and Joe Turner took bronzes, the latter carrying two passengers, a small terrier having a ride on his true passenger's lap.

At the November Motor Cycle Show, HFS added a new model to his range – the Super Sports Aero, describing it as 'destined to break all previous records for automobiles in its class, a very demon on wheels.' The Super Aero, as the car quickly became known, was very similar to Horton's new racer, although production models used a specially tuned 1096cc ohv JAP (LTOWC) engine which allowed the radiator

The Olympia Show Super Sports Aero. (Radio Times Hulton Picture Library)

to be positioned lower, giving a sloping line to the bonnet. Shock absorbers were fitted to the rear forks as standard, the seat squab was staggered, and the chassis was made wider and $2\frac{1}{2}$ inches lower than on the Aero by using the cranked top tube and inverted lug system featured on Horton's car. At the rear the springs were fitted on top of the bevel box angle irons instead of below. Each JAP LTOWC engine was tuned at the Morgan works by Bill Ayrton, and before despatch all Super Aeros were tested to 80 mph on a straight stretch of public road just outside Malvern.

At the Motor Cycle Show HFS also introduced the Commercial model. This had a box body that could be readily fitted or removed from the rear space of a Family body. Certain new developments, applicable to all models, were also announced. Geared steering was made available as an extra, and tapering anti-wobble steering pins were now fitted to the track rod ends. The dynamo was now driven from the cross-shaft by gear wheels, and a starter motor could be fitted in the earlier dynamo position adjacent to the engine.

Just before Brooklands closed down for its winter overhaul, Robin Jackson took out his 1096cc Blackburne Morgan and captured the 2-hour standing start record from Hall at 68.48 mph. We suspect that Jackson was driving his Beart-inspired special, now sporting a body similar to that of the new Super Aero, although of course it had straight crosshead tubes differentiating it from production Super Aeros. Jackson had built this special with shock absorbers all round, the front Hartfords being mounted on his specially cast sliding axles, following the system used by Hawkes and Beart before him.

During 1927, there had been two interesting developments on a more general front. Cecil Jay had moved from Fryers of Hereford to join his previous boss, George Goodall, at Morgans, and the bankrupt Anzani engine company had been transferred from Willesden to Kingston-on-Thames. The latter was due to Archie Frazer-Nash who had taken over Anzanis, incorporating it as the British Anzani Engineering Co Ltd in February 1927. The new factory was adjacent to the Frazer Nash factory, allowing the two companies to share a drawing office and stores. The Anzani CC engine was to be redesigned to eliminate the disaster of the breaking exhaust valves, and was redesignated the M3, to distinguish it from its predecessor. New features were to include modified cam contours, which produced a more gradual valve closure as

Still Faster

well as greater power, and completely redesigned double diameter exhaust valves. Compression was raised slightly by reducing the length of the cylinder barrels, and the valve guides were made detachable.

Robin Jackson had been employed at the new Anzani premises during 1927. He had been working on Claude Temple's ohv Anzani engines, saved by Claude from the old Anzani Company's receiver.

One of the more successful club trials drivers of the 1927 season was GE Swift. He rounded off the year with a gold in the London-Exeter, one of eight Morgan drivers to gain the award, the others including Geoff Harris and HR Taylor, all driving the usual JAP Aeros.

The Southport season recommenced for 1928 on 14th January. Since August 1927 Morgans had been restricted to competing against other three-wheeled cyclecars or sidecars for these events – yet another stimulus to the New Cyclecar Club to reintroduce racing against four-wheelers. The wet sands, a cold breeze and merciless rain played havoc with the programme, but Lones proved faster than Tommy Rhodes for the three-wheeler class. In the sidecar event Edwards's Brough proved considerably faster than Lones, third place going to Ivan Carr's Morgan.

For the 10-mile race Lones and Rhodes were competing against three sidecars. Lones shot into the lead on the first lap, but when he reached the first corner he went straight on, disappearing into the distance like a watershoot. Rhodes finished the course, but came last.

The highlight of the trials year, the Colmore, saw HFS in excellent form, winning the Rhodes cup with his JAP Aero, whilst Goodall won the 'runner up' award, although Horton and Harris retired. When competing in trials, both Goodall and HFS used to fasten some bricks onto the tails of their Aeros, to help the rear wheel with its Parson's chain bite into the surface.

Perhaps the last appearance of Lones with the Blackburne engine was on Black Rock Sands at Portmadoc on 10th March. With his cranked chassis Aero, he proved

Clive and Nel Lones in the dropped chassis Aero at Portmadoc. (Lones collection)

fastest novice in the unlimited sidecar straight mile event, and went on to win the 5-mile sidecar race. Lones had had several ohv Blackburne engines, but latterly had been lucky enough to acquire one of the special racing KMB engines, as used by Norris, Beart and Horton, which featured steel internal flywheels. This particular engine, KMB 216, produced its peak power between 4000 and 4500 rpm running on a 7.2 to 1 compression. Lones had found Blackburnes very difficult to keep in racing trim, suffering many expensive blow-ups. On one occasion, he had broken a conrod at Southport. As he did not have enough money to send the Morgan home by train, he had to drive home on the one remaining cylinder. Clive's wife Nel remembers this well – she actually had time to admire the countryside.

Lones's successes at Southport continued at the April and May meetings when he beat first Syd Keay and then Tom Rhodes to take four firsts and one third in the mile races, and a second place behind Edwards's Brough Superior in the 10-mile races. To negotiate the corners in the 10-mile races Lones had devised a cunning braking system, whereby each front wheel brake had its own lever, the two levers being mounted side by

Freddie James on Bumble Bee hairpin in the Stock Trial. (James scrapbooks)

Still Faster

side on the chassis backbone tube and covered by a piece of bicycle inner tube. By twisting the rubber sleeve as he pulled on the brakes, he could get better braking on one wheel than the other, helping the Morgan to turn.

Two JAP Aeros were entered for the ACU Six Days' Stock Machine Trial in March, UY 2696 being driven by Freddie James and its sister UY 2697 by George Goodall. Both won gold medals, Goodall not losing a single mark. The LTOW JAP proved capable of powering the Aero around Brooklands at 73mph at the conclusion of the trial.

The London-Land's End saw a new name amongst the medal winners – that of Lionel Creed whose family ran the Malvern stone quarries and whom we have previously mentioned in connection with Robin Jackson. He was one of fourteen Morgan gold medal winners with his Blackburne Super Aero.

For the twenty-first London-Edinburgh Trial Hall once again entered 'Julia', his

Goodall attempts the impossible. (Morgan Motor Co)

Horton in the process of taking the Morgan and Jackson cups at Madresfield. (L Creed)

pre-First World War JAP-engined Morgan. He completed the course and won a gold medal. TEA Johnson was driving a Family model with an ohv JAP engine shoehorned under the bonnet, but failed to finish.

Two JAP Aeros competed in the Scottish Six Days' in July. Frank Spouse lost no marks at all to win a silver cup, whilst HFS and Ruth in AB 16 gained a gold after failing Simon's Hill. The hill had three hairpins; whilst reversing to get around the sharpest of these, HFS overturned, though fortunately they both escaped injury.

On Saturday, 14th July 1928 the Madresfield Speed trials were held once more. Instead of the normal standing start, a 15-yard rolling start was used. Horton covered the kilometre in $30\frac{4}{5}$ seconds at an average of 72.6mph to win the Morgan and Jackson cups, setting up the fastest passenger machine speed. Currie's Brough was second in the 1100cc sidecar and three-wheeler class and Cecil Jay drove 'Jim' to third place with a time of $32\frac{2}{5}$ seconds. The faithful Blackburne engine had now been replaced by a JAP JTOR 996cc racing engine. The Morgan 'A' cup went to Lionel Creed's Blackburne Super Aero. CN Taylor's Blackburne Aero was also competing, now fitted with one of the lowered 'wide B' Super Aero-like chassis.

Tommy Rhodes continued to race his Blackburne Aero on the sands. At Middleton sands at Morecambe on 28th July he came second in the novices' section of the two lap sidecar race. In the 20-mile sidecar race he worked steadily through the field, cornering just short of overturning, with the rear forks leaning over at an almost unbelievable angle, again finishing in second place. On 11th August at Southport Tom had to take second place to Clive Lones in the 1-mile sidecar race. Lones's special braking system

122

also helped him to finish a creditable second in the 10-mile sidecar race.

At last the day of the New Cyclecar Club's Brooklands meeting arrived – Saturday, 25th August. Many interesting entries had been received, including a 746cc Coventry Victor three-wheeler, which HJ Vidler, a notable Morgan driver, had been persuaded to drive. Several Super Aeros were also competing, featuring the production models' small, half-moon-shaped cut-out on the bonnet sides behind the radiator, instead of the louvres fitted in Horton's racer when it was delivered in May 1927.

The first race was a two-lap novices' handicap, which Major Gardner in his supercharged Salmson won from scratch. Three Morgans took part, the red Blackburne Aero of HW Baker, a regular trials entrant, B Cooke's JAP Super Aero, and Geoff Harris's pale blue JAP Aero ML 1142 which unfortunately sheared the key to the outside flywheel.

The second race was for three-wheelers only, with seven Morgan entries and the lone Coventry Victor. For this three-lap handicap Robin Jackson had entered his aluminium-bodied special fitted with one of his two 500cc vee twin Blackburne engines bored out to give 546cc. Setting off just after the Coventry Victor he quickly took the

Cecil Jay drives 'Jim' into third position. (L Creed)

Morgan Sweeps the Board

Jackson's aluminium bodied special. (National Motor Museum)

lead and held it till the end, with Horton on scratch coming second and Lones third. Also competing were Tom Rhodes with his Blackburne Aero, Cook and Baker as before and Maskell with his JAP-engined Super Aero, which had a hole cut in the tail to allow the rear wheel to bounce over the track without hitting the tail panel. Lones's third place was achieved with his special lowered chassis, but the old Aero body had now been replaced by a sleek Super Aero body – as Lones was only a short chap, Morgans had made it much lower than standard. The rear top panel, besides being cut away for the deeper than standard staggering to the seat squab, also had a hump in the centre to clear the rear wheel and shock absorber. Testing showed that it failed to give sufficient clearance, so without more ado George Goodall took a hacksaw to the hump in the paddock and cut a hole in it. Lones's engine was his 1926 LTOW dog ear JAP, and his Morgan had Newton telescopic hydraulic shock absorbers on the front wheels to augment the Hartford on the back.

The third race was a three-lap short handicap. No-one challenged Horton, who tore through the field, lapping at 95mph and winning at 92.4mph by a quarter of a mile from Maskell and Lones. Horton too had Newton shock absorbers on the front suspension; a stream condenser adorned the radiator cap, while a new oil tank immediately behind the radiator meant that the louvred bonnet sides had had to be cut into a large D shape for access. The brakes had been modified so that the foot pedal operated the front

Still Faster

brakes via a rod and cable, whilst the outside handbrake applied the rear.

Horton's success provoked Brooklands' handicapper, 'Ebby' Ebblewhite into rehandicapping him for the fourth race over five laps, a fate which also befell Jackson. Horton responded by going yet faster, touching 100mph and lapping at 98mph to beat Jackson and Lones by half a mile at 94.5mph.

Next was the most interesting event of the day, the 50-mile Cyclecar Grand Prix over a special course which included artifical sandbank bends on the Finishing Straight, leading via the banking to the Railway Straight, and then back to the Finishing Straight via the Byfleet Banking. After two laps Horton led Lones and Maskell from Gardner's Salmson but in his fifth lap Horton had to retire with oil on his brakes. Soon afterwards Maskell broke off his gear lever in top gear which allowed Lones to get into a commanding lead. Despite stopping to refill his small radiator he finished the victor from Wilkinson's Riley, Smythe's Amilcar, and Vidler's Coventry Victor. Lones was passengered as usual by Nel, loaded up with nuts and bolts, etc to get her up to the passenger weight minimum. Besides passengering, Nel helped Clive a lot in preparing his car. It was she who lapped in valves and pistons and polished the ports. However, she did not lose her femininity thereby and was annoyed to find that her stockings had got covered in grease. Goodall offered to buy her some replacements, but never did. As well as winning the Light Car and Cyclecar Cup for being the first finisher, Lones also

Ron Horton's amazing racer. (Weeks collection)

Clive Lones about to pass Syd Keay on the Brooklands Finishing Straight. (Autocar)

Alf Slinger helps Syd Keay corner. (Motor Cycle)

won the Greenaway cup for victory in the 1100cc class, and the Jackson cup as the first private owner to finish. Alongside HFS Morgan as he congratulated Lones was his young son, Peter.

One of the stars of the Grand Prix had been Syd Keay, whose Blackburne Aero now had a lowered back end, probably achieved by repositioning the rear springs on top of the bevel box angle irons. Syd and his passenger Alf Slinger impressed all with their Southport-style cornering technique.

The International Six Days' Trial in September saw only one Morgan taking part – the Family Aero of Freddie James. Despite chain trouble and damage to the chassis he went through to win a silver.

At Southport on 6th October Tom Rhodes proved faster than Syd Keay in the straight mile event for cyclecars.

Autumn heralded the start of the record-breaking season once more. On 30th October, Robin Jackson took his aluminium-bodied special onto Brooklands, fitted with his other 500cc Blackburne vee twin engine of standard bore (497cc) and captured further 500cc class records. Out of four records taken, the 1 hour at 71.40mph was the fastest.

Harold Beart's record breaker had been completely rebuilt in the spring to take air-cooled engines, necessitating a redesigned cowl. The chassis was also rebuilt with cranked front cross tubes, similar to Lones's special chassis but much more deeply cranked, considerably widening and lowering the car. All the frame tubes had been polished to show up any cracks that might appear and the rear springs were repositioned Super Aero style above the bevel box angle irons. Two Hartford shock absorbers now held down the rear wheel. The rake of the steering column was reduced, and special hand-finished steering arms were fitted, together with solid rear fork tubes. On 6th, 7th and 9th November, Beart took the car onto Brooklands fitted with one of the special 731cc ohv JAP engines (74 x 85mm) and successfully collected eight records, the fastest being 50 miles at 82.57mph.

Another three-wheeler making a mark on records was the MEB (previously known

Fred James in the International. (James scrapbook)

International Six Days' Trial, 1928.

Wednesday, 12th September.—170½ miles.

MORNING.

Time Schedule. h. m. s.	PLACE.	Mileage. Inter.	Mileage. Total.
	First Competitor leaves at 9 a.m.		
0 0 0	**Harrogate**	0	0
0 10 30	Bridge—Knaresborough	3½	3½
0 33 0	Bridge—Boroughbridge	7½	11
0 48 0	Brafferton	5	16
1 0 0	**20 Mile Notice**	4	20
1 12 45	Cross Roads—Coxwold	4¼	24¼
1 21 45	**White Horse—Observed Hill**	3	27¼
1 27 45	Switch—L.	2	29¼
1 36 45	Sutton—R.	3	32¼
1 47 15	Church—Boltby	3½	35¾
1 48 45	**Boltby Bank—Observed Hill**	½	36¼
2 0 0	**40 Mile Notice**	3¾	40
2 16 30	Square—Helmsley—**Replenishment Control**	5½	45½
2 29 15	Ford	4¼	49¾
2 37 30	Cross Roads—Fadmoor	2¾	52½
3 0 0	**60 Mile Notice**	7½	60
3 0 45	**Blakey—Observed Hill**	¼	60¼
3 31 30	Railway Bridge—Danby End	10¼	70½
3 56 15	Church—Ugthorpe	8¼	78¾
4 0 0	**80 Mile Notice**	1¼	80
4 6 45	Inn—Lythe	2¼	82¼
4 18 45	**Luncheon Control—The Belle and the Talbot Hotels, Whitby**	4	86¼

AFTERNOON.

Time Schedule. h. m. s.	PLACE.	Mileage. Inter.	Mileage. Total.
	First Competitor leaves at 2.30 p.m.		
0 0 0	**Whitby**	0	0
0 6 0	Church—Ruswarp	2	2
0 21 0	**Littlebeck—Observed Hill**	5	7
0 34 30	Railway Crossing—Grosmont	4½	11½
1 0 0	Railway Bridge—Glaisdale **Limber—Observed Hill** **20 Mile Notice**	8½	20
1 7 30	**The Delves—Observed Hill**	2½	22½
1 30 0	**Rosedale—Observed Hill**	7½	30
1 42 45	Fords—Hutton-le-Hole	4¼	34¼
1 54 0	Cross Roads—Kirkby Moorside	3¾	38
2 0 0	**40 Mile Notice**	2	40
2 11 15	Cross Roads—Nunnington—**Replenishment Control**	3¾	43¾
2 45 0	Switch—L.	11¼	55
3 0 0	Cross Roads—Coxwold **60 Mile Notice**	5	60
3 24 45	Brafferton	8¼	68¼
3 39 45	Bridge—Boroughbridge	5	73¼
4 0 0	**80 Mile Notice**	6¾	80
4 2 15	Knaresborough	¾	80¾
4 12 45	**Harrogate**	3½	84¼

Two of Freddie James's logs from the International Six Days' Trial of 1928.

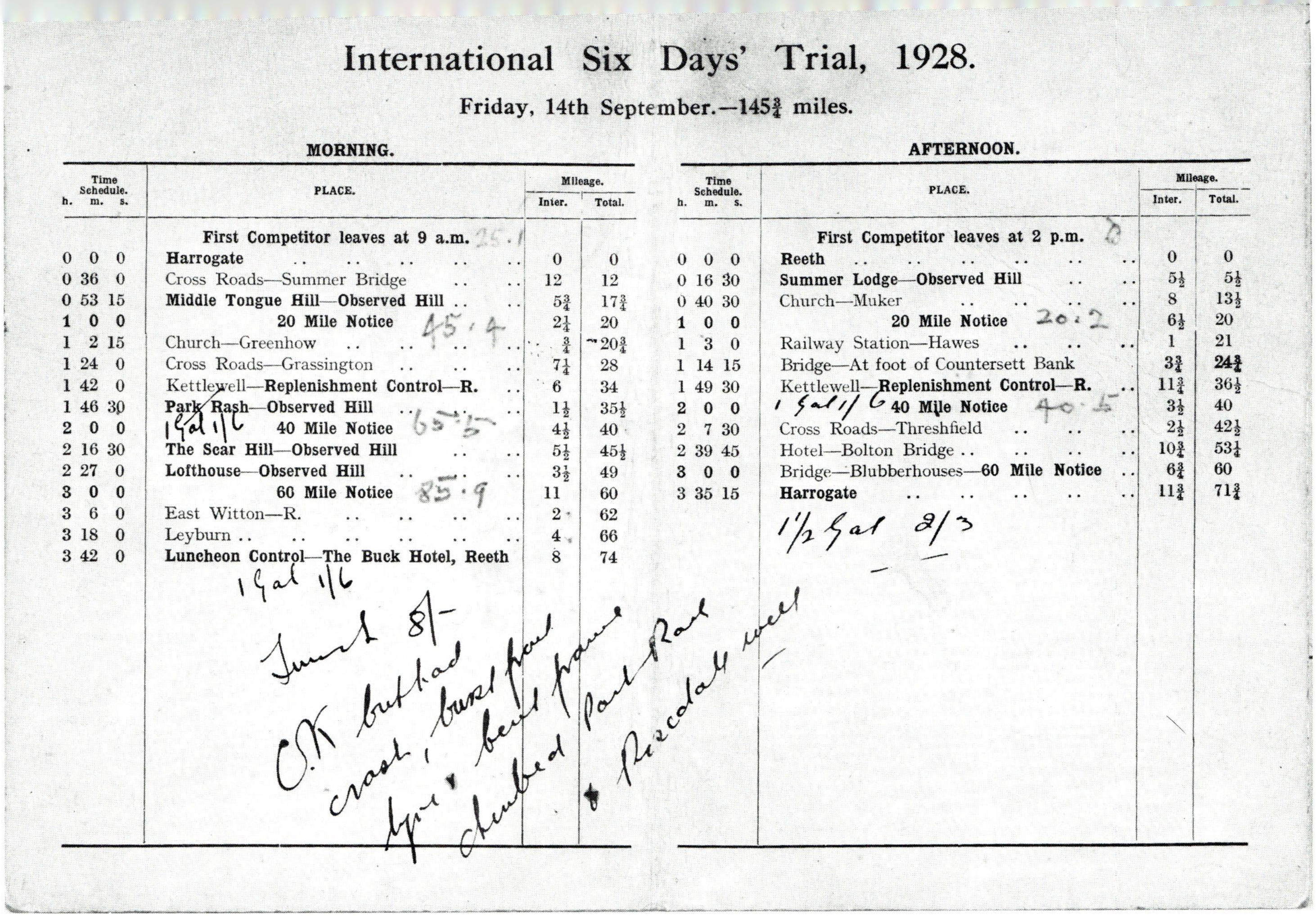

International Six Days' Trial, 1928.

Friday, 14th September.—$145\frac{3}{4}$ miles.

MORNING.

Time Schedule. h. m. s.	PLACE.	Mileage. Inter.	Mileage. Total.
	First Competitor leaves at 9 a.m. 25.1		
0 0 0	**Harrogate**	0	0
0 36 0	Cross Roads—Summer Bridge	12	12
0 53 15	**Middle Tongue Hill—Observed Hill**	$5\frac{3}{4}$	$17\frac{3}{4}$
1 0 0	**20 Mile Notice** 45.4	$2\frac{1}{4}$	20
1 2 15	Church—Greenhow	$\frac{3}{4}$	$20\frac{3}{4}$
1 24 0	Cross Roads—Grassington	$7\frac{1}{4}$	28
1 42 0	Kettlewell—**Replenishment Control—R.** ..	6	34
1 46 30	**Park Rash—Observed Hill**	$1\frac{1}{2}$	$35\frac{1}{2}$
2 0 0	1 Gal 1/6 **40 Mile Notice** 65.5	$4\frac{1}{2}$	40
2 16 30	**The Scar Hill—Observed Hill**	$5\frac{1}{2}$	$45\frac{1}{2}$
2 27 0	**Lofthouse—Observed Hill**	$3\frac{1}{2}$	49
3 0 0	**60 Mile Notice** 85.9	11	60
3 6 0	East Witton—R.	2	62
3 18 0	Leyburn	4	66
3 42 0	**Luncheon Control—The Buck Hotel, Reeth**	8	74

1 Gal 1/6

Lunch 8/-

O.K. but had crash, burst front tyre & bent frame, climbed Park Rash & Riccdall well

AFTERNOON.

Time Schedule. h. m. s.	PLACE.	Mileage. Inter.	Mileage. Total.
	First Competitor leaves at 2 p.m.		
0 0 0	**Reeth**	0	0
0 16 30	**Summer Lodge—Observed Hill**	$5\frac{1}{2}$	$5\frac{1}{2}$
0 40 30	Church—Muker	8	$13\frac{1}{2}$
1 0 0	**20 Mile Notice** 20.2	$6\frac{1}{2}$	20
1 3 0	Railway Station—Hawes	1	21
1 14 15	Bridge—At foot of Countersett Bank	$3\frac{3}{4}$	$24\frac{3}{4}$
1 49 30	Kettlewell—**Replenishment Control—R.** ..	$11\frac{3}{4}$	$36\frac{1}{2}$
2 0 0	1 Gal 1/6 **40 Mile Notice** 40.5	$3\frac{1}{2}$	40
2 7 30	Cross Roads—Threshfield	$2\frac{1}{2}$	$42\frac{1}{2}$
2 39 45	Hotel—Bolton Bridge	$10\frac{3}{4}$	$53\frac{1}{4}$
3 0 0	Bridge—Blubberhouses—**60 Mile Notice** ..	$6\frac{3}{4}$	60
3 35 15	**Harrogate**	$11\frac{3}{4}$	$71\frac{3}{4}$

1½ Gal 2/3

as the Royal Ruby). Since Douglas Hawkes had left Morgan racing in 1923, he had been working as racing manager to Ernest Eldridge, and was involved in preparing his record breakers at the banked Montlhéry Circuit, which had opened near Paris in 1924. Here he had met another contestant on the record-breaking circuit—Gwenda Stewart, a tough young woman who as Mrs Janson had ridden a Trump JAP motorcycle way back in 1922 for a double 12 record at Brooklands. Her present husband, Col RN Stewart, had also been involved with the Trump concern at Byfleet, but when Brooklands had introduced silencers and banned women motorcyclists they had both moved to Paris to race various motorcycles in the freedom of the French track. Trump Motors had meanwhile become the Brooklands Engineering Company, with Gwenda as a director. Two separate accidents then brought Douglas and Gwenda together, one involving Eldridge, who subsequently retired from record breaking, and the other Gwenda herself, who parted company from a Terrot JAP motorcycle when the front tyre came off during practice for a record attempt in 1927. Douglas Hawkes now suggested that she should switch to three wheels, and offered to prepare a Morgan for her. Unfortunately, HFS was not interested, and so Hawkes contacted MEB. They certainly were interested and prepared a car to his requirements. In June Hawkes took short distance 500cc records with an MEB, using a JAP single (80mm x 99mm), and in September Gwenda herself took class I records up to 1 hour from Robin Jackson's Morgan. Although these records were subsequently recaptured by Jackson in October as mentioned above, HFS was not to forget the Stewart/Hawkes threat.

For the MCC High Speed Trial at the end of October, Joe Turner as usual returned his Blackburne engine to Ted Baldwin for overhaul. Once again it proved well worth while as his was the only Morgan to gain a gold medal, covering 73.1 miles in the hour.

Early in November at the Motor Cycle Show HFS introduced his 1929 models. An improved De Luxe model replaced the Standard. Geared steering was now a standard fitment, as were helical cut dynamo gears and a stronger dynamo bracket. Felt oil seals were fitted to the countershaft and rear wheel spindle. Newton front shock absorbers were added to the Super Aero's specification, together with a stay to stiffen the top of the crosshead. A new type of Super Aero body was promised for January, to which a hood could be fitted. This new wider body was to have the oil tank mounted behind the radiator, necessitating large D-shaped cut-outs, and the skirt panel was to be shaped so that it could pass behind the track rod instead of through it.

The last classic trial of 1928, the London-Exeter, was held in pouring rain. This proved too much for Lionel Creed's passenger who refused to get in again after the breakfast stop: he had had enough of being soaked, with rain pouring down from above, and water coming up through the floorboards from below. Creed carried on with his Blackburne Super Aero, and amazingly climbed all the hills. He was told later that if he'd kept to time he would have collected a special award.

Right at the end of the year Gwenda Stewart and Douglas Hawkes took the little MEB onto Montlhéry again, this time fitted with one of the 731cc JAP engines, and broke Harold Beart's recently established records, as well as establishing a further six new ones. This was too much for HFS, who promptly contacted Douglas, offering him a Morgan and help for the forthcoming season.

On the other side of the world, the first Morgan was about to make its mark on the

Still Faster

Australian racing scene. Without an indigenous motor industry of its own, Australia relied on imported cars for motor sport. One of the most popular types of events was short circuit speedway, as opposed to the American style on big ovals. This was introduced in 1923 by John Hoskins at Maitland, New South Wales, predating the craze in England by five years. Early in 1928 Jimmy Thoms of Sydney took a fancy to the new Super Aero, and got his friend Mick Marks to bring a catalogue home from Williams Limited, Sydney motorcycle dealers. The order went in, and the car arrived in a crate in September.

Trials on the road convinced Jimmy that it was a potent machine, and so he entered for the 1929 New Year's Day meeting on Penrith Speedway, an American style 1-mile dirt oval. Mick Marks passengered Thoms, equipping himself with two well padded shirts for which he had reason to be grateful as he spent most of his time hanging out with his face in the dirt. Thoms won his heat in the 1100cc 5-mile car championship, and led from start to finish in the final, making the most of the Morgan's acceleration to beat Donnelly's Fiat and Beasely's Singer at 58 mph—despite a protest from these two that Thoms had taken a short cut when he knocked over some flags.

Thoms won his heat in the Efficiency Motor Schools Cup all-powers event, and went into the final against eight other cars. Mick Marks was all in now, so Cam Fraser took over as passenger for this race. Barnes's 2400cc Frontenac-Ford on scratch proved too fast, catching the Morgan on 28 seconds in the last half lap, after a furious chase through the dust. Braitling's Alvis 12/50, which started 10 seconds too early, was relegated to third place.

Jimmy Thoms and Mick Mark after winning at Penrith. (Wright collection)

Morgan Sweeps the Board

Several Morgan drivers tried the new English speedway tracks. Freddie James was thrown off the Sheffield track for making bad ruts, but another Morgan owner found his Morgan faster than sidecars in the dirt, because he could broadside it in the proper manner. To do this he lowered the gear ratio and added a 60lb lead weight to the nearside of the front crosshead to keep the inside wheel down.

By the January Southport sand meeting Clive Lones had made some modifications to his special Super Aero. A large hump now covered the rear wheel, and he had enlarged the size of the D-shaped cut-outs in the bonnet sides. The colour of the car was also changed—to red. Why red? 'So the blood wouldn't show, but it did', he said recently. Lones came second to Edwards's Brough using his 1096cc JAP engine in the 10-mile sidecar race.

Ron Horton entered his JAP Aero in both the Colmore and the Victory trials in 1929, gaining a gold and a bronze. These were probably the last major trials undertaken by CJ 6343 in Horton's hands, for he was soon to sell it to Malvern enthusiast Lionel Creed. Horton continued to compete in trials, however, driving works Morgans.

Brooklands reopened after its winter repair for the BMCRC meeting on 23rd March. Clive Lones entered for the three-lap novices' handicap, but on the last lap his Morgan caught fire on the Railway Straight. Clive burnt his hands turning off the fuel and so Nel had to apply the handbrake. It was found that the float chamber needle of the Brown and Barlow carburettor had vibrated loose, allowing excess fuel to escape from the flooded carburettor which then ignited. Lones is reported to have thrown the offending article into the River Wey. At the same meeting, Joe Wright used a JTOR engine to lap Brooklands at 113mph in his Zenith, which no doubt impressed Clive.

On 8th March Douglas Hawkes took delivery of an unpainted grey Super Aero, chassis number 1290A, fitted with a JTOR engine, number JTOR/S42395. Basically a standard Super Aero, the car had a tear-shaped hump on the tail and a wind deflector on the driver's side of the scuttle. Engine cooling was assisted by air passing right through the dummy radiator and out through the cockpit. Only front wheel brakes were fitted, operated by a hand lever, although Gwenda was encouraged not to use them. On 25th March she took the Morgan onto Montlhéry taking three time and distance records, the fastest being the 200 mile at 83.68mph. She followed this up with the 50 kilometre on 3rd May, and then the engine was changed. With one of the 1926 731cc engines she took short distance records on 17th May, and records up to 1 hour (taken at 85.22mph) on 21st May.

For 30th May Douglas prepared the JTOR for short distance records, and Gwenda successfully captured the flying start 5 miles at 103.13 mph and the flying start 5 kilometres at 103.4mph—the fastest yet recorded by either a sidecar or an unsupercharged cyclecar. Gwenda lived for excitement. As well as racing motorcycles herself, she had passengered Claude Temple on his ohc Anzani sidecar outfit when he became the first motorcyclist to set a sidecar world record at over 100mph. Fearless by nature, she kept herself very fit, employing a masseur for the purpose. She had many other interests apart from racing, and taking records was for her simply a means of earning money quickly to allow her to pursue them. Douglas would prepare to car for her, helped by the Brooklands Engineering Company for engine pistons and valves,

Douglas, Gwenda and mechanic at Montlhéry, 1929. (Hawkes collection)

and assisted by his Belgian mechanic. When all was ready, Gwenda would take her instructions from Douglas, climb in, keep to Douglas's engine rev limits and take the records.

Meanwhile, trials continued unabated. Freddie James drove his Family Aero W157 to a gold medal in the Leeds £200 trial, despite a delay caused by a broken radiator pipe. In the London-Land's End both Arthur Maskell and GH Marshall competed in Family models, winning a gold and a silver respectively. Maskell travelled with a full complement of passengers, while Marshall's car was fitted with one of the short bonnets finishing behind the LTOW JAP engine. Another keen Morgan trials competitor, Swift, was driving XV 54, a late 1928 Super Aero specially modified for trials work with straight tubes in the front crosshead and rear springs mounted beneath the bevel box angle irons. Since March this method of rear spring mounting had become standard on all new Super Aeros. Whilst Swift won a gold, Lionel Creed driving a factory Super-Aero-JAP failed on Porlock and had to be content with a silver. This factory car was one of the last to have the extra-two speed gearbox behind the engine, giving four speeds. Creed discovered he was in the wrong set of gears halfway up Porlock and stalled when he found it wasn't possible to change from one set to the other whilst moving.

Four Morgans took part in the Scottish Six Days' Trial in May, all JAP Aeros. HFS, passengered by Ruth, and Geoff Harris both won gold medals, whilst RN Reid and RW Wilton, substituting for Frank Spouse who was ill, won silvers.

Lionel Creed used his own immaculate Blackburne Super Aero for the London-Edinburgh, complete with nickel-plated mudguards. He powered his way through to win a gold, as did eight other Morgans, including Swift, Goodall and Maskell in his Family.

133

Lionel Creed in a factory Super Aero on Bluehills Mine. (L Creed)

At Brooklands Clive Lones was the sole Morgan entry in the BMCRC meeting on 1st June. His visits to the JAP stores for parts had enabled him to enter with a 735cc ohv water-cooled twin engine (70mm x 92mm) with which he won the three-lap private owner's handicap at 81.77mph and came third in the passenger event. Later Lones entered the 50-mile handicap for the George Newman cup, but although he beat Baragwanath's Brough he was not amongst the first six to finish. Once again Joe Wright's JTOR-engined Zenith raised the lap record, to 118.86 mph, and once again Lones was impressed—so much so that he arranged with his friend Ted or 'Barry' Baragwanath to try out one of the JTOR engines, namely that from 'Barry's' own sidecar outfit, switching engine plates and flywheel. To his astonishment, Lones found he could now lap faster than with his 1100cc engine, so he asked 'Barry' to get one for him.

The West Kent Club's Dartmoor Trial in July saw a new driver joining the regular club trials drivers of Swift, Broad and Johnson—Sydney Allard, with his JAP-engined Super Aero. On the same day, as they were setting off on the overnight run from London to Exeter, the Morgan speedmen gathered once again at Madresfield for the famous speed trials. Once again a rolling start of 15 yards was used. Apparently Horton did not compete, for Lones's Morgan, named 'Bob' after the family's dog, a black chow, proved the fastest Morgan entrant, powered by the 1100cc JAP engine. A new, more deeply cranked and lowered chassis had now been fitted to 'Bob', which clocked 32 seconds to win both the Morgan and Jackson cups. Second fastest was Lionel Creed, probably using the ex-Horton trials Morgan CJ 6343 which he had recently purchased. He confidently expected to win the Morgan 'A' cup for the fastest amateur but George Goodall objected, reasoning that Creed couldn't be classed as an amateur as he received a 17½ per cent discount off spares from the Morgan Company. Thus the award went to CN Taylor. Cecil Jay was again driving 'Jim', now fitted with the ex-Harold Beart-tuned 731cc JAP engine, with which he won his class.

Just three days later Clive Lones was back at Brooklands, record breaking with his lowered Super Aero. His latest engine from the second-hand JAP store was an ex-

Swift's straight crosshead Super Aero in the Dartmoor Trial. (Wilson collection)

Lones corrects a tail slide to take the Morgan Cup. (Morgan Motor Co)

```
Telephone: AVENUE 0832          4 & 5, High Street, Aldgate,
    Telegrams:
EBBLEWHITE, ALDGATE.                London, E. 1.
ESTABLISHED 1840.
```

A. V. EBBLEWHITE,

Manufacturer and Importer of Musical Instruments.
Gramophones, Records & Supplies. Jazz Band Specialist.
WHOLESALE, RETAIL AND EXPORT.

To the Army and Navy, and the
Honourable East India Company.   PIANOFORTE AND MUSIC SELLER.

19. 6. 1929

Dear Mr. Lones,

Thanks for your letter usually a day or two notice is quite enough, and even then it need not be definite. Usually men who go for Records are down at the track tuning up, and then ringing me up to make the day and time definite. Next week the track will not be available as the J.C.C have it for practice. Looking at the bookings it looks as if the 15th to 26th of July would be the quite clear of fast Cars on Records.

AVEbblewhite

A letter written to Lones by Ebblewhite, the handicapper and starter at Brooklands. (Lones collection)

Freddie Dixon 498cc (80mm x 99mm) single cylinder with which he captured six 500cc class records up to the 50 miles at over 70mph. The following day he completed the session with the longer 2 hours, 3 hours and 200 mile records.

Although Lones was enjoying success, Robin Jackson's record attempts did not always go so smoothly. On one attempt, using a 500cc single Blackburne, Robin had settled down to a steady lap speed and completed around three hours' driving. He passed the timing hut by the Fork as normal, and disappeared onto the Members

Lones's Class I records taken on 23rd July 1929. (Lones Collection)

Banking, only to discover that the steering box had become unsoldered, allowing the wheel to come away in his hands. Shutting the hand throttle, he dropped the wheel and bailed out as the Morgan veered for the trackside railings. However on its way to the ground, the steering wheel knocked the hand throttle open once again, and after glancing off the railings the car resumed its way around the track. Imagine the surprise of Jackson's mechanics when they saw the car appear on the Railway Straight on schedule, but with no driver! At the far end of the Railway Straight the Morgan hit the railings and turned a couple of somersaults, just as Robin appeared, walking around the banking with an injured wrist. Solder also proved to be the undoing of Jackson on another occasion. He was on his way to Syston, passengered by Dick Caesar in his Beart inspired special, when the steering once again went limp. The car ploughed into an ornamental tree surrounded by railings, Dick escaping injury by inches.

On 27th August Clive Lones had yet another engine on 'Bob'. This time it was a 346cc JAP single, with which he captured class records for the flying start 5 kilometres. The following day he once again went for longer distance records, taking the 50 kilometres, 100 miles and 1 hour, the fastest being at 68.15 mph. Obviously with such a small engine, the car was run in as stripped a state as feasible. Lones had fitted beaded-edge front wheels, as these were lighter and caused less friction than the straight-sided wheels he normally used.

On 31st August the New Cyclecar Club ran their second Brooklands race meeting.

Cecil Jay and Charlie Curtis work on 'Jim' in front of the Brooklands tuning sheds. UY 761 is the factory towing vehicle, and on the left is the ex-Jackson special. (Jay collection)

Amongst the non-starters was Lionel Creed who had a broken bevel box following trials damage, for which George Goodall insisted he should pay full price. George himself had entered Cecil Jay to drive the 731cc Beart engined 'Jim', which had received a lowered chassis to Super Aero specification, necessitating a hump on the flat-sided Aero's tail to allow for the rear wheel. The car was towed to the track behind an old trials Standard three-wheeler by factory mechanic Charlie Curtis, who had been with Morgans since 1916 and who was to passenger Jay. During practice on the special Grand Prix course, Jay went too close to one of the sand bank turns in an over-enthusiastic attempt to reduce his braking distance, flipping the Morgan over. Cecil asked Charlie if he could get out. 'Of course I bloody well can't, and when I do I'm not getting back in again either,' was Charlie's reply. True to form, Cecil had to carry sand ballast for the race itself. The steering column was broken in the inversion, and George Goodall's own Morgan had to be stripped of the relevant part to repair the racer.

The first race was a two-lap novices' handicap over the Brooklands outer circuit. Sydney Allard's LTOW Super Aero proved too fast for the rest of the field, racing through from virtual scratch to win at 73.37mph.

The second race was a three-wheeler handicap for the Morgan Cup. Robin Jackson hoped to retain this from the previous year, although he was now racing a different car—his 1096cc Blackburne-engined Beart-inspired special. The opposition included Ron Horton with his racer, fitted with a single shock absorber over the rear wheel and now having a hump on the tail to cover it. Tom Rhodes led from start to finish with his Blackburne Aero, now coloured white and sporting a Super Aero type lowered chassis, despite strong opposition from Clive Lones who finished second in 'Bob' now powered by his newly ordered JTOR engine. Arthur Maskell came third also driving a Super Aero with hump on the tail, his being a 1929 model probably fitted with the tuned LTOW engine he had used the previous year.

Still Faster

Earlier in the year Robin Jackson had advertised his 500cc vee twin Blackburne special for sale. We suspect that Ron Horton drove it in the third race, the three-lap short handicap for the Jackson Cup. He won at 71.15 mph, Clive Lones driving through the field to finish second with the new JTOR.

The fourth race was a five-lap handicap for the Beart Cup and once again Tom Rhodes proved victorious at 89.74mph, despite being rehandicapped after his early win. Horton – driving Jackson's 500cc special, Jackson and Lones all developed trouble and failed to finish.

The finale of the meeting was the Cyclecar Grand Prix. It was run over the same course as in 1928, and the 750cc class was again given three laps' start. This year the sand banks caused quite a few problems to the four-wheelers, an Amilcar and a Salmson nearly overturning and an Austin Seven damaging a wheel. On one lap Arthur Maskell, who had been driving almost brakeless and was suffering from engine trouble, clipped one of the sandbanks, breaking one of the crosshead tubes. Two laps later when he came round to the sandbanks again, the damaged chassis caused him to lose control, mounting another sandbank and finally crashing into the railings lining the track. Here, with considerable understatement, he announced that he had retired! After the race Clive Lones helped Maskell retrieve the car, and drive it back to the paddock.

Maskell announces his retirement! (Wilson collection)

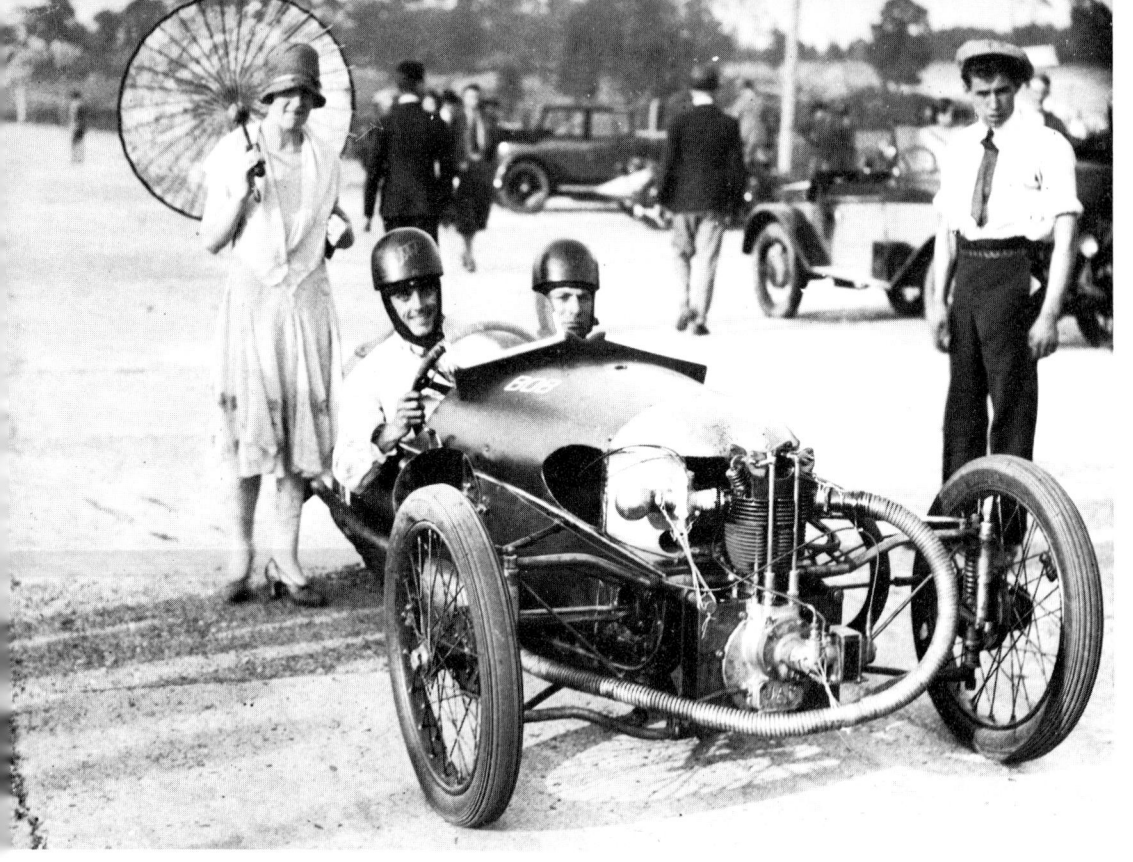

Lones after winning the BMCRC all-comers' handicap. (Motor Cycle)

Meanwhile the race continued. Cecil Jay, cornering very cautiously but neatly, built up quite a lead with his three-lap start, and held it to the end, to take the Light Car and Cyclecar Cup, and also the Mobil Cup for his class win. The next Morgan to finish was Syd Keay's Blackburne Aero which came fifth to win the 850-1100cc class and the JAP cup.

7th September saw Lones back at Brooklands, this time with his 500cc JAP single back in place on 'Bob', running on beaded-edge tyres once more. The bumps of Brooklands had made Clive completely remove the hump on the tail of of his low Super Aero, replacing it, for easier access to the shock absorber, with a canvas cover over a raised metal frame. He won the all-comers' five-lap passenger handicap by nearly half a mile.

On the same day, Gwenda Stewart achieved her target of becoming the first cyclecar driver to put 100 miles into the hour. In fact, she managed 101.55 miles and also captured further 1100cc class records for the 50 kilometres, 100 kilometres, 50 miles and 100 miles. At that time the records for sidecars and cars of 1100cc stood at 89.40mph and 103.24 mph respectively. Douglas had prepared the engine to run on alcohol at 7.2 to 1 compression, giving a consumption of 15 mpg, and told Gwenda to use 4500rpm. As she completed the 1 hour attempt, her engine cut, having run out of fuel. Douglas later admitted that he had not intended to run to such close limits!

Five days later the same combination collected long distance 1100cc records from 7 to 12 hours at 66mph. A higher gear ratio had been substituted, together with much smaller carburettors. Benzole/alcohol fuel was used and Dunlop road racing tyres

Still Faster

substituted for the previous track variety. Fuel consumption now worked out at 36 mph. Over the next two months they continued to take records with both the 996cc and 731cc engines, and on 10th November Gwenda recorded 106.45mph for the flying 5 kilometres, the fastest speed ever accomplished by a three-wheeler cyclecar.

On 14th September the MCC High Speed Trial provided some form of consolation for the failures at the New Cyclecar Club meeting. Maskell led the Morgan contingent, lapping at 80 mph and finishing 6 minutes early, after covering twenty-four laps to win a gold medal. Dennis Welch and TB Raban also took golds, as did Geoff Harris with his KMB Blackburne Super Aero, complete with a hump on its tail.

Speed trials at Southport on 28th September saw Tom Rhodes come second in the 10-mile sidecar race to Buckley's Brough, whilst on 9th November CN Taylor drove his Blackburne Morgan, now rebodied as a 1929 Super Aero with the tall radiator, to make fastest time of the day at the Cambridge University AC Speed Trials near Newmarket.

Just before the Olympia show, JAPs announced modifications to the 1096cc LTOW engine. These included the fitting of fully enclosed push rods together with cast aluminium rocker boxes bolted to redesigned cylinder heads.

At the show itself HFS introduced a new type of chassis known as the 'M' type. It

Rhodes's Morgan at Southport. (Syd Rhodes)

featured for the first time a detachable bevel box in which the mesh of the bevels could be adjusted by threaded rings. The newly designed forged rear fork blades pivoted concentrically with the cross-shaft, which allowed the wheel base to be reduced by around 3 inches. The rear wheel had also been redesigned to take an internally expanding foot brake, and had a knock-out rear spindle and underslung rear springs. The Super Aero was the first to be fitted with the new chassis. In this form, it could be distinguished from earlier Super Aeros in that the front crosshead was lowered by cranking both tubes—rather on the pattern adopted by Lones, as opposed to the inverted lower lug and cranked top tube of the 'B' type. Shock absorbers were fitted to the front wheels only. Although the 'M' type was made the standard Super Aero chassis from the time of the show, a few 'wide B' chassis models were produced with the inverted lower chassis lug.

Although the 996cc and 731cc engines produced the most interesting records for Gwenda Stewart in 1929, she also used a 500cc single JAP and even a 350cc single (70 x

Creed has trouble with Parson's chains on the ex-Horton Aero. (L Creed)

Still Faster

90mm) for some attempts. She had covered over 5000 miles on the Montlhéry track in the Morgan, of which 1000 were at over 100mph—an impressive feat when one realizes that she had never even driven one on a road! Now that the record year was over, Douglas returned the Morgan to HFS for overhaul, and at long last for its first coat of paint. At the same time he asked HFS for a special single-seater, especially designed for short-distance records. HFS wasn't very keen. After all, the previous records had been obtained with a virtually standard Super Aero, which he was able to advertise to his advantage, but eventually he agreed to Douglas's demands and gave the go ahead for a special.

The year of 1930 opened with the New Cyclecar Club changing its name to the Light Car Club. Membership was now extended to cars of up to 1500cc, whereas the previous limit had been 1100cc.

In the Colmore Cup Trial in February Ron Horton, now driving a factory JAP Aero, UY 5068, took the Rhode Cup for the best car, whilst HFS and Ruth in JAP Aero AB 16 and George Goodall in another JAP Aero GC 4 took gold medals. Lionel Creed entered with Horton's old Aero CJ6343, which must have done more major trials than any other Morgan, but lost any chance of a medal when his driving chain tangled with the Parson's chains. Creed had experienced this type of problem before and had wondered whether the Parson's chain could be dispensed with altogether by having a greater tyre area on the rear driving wheel. Theoretically, the extra grip this should give would make up for the loss of the chains. In late 1929 Lionel wrote to Dunlop asking whether they could produce a special rear wheel for him, consisting of two wheel rims slung side by side on a single hub. He got as far as getting blueprints produced by Dunlop before telling HFS what he was up to. 'The old man' thereupon agreed to try out the idea, of which more later.

In March 1930 Gwenda Stewart was entertained by HFS to a luncheon in Malvern, in honour of her magnificent 101.55 miles in the hour. She was presented with a gold chronograph, which had been subscribed by the manufacturers of Amal Carburettors, Coventry chains, Dunlop tyres, M-L magnetos, JAP engines, Lissen plugs, Castrol oil and of course by HFS himself. After the meal Gwenda was taken to HFS's home. Although Peter Morgan had by now been sent to bed, she went upstairs to talk to her young admirer.

Back at Montlhéry on 21st March, Gwenda took to the track to collect middle-distance records. The Morgan was powered by a new JAP engine, one of the rare 1096cc air-cooled racing JAPs developed by lengthening the stroke of the JTOR (80 x 109mm).

On the same day, back on the trials hills, Freddie James drove CJ 743, a factory Aero with high level exhaust pipes and a single D cut-out instead of louvres in the bonnet side, for the Leeds £200 trial. Foul bitter weather enveloped the London-Land's End Trial in April, in which Geoff Harris was one of eleven Morgan gold medal winners, driving what was probably the works JAP Aero that Freddie had just used, but carrying the registration ML 1142, fitted with high level exhaust pipes and flanged cycle type mudguards. High level pipes were becoming popular for trials as they were less vulnerable to rock damage. Among the other gold medal winners were Marshall with his LTOW-engined Family, Harry Jones—Morgan's service manager in his first MCC trial, and George Goodall. Goodall was driving his usual registration plate, GC4,

Mr and Mrs Goodall in their prototype Sports Family. (Goodall scrapbooks)

but the Morgan was in all probability a prototype Sports Family using the double cranked lowered M type chassis. High exhaust pipes were once again in use, and a single D cut-out behind the radiator gave access to the oil tank. The windscreen was one of the new Pearce V-screens, as used by HFS in the Colmore.

The ex-Robin Jackson aluminium-bodied special had been eventually purchased by Clive Lones, the 500cc Blackburne engine passing to Ron Horton. For record attempts Clive always used Shell oil. One day, whilst joking at their premises, he was offered a Chater Lea 350cc single engine. He collected it from Letchford and fitted it to the ex-Jackson special, which had been painted black in 1929. Lones entered the newly engined special for the opening BMCRC meeting in April, but after leading the first lap of the three-lap passenger handicap he finished in fourth place behind winner Baragwanath's Brough.

In May Geoff Harris drove his usual JAP Aero ML 1142 to win a silver cup in the Scottish Six Days' Trial, without losing a single mark. Obviously a master of the trials art, he ran with gears of $5\frac{1}{4}$ to 1 top and 11 to 1 bottom, with the rear tyre (27 x 4 Dunlop Sports) inflated to only 12 to 15 lb per square inch. Parson's chains were fitted for each observed hill, taking around 90 seconds to fit, and 30 to remove. He took each hill at speed, making corrections on the throttle.

On 15th May, Gwenda Stewart and Douglas Hawkes were joined by their friend and fellow racing driver 'Sammy' Davis for an attack on the 24 hour record with the long stroke 1096cc engine. Sammy had never driven a Morgan before, and found that it ran with a slight snake. For record attempts Hawkes arranged his own oil supplies to the vital parts. Each had its own drip indicator which had to be checked, to make sure that the colourless Castrol racing oil was still dripping through, and there was also a pressure gauge and an ammeter to keep an eye on. Sammy was quite worried by the oil indicators, though Gwenda herself recently confided that she never bothered to look at them, having far too much to do just driving. One wonders whether Douglas ever knew this, as no less than three were fitted. The passenger compartment was now fitted with extra fuel tanks for the long distance to be attempted. Driving spells were to be of three hours, shared between Gwenda and Sammy. On Sammy's second spell, the nearside piston seized and the Morgan stopped. Nonplussed, Hawkes merely sent the drivers off for a rest, fitted another engine, and restarted the record bid. Despite a broken front suspension spring, after 21 hours' driving the records were in the bag. As Douglas, his chief mechanic Jean, and Parks of Dunlops had been on duty for 31 hours they stopped the attempt then—to go on would only serve to raise the 24 hour record they had made on distance anyway.

Goodall drove his dropped chassis Sports Family in the June London-Edinburgh, and was one of six Morgan gold winners, including RD Smith who was still regularly competing with his Anzani special. Dennis Welch, a motorcycle trials competitor of some experience, drove AB 16, a factory JAP Aero with the new type of Pearce windscreen fitted. GE Swift wasn't entered for this event, but now had one of the new M type Super Aeros converted for trials work with straight front crosshead tubes, as on his previous car. He retained the registration number XV 54, and used one of the latest rocker box JAP LTOW engines.

For the June BMCRC meeting, Clive Lones entered both his racers. With the flat cam ohc 348cc Chater Lea engine on his ex-Jackson Morgan he won the three-lap non-trade handicap by 100 yards at 64.42 mph, after creating a large oil smokescreen. He used the same car for the passenger handicap but retired with bearing trouble on the first lap. The Chater Lea was a good, well-made little engine, but was prone to bad vibration at around 6000 rpm—making Clive's hands go quite numb.

The following race, the 350cc to 1100cc three-lap passenger handicap, saw Lones back in 'Bob', fitted with his ex-Dixon 498cc JAP engine. He beat Cox's 1096cc JAP Morgan to finish first.

Madresfield was held on 19th July in fine weather. With his JTOR engine installed in 'Bob', Clive Lones won the Morgan Cup for the fastest Morgan. He also had the ex-Dixon engine in attendance on the ex-Jackson car, and with this he came third in the 500cc sidecar class. In the 1100cc Morgan class only Jay, using a 1096cc engine, and JA Stinton with a similar engine competed against Clive Lones. One of the entrants for the car classes was Lionel Creed with his Brooklands Austin. 'You'd have won the Morgan class if you'd entered', HFS told him. 'You know why I didn't', Lionel replied. This was an oblique reference to George Goodall's often inflexible approach to the costs incurred in racing. Although responsible for much that Morgans could be grateful for, he was considered by many of the racing men, and some agents, as being a bit too uncharitable towards them; after all, their achievements did give Morgans good publicity. On one occassion, for example, Clive Lones, a world record holder, received a bill for just two pence!

One week later the Light Car Club, previously known as the New Cyclecar Club, held its annual Brooklands race meeting. The first race was for novices, with no

Robin Jackson in his Beart-inspired special carries ballast instead of a passenger, at The Light Car Club meeting. (Autocar)

Sydney Allard and Cecil Jay leave the start in the three-wheeler handicap. (Motor Cycle)

```
MORGAN MOTOR CO., LTD.,          January 29th, 1930
    MALVERN LINK.

    Mr. H. L. Creed,
              Lynx Motors
              Newtown Road,
                        Malvern
                    INVOICE                              PRICE

    YOUR ORDER No.

    2 Parsons Chains
    1 Track Rod
    2 Spring Shackles
    1. 48.T. Sprocket
    2. H.L. Plugs

    2 ft of Rubber Petrol Pipe                       1    6
    2 ft of    "       Oil                           1    8

                                                     3    2
              Less 17½%                                   6

                                                     2    8
    1 Tin of Hermetiool            Nett              2    0

                                                     4    8

    DESPATCHED

    PER
```

The factory discount given to enthusiasts.

Morgan entrants, but in the second, the three-wheeler handicap over three laps of the Brooklands Outer Circuit, there were six. On scratch was Ron Horton with his usual Blackburne racer, recently rebuilt by Best and Bowen, Morgan tuning specialists. His chassis was now fitted with double drop front crosshead tubes in current Super Aero style but supported by a double tie rod, and twin Hartfords had been fitted to the rear wheel, the anchorage helping to strengthen the bevel box. Of the other entrants only three came to join Horton in facing the starter: Robin Jackson in his 1096cc Blackburne-powered Beart-inspired special, Cecil Jay in the 731cc JAP-engined 'Jim',

Morgan Sweeps the Board

now having D-shaped cut-outs where the Aero's bonnet louvres had been, and Sydney Allard with his 1096cc JAP Super Aero carrying the name of 'Snail'. Allard made an excellent start to take the lead, as Jay suffered from a reluctant engine and Jackson also had engine problems. Horton was reported to have lapped at 104 mph in practice but had to retire with a pulled-off nipple on the magneto control wire. Jay followed on the second lap, allowing Allard an early victory from Jackson at 83mph.

The third race was a long handicap over five laps. All the places were taken by the car entrants, as Jackson and Allard both found five laps a bit too far.

This year the Grand Prix was to be run differently from the events of the previous two years, in that each class had a heat event before the grand finale. The course was different too, utilizing the Brooklands Mountain circuit (Finishing Straight to Members Banking to hairpin bend at the Fork and back onto the Finishing Straight), without any sandbanked artificial bends.

The first heat for cars under 850cc saw only one Morgan compete, that of Cecil Jay. He went into an early lead, but then fell back and finally stopped on the eighth of the twenty laps with a twisted bevel box countershaft, following a too enthusiastic gear change.

The second heat for 850cc to 1100cc saw the fastest Morgans pitted against the cars. Horton, Lones and Maskell started together and completed their first lap still abreast. After going into the lead, Horton slowed on the eighth lap, accelerated again, stopped on the tenth to change plugs, and eventually retired on the fifteenth lap. Lones then took up the lead but finished second to Bartlett's supercharged Salmson. His was the only Morgan to qualify for the final as Keay, Allard and Maskell did not feature in the first five.

Before the final Lones readjusted his brakes, and elected to be push-started. He was leading all the cars in his class by the end of the first lap and kept his position to the end,

Cecil Jay corners at the Fork Hairpin. (Motor Cycle)

Still Faster

to become an easy winner at 58.1 mph from Bartlett's Salmson and Aldington's Frazer Nash, winning the Light Car and Cyclecar Cup once more. Obviously the JAP JTOR engine was going to revolutionize future Morgan racing, having proved to be both reliable and fast in its first Brooklands victory in a Morgan.

Propshaft whip was a serious problem at such high Morgan speeds. We have already mentioned that Jackson attacked the problem in a very simple manner, turning a piece of ash to put inside the propshaft. Lionel Creed went one step simpler by using a broom handle in place of turned ash. Ron Horton had his propshaft balanced by Harry Andrews of the Andrews Crankshaft Grinding Company of Birmingham, and also claimed success. Lones tried to balance his himself, running it at 6000rpm in a lathe and adding solder to the lightest part of the wall. However, when he was discussing the problem with HFS one day, they decided that splitting the propshaft in two might prove the real answer. A shaft was duly cut in half, joined by a male and female square joint and supported by a bearing slid along the backbone tube. The ball race needed replacing every 1000 miles due to lack of lubrication, but the experiment proved successful and development continued at the factory along these lines.

Propshaft whip could have been no greater problem than to the Douglas Hawkes/Gwenda Stewart record-breaking team with their very high speeds. Not surprisingly, the special single-seater built for them by HFS was equipped with a split propshaft, the simple universal joint being supported by a bearing within a bearing housing specially let into the chassis backbone tube, some 18 inches from the bevel box. Like Hawkes's own special single seater 'Flying Spider' which he had used in the 1920s, the new single-seater was tailor-made for its driver, in this case, Gwenda. The chassis, number M262, was very similar to a normal 'M' type, having a double dropped front crosshead, although the pinion shaft fitted into the bevel box was much longer than standard, extending up to the propshaft-bearing housing. The seat was partly fashioned from two 10-gallon fuel tanks on either side of the backbone tube and was positioned fairly high, being above this tube rather than alongside it as in a Super Aero. To compensate, the rear springs were specially made to lower the height of the car's rear end. The all-aluminium bodywork was to Super Aero style, but much slimmer. The entire tail portion could be removed for access to the rear wheel and transmission. As usual a battery of drip feed lubricators supplied Castrol 'R' to the vital parts, although of the five fitted only three were used. The fuel was pressure-fed from a hand pump close to the driver's left hand. Once again Gwenda was encouraged not to use the single handbrake.

The new car was handed over to the team in July, and on 6th August Gwenda took it out for its debut on Montlhéry track. The engine was the long stroke JTOR of 1096cc (80 x 109mm), made for Hawkes by JAPs; to it was fitted a duraluminium outside flywheel. A squally wind delayed the record attempt until late in the evening but Gwenda still managed two full laps on full throttle, taking the 5 kilometres record at 113.52mph and the 5 miles at 107.51mph.

M262 next appeared at Arpajon, a few miles from the Montlhéry track, for attempts on the flying kilometre and mile records. The Arpajon course was a narrow, heavily cambered road lined by poplar trees. As one can imagine, the camber played havoc with the Morgan's rear wheel, which couldn't decide which side it wished to be on, crab

Gwenda sets off in the 731cc two-seater at Arpajon. (Motor Cycle)

tracking its way along at full throttle. Gwenda was unable to do much more than hang on, whilst the crowd scattered for protection behind the trees. Her first runs were with the 731cc-engined two-seater, with which she just failed to beat the 100mph barrier over the flying kilometre at 99.11 mph. Then, after a few motorcycles, Gwenda came screaming through in the 1096cc single-seater, snaking from one side of the road to the other. She recently described this as the most frightening drive of her life, as the Morgan became virtually uncontrollable in its snaking. She believes that Douglas purposely made the hand throttle so stiff that she couldn't attempt to modify her speed. She hung on, however, and was well content with a time over the flying kilometre equivalent to an average of 115.66 mph, a record that was to stand for very many years to come.

Not satisfied with their 750cc class records Gwenda and Douglas returned to

Still Faster

The single-seater screams between the trees. (Motor Cycle)
Gwenda hangs on at 115 mph. (Motor Cycle)

Unretouched photograph of the single-seater cockpit. Only three of the five drip feeds are in use. Note the rubber band on the steering wheel, used to advance the ignition. (Motor Cycle)

Montlhéry just one week later to try to break the 100 mph barrier. This time the engine was fitted to the single-seater. They succeeded, becoming the first to take a world 750cc record at over 100mph in a car or three-wheeler when Gwenda recorded 100.64mph over the flying 5 kilometres. Just up the road at Arpajon, Joe Wright's supercharged JTOR-engined OEC Temple JAP took the world motorcycle maximum speed record at just over 137mph.

Back in England on 16th August the BMCRC ran a ten-lap three-wheeler handicap open to members of the Light Car Club. Four Morgans entered, but one of these, Ron Horton's, did not compete. He had now developed ambitions for four-wheeler racing and had gone over to Ireland for the Ulster TT with his Riley. He was soon to sell his famous Blackburne racer to Robin Jackson, who was proposing to set up a business as a car tuner in premises inside Brooklands track, adjacent to the Paddock.

The starters were Lones, Allard and Maskell, and the circuit was the Brooklands Mountain circuit, but with artificial sand bank bends opposite the Paddock grandstand and under the Members Bridge. Maskell started first, driving his 'M' type Super Aero with his 1926 tuned LTOW JAP engine. He needed pushing for some distance before the engine fired. To help keep his passenger on board Maskell had fitted a steel hoop high over the tail panel for him to grab hold of.

Twenty-nine seconds later Sydney Herbert Allard set off with his 1929 'dog ear' JAP Super Aero. Since 1929, Allard had been trading as a motor trader from premises in Keswick Road, Putney, under the supervision of his father. He had coined the pet

Still Faster

name of 'The Snail' for his Morgan.

Nine seconds after Allard, Clive Lones set off in his JTOR-engined 'Bob'. He was unable to make any impression on the other two and it seemed as if the three Morgans would finish in their starting order. But then the nearside barrel of Allard's JAP broke loose, shedding debris over the Paddock bend, and forcing him to retire on the ninth lap. Maskell thus won at 53.32 mph from Clive Lones.

On 12th September Gwenda returned to Montlhéry, this time using the standard stroke JTOR engine (996cc), with which she took several 100mph records for medium distance, including the 50 miles at 102.64mph.

At that year's MCC High Speed Trial on 27th September only Maskell represented Morgans. Timed flying laps of the outer circuit were included in the programme but Maskell developed propellor shaft trouble and withdrew. Although he started in the third of the high speed trials, the trouble recurred and he retired once more. He may well have been using the factory's 'Jim' for these events.

Clive Lones took his JTOR-engined 'Bob' to Southport on 4th October. He came first in his class, and shattered Horton's flying kilometre sand record by recording 93.99mph. For these short-distance speed trials, Clive found he could raise the compression to 12 to 1 for the cylinder on the driver's side and use the lower figure of 11 to 1 on the passenger side, as this cylinder received less lubrication than its sister. For his 1925 Amac TT twin carburettors he used a 69 jet for the driver's side and 71 for the other, and ran on RD1 fuel (a methanol-based fuel also containing some acetone and benzole). Ignition advance could be as much as 60 degrees.

One week later the final BMCRC race of the year took place. For some time Robin Jackson had desperately wanted to acquire a BMCRC 'Gold Star', awarded for a 100 mph lap during a BMCRC race, and he felt that this meeting could be his last chance — Burney and Blackburne Ltd ceased production of twin engines in 1927 and could no longer supply racing spare parts for their old KMB and KMC power units.

Earlier in the year Jackson had purchased Ron Horton's Blackburne racer when Horton decided to switch from three to four wheels. Unfortunately, the famous ex-Beart engine was no longer in use, having suffered an expensive blow-up. However, Jackson managed to build up a very fast KMB unit from spares, and when he fitted it to Horton's car he found that it would consistently produce 100mph laps, something Horton had never managed with his own engine. He decided to enter this Morgan for the BMCRC meeting, and meanwhile continued experiments with supercharging a KMC engine fitted to his own Beart-inspired Special. He found that this too could lap at over 100mph, but was unsure of its strength when supercharged. As the KMC was a production engine, Blackburnes would not have fitted strengthened components as on racing engines such as the KMB.

Way back in 1927 Jackson and Harry Hatch, the Blackburne designer, had started work on designing a replacement racing engine to succeed the KMB, basically by using two of the efficient Blackburne 500cc air-cooled single barrels and heads fitted on to a vee twin crankcase. However there was no way in which this potentially very fast engine could be ready in time for this meeting, and so Jackson continued to prepare the Horton car with the KMB. Unfortunately a mere ten days before the event he blew up the KMB in a very complete way, and thus was forced to enter the special with the 'blown' engine. Now very low on spares, Jackson dare not test it any further, although it had done only one or two 100mph laps. On the day of the meeting he set up a signalling station just after the Hennebique bridge, where his mechanics could see the Fork for timing purposes. From this position they were able to put out a signal for Jackson, to let him know if he was going fast enough to achieve a Gold Star lap. The supercharger was fitted low down on the nearside of the engine, driven from a sprocket mounted on the flywheel, and was fed by a 48mm Solex carburettor. Jackson found this easier to tune than a track type Amal—and he also knew Jack Lawson of Solex quite well.

In the three-lap private owners' handicap for the Phillips Cup, Lones managed to beat Jackson to a Gold Star, lapping at over 100mph with his JTOR engine on 'Bob' to finish second. Just 20 minutes later both Lones and Jackson started in the five-lap all-comers' passenger handicap for the Wakefield Cup, Lones off 15 seconds and Jackson on scratch. In spite of a constant misfire, Jackson's blown Blackburne held together to achieve a lap at 101.85mph and finished third. Lones in fact won the event at 97.65mph and also took the 1930 Brooklands 1100cc Cyclecar Championship Trophy, once again lapping at over 100mph. During one of the races Lones set up a new Morgan outer circuit lap record of 102.48 mph.

Lapping Brooklands at 100mph may not seem all that impressive when compared with Gwenda Stewart's 100 miles at over 100mph at Montlhéry, but then Brooklands was a rather different proposition to Montlhéry. The famous bumps made the journey distinctly uncomfortable. 'Ermintrude', the bump over the Hennebique Bridge, would throw a car a good 30 feet before it landed, so that the engine had first to be cut with a magneto cut-out or throttled back, to avoid a blow-up. The Railway Straight was the fastest part of the circuit, up to 116mph being reached on a 100mph lap. Then came the Byfleet Banking, needing reduced throttle, and then the very difficult reverse camber bend at the Fork, which was often taken on two wheels. Clive Lones sometimes used a rubber band to hold the throttle open, so that he had both hands free to control the steering.

On 5th November Gwenda Stewart was out at Montlhéry for what was probably her last drive in the Morgan before she switched to driving Derby cars, produced at Douglas Hawkes's little French car factory. She successfully captured the 200-mile 1100cc class records previously held by Sandford's Sandford, at a new speed of 88.82 mph, and improved on her own 2 hour record with a speed of 88.61mph. She now held every 1100cc class record and all but three of the 750cc records, while many of her 350cc records still stood from 1929.

At the Olympia Motor Cycle Show in November, Morgans introduced the Sports Family four-seater. This was fitted with the latest 'M' type chassis, lowered in the same way as the Super Aero but 4 inches longer and incorporating a divided propshaft as used on the Hawkes/Stewart single-seater earlier in the year. Although carrying an 'M' type chassis number, this new divided propshaft chassis became known as the 'C' type. This may have been an abbreviation for 'Competition' as the divided propshaft would be of the greatest advantage in speed events. The front end of the Sports Family body was the same as a normal Aero: behind the Pearce windscreen, the body sides turned inwards to terminate in a boat-like tail.

Still Faster

The London-Gloucester Trial started from Staines on Friday 11th December. For this event, Lionel Creed borrowed a works Aero, AB 16, with a rocker box LTOW JAP. Despite Bushcombe Hill causing no end of trouble with its restarting test, Creed made a spendid climb.

The London-Exeter was held later in the month, on Boxing Day. Starting from Virginia Water, it finished at Shaftesbury the following day, after 253 miles and five observed hills. Six Morgans competed, the fastest being Swift, who won a gold in company with Kingdon's 980cc Morgan and Joe Turner, still regularly competing in trials with his Blackburne Aero. Dennis Welch was driving a works JAP Aero AB16, and failed on Devonish Pit Hill with wheelspin, gaining a silver. Dennis reported back to George Goodall after the trial, suggesting that twin rear wheels fitted within the rear forks might solve the wheelslip problem. Unbeknown to him, the factory were already working on Lionel Creed's similar idea.

Development of the twin rear-wheel car had struck many problems. When the two rear rims were laced onto a single hub they placed extreme strain on the bevel box, and Morgans had to try several designs before they found one sufficiently robust. Basically, a standard width 'C' type bevel box was used, but the bearing housings for the cross shaft bearings, which also served as the rear fork pivots, were extended outwards. The cross shaft was thus made wider than standard, and was now mounted in four 1 inch x $2\frac{1}{4}$ inch bearings, there being two inside each extended bevel box bearing housing instead of the usual one. Standard Morgan 'C' type fork blades were pivoted on the outside of the extended bearing housings, spaced to the outer edge by a steel spacer ring sweated onto the bearing boss. This gave a much wider space for the rear wheel hub within the fork blades, such that it could be increased from the standard 9 inches or so to $13\frac{3}{8}$ inches. The special rear wheel had a one-piece bronze hub with two outer spoke flanges on each side and a single inner one in the centre. From this were laced two 19 inch rims spaced on $4\frac{3}{4}$ inch centres. The steel spacers fitted to the bearing housings also strengthened the bevel box by virtue of a T section welded onto the side of each, which was then extended forwards and fastened by a set screw into the front of the bevel box castings.

The first Morgan to receive the twin rear wheel arrangement was a fairly standard Aero, with louvred bonnet sides, registered UY 9862. Originally fitted with a standard low level exhaust system, it was tested by 'Jim' Goodall, George Goodall's son, in minor local trials. This Morgan, incidentally, was fitted with a special 1096cc LTOW rocker box JAP engine, but rather unusually had coil ignition.

When this special Morgan had shown itself to be fairly reliable, a second twin rear wheel Aero was constructed. Luckily for the historian, this had a single 'D' cut-out in the bonnet side instead of the louvres. A dummy radiator was fitted as George Goodall, who was to drive it, was now using a racing 996cc air-cooled JAP twin, fitted with compression plates to make it suitable for trials.

The first major appearance of these twin rear wheel Morgans was in the 1931 Colmore in February. Three Morgans were entered, the prototype twin rear wheel with water-cooled engine being handled by Geoff Harris, and the air-cooled one by George Goodall. Joe Turner was driving his usual Aero Blackburne. That the twin rear wheel idea had got something was shown by the results: Harris won the Carr Cup for the best

Morgan Sweeps the Board

'Jim' Goodall in the first twin rear wheel car. (Goodall scrapbooks)
Goodall takes the second twin rear wheel car up Ferriscourt in the Cotswolds. (Autocar)

Still Faster

performance by a three-wheeler, whilst Goodall won a silver medal.

Back at Brooklands Robin Jackson was continuing the development of his two Morgans, the ex-Horton car, and his Beart-inspired special. He had now built up another fast Blackburne for the Horton car, fitted with twin carburettors, something Horton had used only during his last year with the car. For the special, Jackson was nearing completion of the special 1087cc air-cooled Blackburne vee-twin he was building with Harry Hatch, but pressure of work at his Brooklands premises (known as the Robinery) was restricting his time. Jackson was experimenting with chassis tuning on his Morgans for Brooklands use. Firstly, the centre pins were inclined backwards by 2 degrees, which improved the handling considerably. Secondly, Jackson tried to improve the front suspension. He modified his special's Hartford shock absorbers to give variable rate damping, replacing the flat side plates by plates with cammed faces, so that as the arms moved away from the setting the tension increased. Unfortunately, when this was combined with soft front springs, Jackson found that he got considerable kick-back at the steering wheel. He therefore lengthened the steering link from the end of the drag link, moving it from its original site on the right-hand steering arm to a point on the nearside of the track rod. Increasing its length allowed a much greater suspension movement with less reaction at the wheel.

The ex-Horton car had Newton shock absorbers. We know that it, too, had the long steering linkage when Jackson drove it to a class win in the Intervarsity Hill Climb, held at Ewelme Down near Oxford on 28th February, so presumably it also had soft springs.

The Cotswold Trial held on 7th March gave George Goodall another chance to test the air-cooled twin rear wheel Morgan. This second twin rear wheel Morgan was not registered for the road, and so all sorts of registration plates were used on it. It carried Goodall's favourite GC4 for this event. On Coldfeet, which was more like a river bed than a hill, Goodall turned it over, though he did win a third class award. High level

Jackson in the ex-Horton racer at Ewelme Down. (Autocar)

Lones about to overtake Archer at the Fork Hairpin. (Autocar)

exhaust pipes had been fitted to Goodall's car, and the other twin rear wheel car, UY 9862, soon followed suit. Two silencers were fitted to each exhaust pipe to give the extra muffling required for those trials which contained a silencer test. On UY 9862 the final silencer had an integral fishtail incorporated into it.

During the Brooklands close season Clive Lones had been sprucing up his tired Super Aero body. When it reappeared at the BMCRC opening meeting on 28th March it had a new lower body panel to the latest Super Aero style. Lones started off the season well, for he won the ten lap 'Round the Mountain' race with his JTOR engine at 56.28 mph from Archer's New Imperial sidecar. For the tricky Mountain Circuit he used gear ratios of 5 to 1 top and 8 to 1 bottom, giving him a useful maximum of 90mph 'down the hill' to the Fork hairpin. Nel gave up passengering Clive at the end of the 1920s and his regular passenger then became Tom Clarke, who worked at the same power station. Working in a power station gave Clive an 'ear' for turbine speeds and so, like Ron Horton, he never fitted a rev counter to his engine—he reckoned that he could always tell the engine speed just by its sound. His car was now painted yellow, and soon became known as the 'Flying Banana'.

One of the competitors in the London-Exeter trial had been John Hooper, a Walsall leather worker, who had driven his stepfather's Calcott car. For the London-Land's End he entered his new black JAP Aero with an 'M' type chassis, recently received from the Colmore Depot, registered DH 8602. Unfortunately, he retired. The other new Morgan competitor was Henry Laird, a grandson of the founder of the Cammell Laird shipbuilding company. Passengered by his wife Barbara, he drove through the trial to a gold medal with an 'M' type Super Aero, CK 4187. This was not Henry's first Morgan, which he had purchased way back in 1927. A 1925 side-valve JAP Aero, it had been promptly christened 'Johnny' by Henry's father, after a line in an old music hall song which read 'Johnny Morgan plays his organ'. Henry was now on 'Johnny IV', purchased to celebrate his engagement to Barbara in 1929: she had been given the choice of an engagement ring or a new Morgan and chose the latter. In 1931 Henry joined MA McEvoy in his motor engineering venture at Derby, where he was involved in the tuning business.

FLM Harris, of *Light Car and Cyclecar* magazine, drove AB16, a 'C' type Super Aero, to another gold medal, as did Swift in his 'M' type Super-Aero. Another gold was won by JR Hebditch, who actually finished on two wheels. Incredible as it seems, his nearside front wheel collapsed a mile or so before the finish when he went into a ditch. He carried on, driving the last mile without the wheel at a good 20mph. The brake drum and frame members had been bent back and doubled under, and on this the car skidded and bashed its way along, steering on the one remaining front wheel.

Two days later Jack Sylvester entered Reg Baker for the Syston Park Grand Prix races. He went down to the factory to borrow 'Jim', as arranged with Goodall, but found that the car had not been prepared. The gear ratios were still as for Brooklands, and the rear sprocket holes were oval from long use. Reg unfortunately had to retire in the sidecar event when the sprocket bolts began to sheer. In any case, the 731cc engine was not really suitable for such a circuit.

Sydney Allard was the sole Morgan entrant in the April BMCRC meeting, driving his 'B' type Super Aero which now had an 80 x 99mm air-cooled racing JTOR JAP on the front. Unfortunately he suffered from fuel feed problems, and retired in both the events he entered: though he did manage one lap at 96.71mph.

At Whitsun a month later, the London-Edinburgh got underway from Wrotham Park near Barnet. Park Rash was again one of the trials hills to be included. All five Morgans simply flew up it, in contrast to the sixty-two cars and eight of the nine sidecars which all failed dismally. Unfortunately Hooper went outside the time limit in the stop and restart test on Tan Hill and so had to settle for a silver medal. Golds were won by Goodall, Harry Jones, Laird and Kingdon.

Reg Baker in 'Jim' at Syston Park. (Morgan Motor Co)

Geoff Harris's faithful Aero in the Scottish. (Motor Cycle)

Geoff Harris, meanwhile, was the sole Morgan driver entered in the Scottish Six Days' Trial. His amazing skill in handling his Aero ML 1142 as it leapt over the rocks brought him a gold medal. Modifications to his Aero included a new rocker box LTOW JAP engine. He tied the tie rod with tape to the chassis behind the engine to keep it in position when the chassis flexed. He had replaced the standard $\frac{1}{4}$ inch tie rod with one of $\frac{3}{8}$ inch made of high tensile steel to reduce the risk of breakage. Gear ratios were $5\frac{1}{4}$ to 1 top and 11 to 1 bottom.

At the beginning of the year, the Light Car Club had announced a new type of race meeting to replace their Grand Prix. This was to be a relay race over ninety laps of the Brooklands Outer Circuit, each team of three cars being collectively handicapped. The fastest car of each team had to go first: if it failed to cover its thirty laps, the second fastest could complete them, before starting on its own set, and so on. Naturally this novel way of competing against four wheels had a strong appeal for the Morgan contingent.

The race was held on Saturday, 25th July. George Goodall had entered a team of three Morgans—Lones in his JTOR-engined racer, Maskell in 'Jim'—now fitted with a

Still Faster

JTOR engine, and Tommy Rhodes in his Aero which had been rebodied by Morgans to the latest Super Aero pattern, with a hump on the tail to cover the rear wheel. Also at Goodall's insistence, the KMC Blackburne was replaced by a JAP racing engine and Tommy's brother, Syd, believes this to be one of the special long-stroke 1096cc air-cooled engines. Unfortunately, during practice this engine seized on the Byfleet banking at around 90mph, sending Rhodes into a spin. This may have moved the team from scratch to 5 minutes, but they still found themselves conceding over 3 minutes to the supercharged MG Midgets, and over 6 minutes to the works Austin Sevens.

The 'A' car and fastest of the team was Clive Lones's JTOR Morgan. He set a fine pace by lapping at just under 93mph, often with all three wheels in the air, as he began to cut into the nineteen lap lead of the limit man, travelling high on the bankings. All looked well for a good battle, but then came the rains—just before Lones completed his thirty laps and handed over to Arthur Maskell in 'Jim', also with JAP JTOR power. Soon the rain became a deluge, and poor Maskell was forced to drop his lap speed to the 80s in such poor visibility, becoming a frequent visitor to the pits with his engine spluttering in the wet. As a result, instead of making up their handicap the Morgan team were losing to the leaders. Rhodes was the final Morgan member to take to the track. After lapping at 87mph the rain and water from the flooded track reduced him to one cylinder and he limped round to complete the ninety laps. The Morgan team were the last to finish within the time limit and were placed twelfth. Despite the weather the race itself had been a success and everyone looked forward to the next year's event.

The following month Lones returned to Brooklands for the BMCRC fifth meeting. He was the only cyclecar competitor, entering two events and winning the second, a passenger handicap, at 90.06mph with the JTOR engine. For this type of short Brooklands event, Clive used a compression of 9 to 1 on the driver's-side cylinder, and 8.8 to 1 for the oil-starved near-side. The fuel was methanol based RD1, and the ignition was advanced 55 degrees.

Madresfield was host to the annual speed trials on 29th August. With the marriage of Cecil Jay and his subsequent retirement from racing, George Goodall had been nominating other drivers for 'Jim' during the year, but for Madresfield he decided to drive his old racer himself. The engine was a highly tuned JTOR, claiming 64bhp at 5400 revs per minute—a combination that proved fast enough to give Goodall the Morgan cup in $32\frac{1}{5}$ seconds. This year there was also a team award, which went to Goodall's team of himself, Lones and Rhodes. Despite Goodall's success it is interesting that Horton's time of $30\frac{4}{5}$ seconds, achieved in 1928, was still unbeaten by any other Morgan.

Tommy Rhodes now took his Morgan back up north to Southport for the Championship meeting on the sands on 19th September, where he entered the 10-mile sidecar and three-wheeler race in company with Syd Keay. A fast pace soon split the field, and Keay's Blackburne-engined Morgan was soon boiling. Rhodes finally pushed his Morgan home to victory, whilst Keay came third.

The MCC High Speed Trial this year had the usual high speed 'hour blinds', separated by a series of two-lap sprint races. In the three-wheeler event, Arthur Maskell drove his 'dog ear' JAP-engined 'M' type Super Aero to a comfortable victory

Henry and 'Barbie' with 'Johnny V' at the MCC Brooklands meeting. (Laird scrapbooks)

at 69.08 mph. 'Touring' equipment was required for MCC events, and so Maskell had fitted some circa 1924 Aero mudguards to his racer. When the one hour 'blind' for three-wheelers was run off, Maskell covered over 70 miles to win a gold. One fellow contestant who was obviously impressed by this demonstration of speed was Henry Laird. He had entered in 'Johnny V', a primrose-coloured C-type Super Aero registered VN 2810, but failed to gain an award.

The following month Henry and Barbara Laird were once again in 'Johnny V', but this time they were competing in the type of event for which it would soon be famous—trials work. The event was the MCC Sporting Trial and the Morgan star proved to be Geoff Harris, driving a twin rear wheel factory car. He won a first class award, whilst Swift and Laird gained silver medals. Laird's Morgan had a very shallow vee windscreen so that he could look over the top, a future 'trademark' of this car.

Whilst Morgans had had a fairly successful sporting year, the ordinary motorist was demanding improvements—in particular the provision of a reverse gear to eliminate the need to get out and push the car backwards in traffic, and also a spare wheel. Furthermore, although the engine was excellent as regards performance, it could be difficult to start and was not very smooth in action. Morgans were taking these criticisms seriously and development at Malvern continued.

The Three-Speeder Era

The Motor Cycle Show of November 1931 was important in that Morgan announced the first of their improved models for the ordinary motorist. The new chassis featured a rear-mounted aluminium three-speed and reverse gearbox fitted in place of a bevel box. The output shaft of the gearbox was connected to a worm gear, which meshed with a phosphor-bronze worm wheel attached to a cross shaft. On one end of the cross shaft was a sprocket which allowed a single chain to take the drive to the rear wheel, whilst the other end of the cross shaft held the dynamo drive gear. Like the earlier 'C' type, the new three-speed chassis had a split propshaft running in bearings.

With this new chassis it was no longer practical to start the Morgan by winding on the cross shaft, as it was now at all times connected to the rear wheel, there being no dog system. To accommodate this change, JAPs had been persuaded to redesign their LTOW engine. The new water-cooled engine was designed for smoothness, and the cylinder angle was increased from a 50 to 60 degree angle. The engine was equipped with dry sump lubrication, using a duplex Pilgrim pump to deliver and return oil from the engine. A starter dog was fitted to engage with one of the two camshafts—a weak point in the new engine's design, together with coil ignition to give easier starting. The new engine was coded LTOWZ by JAPs, the 'Z' referring to dry sump. Its capacity was unchanged at 1096cc (85.7mm x 95mm).

A side-valve version of the new engine was also produced in both air- and water water-cooled forms. It too was of 1096cc, the first time this capacity had been used in a JAP side-valve fitted to a production Morgan. The LTZ air-cooled version had detachable heads.

The Super Aero switched completely to the new 'R' chassis (so called because the

Ron Horton storms Ham Mill in the London-Gloucester with the first twin rear wheel Morgan. (Horton collection)

gearbox was designed to run on Castrol R) and became known as the three-speed Super Sports. The Sports Family also changed over completely, but the Family and Aero models, including the new two-seater Family, could still be ordered with the two-speed chassis. The Family range had been made more modern-looking for 1931 and was further improved for the coming year. Morgans were hoping to recapture a larger share of the small-car market in these years of depression, at the expense of models such as the Austin Seven.

On 28th November at the Cambridge University hill climb at Kimbolton Castle in Huntingdonshire, Robin Jackson showed that the old ex-Horton Blackburne Super Aero was still a force to be reckoned with. Snaking along the badly cut up and loosely surfaced road, he beat the cars and sidecars, to become the fastest passenger machine. The car now featured normal Morgan steering connections.

The London-Gloucester Trial in December saw both twin rear wheel Morgans in action. Ron Horton was driving UY 9862 and Harris its sister car, both making the best ascents of the day on Ham Mill.

In the London-Exeter Trial, held later that month, the two twin rear wheel Morgans once again took part. Swift drove UY 9862, and Harris its sister once again, running it as GT 37. Harris won a gold, in company with Laird in 'Johnny V', Goodall, Clarke and Lowe, whilst Joe Turner won a silver with his Blackburne Aero in company with Hooper and Maskell. Poor Swift failed to keep to the time schedule.

George Goodall completed the trial with one of the new 60 degree ohv JAP-engined three-speed Morgans. This particular car appears to have been a prototype Sports

Swift tackles Ibberton with a twin rear wheel Morgan. (Morgan Motor Co)

Goodall with the three-speeder. (Morgan Motor Co)

Morgan Sweeps the Board

model featuring headlamps fitted to the top of the mudguard stays, in the position they were to occupy on the production models introduced the following spring. The body had a boat-tailed rear end and sported one of Goodall's favourite flat windscreens. Interestingly, it also featured short lower engine bearing tubes, as on Goodall's earlier two-speeder.

Clive Lones took delivery of a new chassis early in 1932. This was not one of the new three-speed chassis, but a two-speed 'C' type, 4 inches wider than the Super Sports, 3 inches longer and 2½ inches lower, with a between centre pin width of 47 inches. Clive's father was a metals analyst, and he had been able to get a special bevel box made through his father's contacts at Deutch and Brenner. The bevels themselves were the noisy straight-cut type, specially made by Moss Gears of Birmingham. The chassis was silver soldered together on the factory jigs using Accles and Pollock tubing, making it as strong as possible. Clive transferred the bodywork from his previous racer and improved the front brakes by incorporating Amilcar drums. As he had already won a Gold Star for his 996cc engine, Clive now hoped to develop the 731cc engine he had received with the Avon JAP and repeat his success. The Avon JAP was a four-wheeler sprint car originally built by HM Walters of Jappic fame and Vivian Prestwich of JAPs, for Kaye Don to use for record attempts. In the late 1920s Clive had purchased it and sprinted it with some effect. Clive had tried out the engine in his Morgan the previous summer at Brooklands on 27th July, entering three races and winning one, a three-lap handicap, at 71.76 mph.

For the 1932 Colmore Trial Ron Horton once again drove the twin rear wheel UY 9862, finishing the trial successfully with a second class award. WH Atkins in his Morgan failed hopelessly on Blockley Hill and Guiting Wood Hill: he was incorrectly geared for the event, and later turned over.

Robin Jackson supported Cambridge as usual in the Intervarsity Speed Trials held

Clive Lones's new chassis. (Lones collection)

The Three-speeder Era

on 20th February at Hexton, near Hitchin, probably using his ex-Horton car. Two weeks later he was at the Oxford University event on the unopened Eynsham bypass. The surface was not yet finished, and Jackson threw up stones from his rear wheel to come second in the passenger event to Collett's Norton. Also driving a Morgan for Cambridge was young Jan Breyer, rushing to the event straight from the examination room. His efforts proved in vain for the timing apparatus broke down on his only run, and then his magneto packed up. Varsity events were like that.

Jan Breyer's Morgan had started life as a 1928 Aero. He acquired it in 1931 and soon afterwards replaced the water-cooled side-valve JAP with a 4-cam KTCY unit from a Coventry-Eagle motorcycle. When the chassis fractured Jan drove it gingerly to Harold Beart's premises where the rear end was lowered by the usual method of mounting the springs on top of the bevel box angle irons. The front crosshead was widened and given a double drop to current racing Super Aero style, and beefed-up Beart steering connections were used. In this form Tommy Sulman had driven it to Eynsham for Jan to drive. Sulman had recently arrived in England from Australia enthusing about speedway, and wishing to get involved in this as yet young sport in this country. Jan swapped Tom a special GN chassis with two countershafts known as 'Hank', a water-cooled Blackburne engine and other assorted parts, in return for parts Tom had previously used to convert a similar Morgan to Jan's into a four-wheeler (basically using a GN back axle and rear springs). Jan then converted his own Morgan into a four-wheeler and took it onto the Crystal Palace Speedway. However, the sideways 'G' forces played havoc with the chassis, even twisting the cross shaft, and he decided that for him, at any rate, speedway was over. When the chassis was later stripped for rebuilding he removed the tired Aero body to make a Shelsley special, with which he had considerable success in the mid-1930s. He called this 'Salome', in consideration of the numerous changes it had undergone. Jan knew Robin Jackson quite well, and used sprockets to his design. He was also lucky enough to acquire one of Eric Fernihough's steel flywheels, still with his timing marks on it, to replace the standard Morgan cast-iron type.

On 19th March the BMCRC ran its clubman's Brooklands race meeting. Clive Lones entered his racer on its new 'C' type chassis in the class J one-lap all-comers' flying start sprint, recording 95.78 mph, and also in the five-lap all-comers' 'Mountain' handicap. The mounting of the rear shock absorber to the bevel box wasn't up to the job and eventually fractured, giving the occupants a very bumpy ride. On the third lap Clive took the lead, and held it to the end, although he was challenged by a motorcycle he had already passed. Clive was using his 731cc (74mm x 85mm) ohv water-cooled JAP engine, ex Avon JAP.

The London-Land's End Trial started on Good Friday. GE Swift now had one of the new three-speed Super Sports, registration GW 35, whilst George Goodall drove his prototype three-speeder GC 4 as used by him in the Exeter, and now sporting a 'Freddie James' stork mascot. Both twin rear wheel two-speeders were entered, Harry Jones driving UY 9862 and WAG 'Jim' Goodall its sister, now carrying CJ 743, in his first MCC trial. Bluehills Mine provided the excitement when John Hooper in his usual JAP Aero took the hill at speed on advice from a car owner. He approached the corner far too fast and cannoned into the rock wall, mounting it and nearly capsizing

Launceston control—CJ 743 and UY 9862 are the two rear wheel cars whilst Swift is in his new Super Sports GW 35. (Harry Jones scrapbooks)

before returning to the other side of the track where the fence finally stopped him. The only damage was a battered mudguard and a broken plug lead, and he was soon on his way again to gain a silver medal.

In April the Wye Valley Clubs ran their annual trial. As these mud-pluggers were held on home territory, they were naturally popular with Morgans. George Goodall drove the later of the two twin rear wheel cars, this time running on trade plates, to a second class award.

The London-Land's End was the last MCC event for UY 9862 in the hands of factory drivers, for in April it was sold to RJ Cole, re-registered as WP 1831 and being given a new chassis number for the occasion (M 670). Cole immediately entered it for the London-Edinburgh Trial in May. The other twin rear wheel Morgan, now carrying ML 1142, was entered by Geoff Harris, who intended to take it through the Scottish Six Days' when he arrived in Edinburgh. George Goodall was driving his boat-tailed three-speeder GC 4, and HFS Morgan was making a welcome return to trials driving with WP 1898, an LTOWZ-engined three-speed Sports model. The Sports model was introduced in the spring to replace the Aero. It was similar in concept to the Sports Family, having a boat tail and headlamps mounted on the mudguard stays, but with a luggage locker behind the two seats.

Premier awards were awarded to Cole and Goodall, and also to Welch, Hooper, and Whitnall, whilst Harris, Creed, HFS and Marshall—still driving his LTOW JAP two-speed Family with the short bonnet—all gained silvers.

Geoff Harris once again gave an outstanding performance in the Scottish Six Days' Trial to win a gold medal. On the fourth day, Weem hill caused many failures. Indeed when Harris reached it he rammed and was stopped by a huge boulder. Restarting, he then tore up the hill, bouncing and leaping over the rugged surface, the twin rears

HFS takes a Sports through the Edinburgh. (Wilson collection)

hurling mud behind him. As he crested the top, the offside front tyre tore off. On the very next day, however, he made no mistake, making the only clean ascent of the day. Harris was using 10 lb pressure for each rear tyre, and 20 lb for the front.

Back at Brooklands Clive Lones contested the five-lap Passenger Grand Prix Handicap, one of five starters. Lones was on scratch and only just failed to catch Archer's Velocette, finishing second. He was using his JTOR engine, but he had now fitted an internal flywheel assembly having an extra 10 mm of stroke to give 1096cc. Although theoretically it should have been a more powerful engine than the standard 996cc JTOR, the extra capacity had little effect on power. Clive now had a long range fuel tank fitted under the bonnet in readiness for the future Relay Race.

16th July saw the Light Car Club's second Relay Race take place on Brooklands. Once again Morgans had entered a team of three cars. The 'A' car, and fastest, was Clive Lones's with its 1096cc long stroke modified JTOR engine. The 'B' car was Tommy Rhodes's Super Aero, fitted with his own long stroke JTOR JAP engine which sported the rocker boxes and push rod tubes fitted to these engines since 1930. This engine had been tuned for Tom by 'Barry' Baragwanath who, as well as being on a retainer from Brough, ran a tuning business in London. One of Baragwanath's secrets was to increase the big end clearances, as he believed that the connecting rods bent under load and were then likely to be nipped by the flywheels. He also tuned each cylinder separately.

Clive Lones also learnt a lot from his friend 'Barry', which doubtless helped him on his way to virtual supremacy with his own JTOR engine, in either 996 or 1096cc form.

The Morgan team: 2A Lones, 2B Rhodes, 2C Harris. Harris's engine receives attention. (Syd Rhodes collection)

At the limit of its development, Lones estimated its output as 70 bhp. On the advice of Baragwaneth, he had special side-by-side rods made, instead of the JAP forked and plain type. He used steel supplied through his father's contacts at Hughes Johnson near Birmingham, and had them heat-treated at Deutch and Brenner. He used special Norton pattern pistons, and as side-by-side rods produced an eccentrically mounted piston the barrels were offset slightly to allow the piston to sit more squarely on the end of the con rod. 'Barry' did quite a lot of work on Lones's big engine. Clive would leave an old benzole can outside his house if he wanted an engine picked up by a passing lorry for delivery to 'Barry's' tuning shop in London.

The last member of the team was Geoff Harris driving the ex-Gwenda Stewart long-stroke JTOR-engined Super Aero. Charlie Curtis, the Morgan mechanic, was in attendance during practice when Geoff was testing the engine. He remembers seeing a JAP mechanic waving at Harris as he passed beneath one of the Brooklands bridges. Harris put on speed and blew up the engine, and it was only then that he realized that the JAP man was trying to tell him to slow down, not speed up.

Robin Jackson was the 'A' member for the Cambridge University team, probably using Horton's car, the B and C cars being an Alvis and MG respectively. Michael

The Three-speeder Era

Clive Lones with 2A (Syd Rhodes collection)

McEvoy had also entered a team, which included Henry Laird. He had forsaken his Morgan to drive a McEvoy special—a modified Wolseley Hornet, this being the 'C' car to an Austin and another McEvoy Special. Harold Beart, who also held the Wolseley agency, drove a Wolseley Hornet special as the 'B' car in Vic Derrington's team.

Robin Jackson's was one of the first teams to start, but he himself completed only five thunderous laps before the Blackburne engine broke a valve. The Morgan team was heavily handicapped and did not set off until nearly one hour after the limit team. Lones soon got down to business, carrying 10 gallons of fuel for his allotted thirty laps, lapping at over 94 mph, and half an hour later increasing this to 98 mph. Just when all seemed well, Lones smashed his big end after one and a half hours and had to hand over to Tom Rhodes. He too suffered misfortune and broke a valve rocker. Geoff Harris took over, and drove for a mere twelve minutes before the same thing happened to him. The supercharged Austin Seven team on scratch showed remarkable speed and reliability, finishing fourth behind the winning Wolseley Hornet team. These 'dutch clog' Austins had averaged 91.13 mph.

One week later Clive Lones was back at Brooklands for the three-lap 'Junior' Handicap, using a special 492cc twin JAP engine. This engine had been designed for Joe Wright to use for record breaking and claimed 38 bhp at 6000 rpm. Clive considered supercharging it with a Cozette supercharger, but did not make much progress as the pistons continually burnt through.

Laird was using 'Johnny V' as his everyday transport, but as the trials bug began to bite he decided to modify it to make it more suitable. He therefore fitted straight front crosshead tubes instead of the cranked Super Aero type to increase ground clearance, and the latest 'Sports' type three-speeder centre pins, allowing the headlamps to be mounted on the mudguard stay.

On 28th July the MCC introduced their first London-Scarborough Trial. Laird was one of the competitors with VN 2810 or 'Johnny V'. Near Retford, he broke a mudguard support early in the morning, but luckily found a garage where the mechanic in pyjamas and mackintosh made an excellent welding repair. He won a premier award, as did Hooper, and Hicks, the latter driving a three-speed Sports with the optional 'Goodall style' flat windscreen. A fourth Morgan premier award was taken home by Brand, driving what appears to be a home-made Morgan special fitted with an ohv 980cc JAP engine, presumably a detuned KTOR.

On August Bank Holiday Monday the action turned to Donington Park for the first day of a two-day meeting on this delightful road circuit outside Derby. This was the first meeting to use the newly resurfaced motorcycle racing track. Lones had now rebuilt his JTOR engine, but had again chosen the standard capacity of 996cc, finding the 1096cc conversion of little benefit. He won the three-wheeler event from Tommy Rhodes who was driving his own Super Aero with his 1096cc long-stroke JTOR engine. A late entry was Henry Laird, who lived close by at Duffield. He finished within the specified time after the winner which entitled him to a replica award.

When the second day's events were run off Tom Rhodes found he could lap slightly faster than 'Kim' Collett's Norton sidecar. He hounded him relentlessly, nearly forcing him into a mistake when he tried to pass Laird's Morgan by taking to the grass. Unfortunately Rhodes's engine then went onto one cylinder, so Collett beat him into second place with Laird coming third. Laird was pleased with the performance put up by his 'trials' Morgan and considered whether he should now take racing seriously.

Back at Brooklands the BMCRC ran their 'Cup Day' Meeting on 27th August. Tommy Rhodes entered his 1096cc long stroke JTOR JAP-engined Super Aero in the three-lap all-comers' handicap for the Prestwich Cup. Lapping at just under 99 mph, he threaded his way through the field but retired on the last lap. In the Cox Cup Consolation Handicap, B Lambert's 1096cc long stroke JTOR JAP-engined Morgan started on 3 seconds handicap and won at 88.46 mph from Brook's Norton and Bishop's Excelsior-JAP. During Lambert's earlier Brooklands exploits in May and June his Morgan had been powered by a 996cc JTOR engine, but now like Lones before him, he had switched to trying out the long stroke 1096cc version.

Brooklands was also the venue of the eighth annual MCC High Speed Trials on Saturday, 3rd September. As well as the usual 'hour blind' this year there were several two-lap handicaps and team relay races. Hooper won the sidecar and three-wheeler handicap in DH 8602 from Twitchett's Morgan, whilst a newcomer to Morgan competition, EP 'Joe' Huxham, came third. 'Joe' was the recently appointed Bournemouth agent, a real Morgan character, who enjoyed a beer. Being an agent was to him almost synonymous with being a competitor and so on 29th June he had purchased a black and cream 1932 Super Sports, chassis R 260. The car was modified for extra legroom and also featured a stainless steel radiator shell, two doors, an Andre

The Three speeder Era

bumper bar, a shortened gear lever and a 19-tooth gearbox sprocket.

For the High Speed Trial HFS had asked Lionel Creed to compete with one of the most unlikely vehicles, the factory-owned twin rear wheel Morgan. Creed dutifully took the car to the track but was told that despite the two Ghost silencers per exhaust he still needed the regulation fishtails to pass scrutineering. He hunted around the track workshops and managed to find two, one from Robin Jackson and the other from Thomson and Taylor, arriving at the start just as the field was leaving. He managed to cover 67.30 miles in the hour with the 'C' chassis Morgan.

Hurtling around the banking after his handicap win was John Hooper in his 'M' type Aero. He averaged a remarkable 76.85 mph. His mechanic was Bertie Le Man, a wizard with engines who prepared his LTOW JAP for this and other events, and passengered for him. The compression was raised slightly and the engine was given stronger valve springs and polished ports but was otherwise fairly standard. Oil was supplied to the cylinder bores by direct hand pump as Le Man considered the JAP system inadequate.

Of the other Morgan entries, 'Joe' Huxham covered 68.22 miles but poor Twitchett burst a rear tyre at 70 mph as he came off the banking; he finally turned over though without injury to the occupants. Lowe's Morgan covered 57.25 miles which gave him a silver instead of the golds awarded to the others, while RJ Cole failed to start with the other twin rear car, WP 1831.

Tom Rhodes returned to Southport Sands on 10th September for the Championship meeting. He eventually passed Wood's Douglas sidecar to win the ten-lap sidecar event with his 1096cc long stroke air-cooled racing JAP.

At the beginning of October, the BMCRC ran a 100-mile handicap race, for the £200 Hutchinson Challenge Cup. Clive Lones refitted his 731cc JAP engine to his Super Aero racer but shortly before the race he discovered a leaking cylinder head gasket. As he was unable to obtain a replacement, he was driven to the drastic course of reducing the cylinder spigot with a large file in order to get more pressure on the gasket. In the race Lones retired after four laps when the carburettor stub snapped clean off.

The 1932 Olympia Motor Cycle Show revealed another concession to the ordinary Morgan motorist, the introduction of interchangable 18 inch Dunlop Magna wheels. Spare wheels were now available, and the Sports model accordingly lost its boat-style back end in favour of a flat one on which the spare could be mounted. The Super Sports model now used the same chassis as the other models, with a standardized 1-inch drop, and carried its spare on the tail at an angle of 45 degrees; this was later changed so that it lay flat. The Family Morgan was completely redesigned, and like the Sports, given a flat-ended tail on which the spare wheel was mounted. The bonnet was also improved and fitted with a small sliding door allowing access to the petrol filler cap without lifting the bonnet.

Plate clutches had replaced the cone type the previous June, and the LTOWZ engine now had a redesigned waterproof distributor and a water-heated manifold, all making for easier starting and control.

Trials continued with Atkins borrowing the twin rear wheel Morgan for the LCC Buxton to Buxton Trial in September. In October Creed gained a premier award in the

Morgan Sweeps the Board

MCC Sporting One Day Trial whilst Hooper and Brand with his special gained silvers. Cole's twin rear wheel Morgan retired.

Down at Putney two years of experimenting were drawing to a close as Sydney Allard unveiled his first trials special. This was a four-wheeler, the front of which was virtually standard Morgan with the old LTOW engine from his racing Morgan days providing the power. The rear contained a modified BSA three-wheeler front axle which transmitted the power, and a Moss four-speed and reverse gearbox was fitted centrally within the propshaft. Allard entered his new construction (JJ 761) for the forthcoming London-Exeter Trial, and named this special 'Millie the Moocher'.

Both twin rear wheel Morgans took part in this event—RJ Cole in WP 1831 and Dennis Welch in the factory car now carrying AB 16—and both gained premier awards. 'Joe' Huxham collected a silver with his Super Sports, as did Atkins, now in his three-speed Super Sports. Poor Allard came to rest on Fingle Bridge with a stripped final drive pinion forcing his retirement, but his all independent suspension special created a great deal of interest. AB 16 also caused interest, unfortunately of the police sort: the twin rear wheel Morgan's claim to be a three-wheeler when it had four tyres came under rigorous questioning at Shaftesbury Court. Happily the case was dismissed when Goodall explained that it did have only three wheels, as the two tyres on the rear were laced to a single hub. Thus it could not possibly be rated as a four-wheeler, with the resulting higher road tax.

Cole with the ex-factory twin rear wheel Morgan. (Wilson collection)

The Three speeder Era

The 1933 Colmore as usual brought out many interesting Morgans. Henry Laird and Barbara were in 'Johnny V', the only Morgan to be entered with a single rim rear wheel, for no less than three twin rear wheel Morgans turned up. Cole entered his ex-factory car WP 1831, Lionel Creed its sister car, and the third contender was a newly built factory twin rear wheel car which usually carried the registration WP 2928.

This, the first of the three-speed twin rear wheel cars, was a Sports two-seater fitted with a LTOWZ JAP engine. When W Derek Evans worked at the Morgan Motor Co, during the 1930s he used WP 2928 on many occasions, such as taking the cashier to the bank or delivering spares to the Station. He recalls that driving it on the road was like driving a Morgan with a garden roller for a rear wheel.

The Victory Cup Trial this year was a very muddy affair, so bad in fact that Laird could do no more than look at Red Marley hill. He sank axle deep with VN 2810 but still managed to collect a third class award.

The following weekend, on 11th March, Henry did rather better, running 'Johnny V' without its hood and passengered by Barbara as usual, to collect the *News of the World* Cup in the East Midland Centre 'Bemrose Trial'.

For the Wye Valley Trial on 8th April Lionel Creed found that he had been selected to drive the factory two-speed twin rear wheel car, still with Brooklands fish tails in place, instead of George Goodall. He collected the Morgan from the factory the day before the event, but the next morning was confronted by a flat rear tyre. Calling in at the factory for a replacement tube, he was somewhat surprised to find that they hadn't got any! He thus had no option but to set off with the other tyre blown up hard. On one of the rocky hills he punctured a front tyre—it eventually came off completely—but he did manage to get out of the observed section without penalty. Henry Laird came up

Henry Laird attacks Little Cwm in the Wye Valley Trial. (Laird scrapbooks)

Morgan Sweeps the Board

next with 'Johnny V', with two punctured tyres—the rear and one front. He sportingly agreed to give his remaining good front wheel to Lionel, but when they came to take off the factory car's damaged wheel they couldn't shift it, as the nut was cross threaded! Henry carried on, his tally of tyre problems reaching three bursts and a single puncture by the finish.

For some time the Morgan factory had been looking at alternative engines to the now fairly expensive and comparatively rough JAP. Since 1929 they had been experimenting with four-cylinder engines in a modified chassis, but that is a separate story, of which more later. JAPs themselves had offered several new engines for Morgans to try out, but they had all seemed worse than the present type—indeed 'Jim' Goodall remembers that the vibration from one of these was so bad that the windscreen shattered.

For the London-Land's End Trial which started on Good Friday a new side-valve water-cooled engine made its competition debut. This was the 990cc (85.5mm x 85.5mm) Matchless MX engine designed under the supervision of Mr Heather at the

Harry and Lola Jones in the three-speed twin rear wheel car on Gooseham. (Harry Jones scrapbook)

The Three-speeder Era

Matchless works in Plumstead, London. It was basically a water-cooled version of the air-cooled engine used by Matchless themselves in their Model X motorcycle. Lubrication was by dry sump, with the valve gear totally enclosed within a compartment on the cylinder casting. Despite being a 50 degree vee twin, it produced negligible vibration and possessed a remarkably slow tickover. It was very easy to start via the starting handle which engaged directly onto the front main shaft or by the electric starter. A single three-lobed camshaft operated the four cam levers and the power output was 27.5 bhp at 4000rpm. Two Morgans were equipped with these engines for the Land's End: George Goodall had one fitted to a Sports two-seater, carrying the old registration UY 9862, and Bradshaw had one on his Morgan. They appeared underpowered for trials use, as both needed to be pushed on Doverhay hill whereas most of the other Morgans with their JAP engines were successful.

Premier awards were won by Harry Jones, driving the three-speed twin rear wheel Morgan, Elliott, Hooper, Cole with his old two-speed twin rear wheel car, and Brand now driving his new three-speed Sports model. 'Joe' Huxham, 'Jim' Goodall, George Goodall, Atkins and Bradshaw gained silvers. Lionel Creed came unstuck on Bluehills Mine when he tried to slide the factory two-speed twin rear wheel car round the bend, found he couldn't, lifted a front wheel and went into the rocks, badly damaging the wheel. Lionel managed to obtain a replacement wheel from the Cornwall Morgan agent, and carried on later, but with no chance of an award.

As cars were to compete on Donington during the 1933 season the track had been considerably widened before the Easter meeting. Clive Lones had been working on his 731cc engine through the autumn and winter and refitted this engine to his Super Aero racer. His was the only Morgan in the 750cc ten-lap event, but despite a bad start he worked through the field to finish second to Collett's Norton.

The last event on Easter Monday was the 1100cc ten-lap event. Collett walked this one, to win from Laird in 'Johnny V'. Lones held a comfortable second place for a good portion of the race but he finished on one cylinder, too late for a replica award. Tom Rhodes, with his 1096cc air-cooled JAP, had even worse luck, turning his Morgan over at Starkey corner. Although he was trapped beneath the car, he suffered only the minor injury of a skinned elbow.

Way back in August 1932 Arthur Maskell had sold the racing Super Aero he had used in 1930 to a student, complete with his tuned 1096cc JAP LTOW engine. He himself had by then received his newly ordered personal Morgan, a very late Super Aero, chassis number M672. Henry Laird's current interest in racing prompted Maskell to return to see the student, John Palmer, and he persuaded him to sell it to Laird. Now tiring of his Johnny numbers, Laird called the car 'Johnny Red', while his previous 'Johnny V' became 'Johnny Yellow'. He soon started to omit the Johnny prefix, calling his two Morgans simply 'Red' and 'Yellow'. The ex-Palmer car was still fitted with Maskell's tuned racing 1926 engine, LTOW/T64353/W, and was generally little altered from its Brooklands days, except for a matching wind scallop mounted on the passenger side of the scuttle and a Bentley and Draper steering damper. Even the holes on the tail for the hoop used by Maskell's acrobatic passenger in 1930 were still there.

Henry made his track debut with 'Red' at Whitsun in the passenger machine event at Donington. After leading the first lap by 100 yards he retired with slipped magneto timing. John Hooper's black Aero, also making its Donington debut, upheld Morgan honour by finishing third behind the Norton sidecars of Taylor and Tozer.

Clive Lones had a serious accident during practice for this event. He overturned his Morgan when braking hard to avoid Goodman, a motorcyclist, who pushed his Sunbeam motorcycle across the track in front of him on the flat-out downhill straight towards Starkey corner. Clive needed hospitalization and as Morgans hoped to include him in their team for the forthcoming Brooklands Light Car Relay Race, the Morgan was taken to the factory for straightening out and overhaul.

The twenty-sixth London-Edinburgh Trial was also held at Whitsun, this year in fine weather. Premier awards were won by Harry Jones and RJ Cole with their three-speed and two-speed twin rear wheel cars, and also by GB Brand's Sports model.

In March 'Joe' Huxham had held one of his 'Huxham's Rallies', basically a social gathering of enthusiasts with some minor competition followed by retirement to the pub for a few jugs of beer and a singsong. Morgans had supported their new agents, with 'Uncle' George Goodall, 'Cousin' Harry Jones and Stuart Spring, the factory sales representative, all taking part down at Bournemouth. Goodall drove a 'new' GC 4, a Sports model with Magna wheels and high level exhaust pipes (these were fitted to the Super Sports model from the 1932 show, but were not fitted to the Sports as standard). The engine was a special ohv air-cooled JAP, one of the JAP prototypes being tested at this period.

By the time the 1933 London-Scarborough Trial came round in July another air-cooled ohv engine had been fitted to GC 4. This was of Matchless manufacture, and was a prototype MX2 unit.

As with the MX engine, its capacity was 990cc, with 'square' dimensions (85.5mm x 85.5mm). The crankcase and bottom end were virtually identical to the side-valve equivalent, but air-cooled cylinders and heads and ohv rocker gear were fitted, similar to that used on the 495cc Matchless motorcycle single later in the year. The rocker gear was totally enclosed and mechanically lubricated, developed from the system used on AJS motorcycles (AJS had been taken over by Matchless in the autumn of 1931). Rollers were fitted to the cam levers to take the extra strain of the ohv system, and an adjustable oil feed supplied the inlet valve guides. With compression of 6.2 to 1, 39.1 bhp was claimed at 4600 rpm.

The engine proved successful, powering Goodall's attractive sky-blue Sports with dark blue wings to a premier award. He also won the three-wheeler appearance prize for having such a smart vehicle.

With the increasing popularity of the Light Car Club's Relay Race, the support by the factory and accessory manufacturers was considerable. Before this year's event on 22nd July, HFS recalled the Morgans owned by his team of Rhodes ('A'), Laird ('B'), and Lones ('C') for overhaul, repainting them all in the new 'team' colours of red with cream wheels. Lones's and Rhodes's Morgans were fitted with well base rims in place of the split rim type previously used: this may have been a direct result of Rhodes's experience during practice for a previous Relay Race, when a split rim came adrift and sent him into a high-speed spin. Lones's car now sported a scuttle wind deflector instead of the previous Aero screen, and he was to use his highly tuned 731cc water-cooled JAP engine.

The Three speeder Era

Mr and Mrs Goodall with the MX2 Sports at Scarborough. (Goodall scrapbooks)

Henry Laird must have felt highly honoured to have his Morgan picked as the 'B' car as he had raced it so little. A double disc Andre Hartford shock absorber was installed over the rear wheel; as this demanded extra clearance the tail panel was cut away and replaced by a canvas covering to the Lones pattern. Although the ex-Maskell LTOW engine was fast, JAPs fitted a JTOR engine for this event, and so a red dummy radiator replaced the water-cooled radiator.

Tommy Rhodes's Morgan was also equipped with a canvas cover over the rear shock absorber, replacing the previous hump. He too had a new engine, a specially tuned 996cc JTOR JAP, a sister engine to one being developed by Eric Fernihough, tuned by Booker and Millington at the JAP factory to run on RDl fuel.

Michael McEvoy, Laird's business partner, also entered a team in the Relay Race, comprising his own McEvoy special Wolseley Hornet, Greaves's Frazer Nash, and John Hooper in his old 1931 'M' type Aero with a tuned LTOW JAP engine.

Practice was enlivened by an abortive attempt at radio contact through loudspeakers installed in the Morgans. This caused much press interest, and lost them valuable time. Charlie Curtis was in attendance as general mechanic, together with the JAP mechanics, and Davenport of Amal Carburettors.

The Morgans were heavily handicapped once again and thus a high lap speed was essential. True to form, Tommy Rhodes was soon lapping at around the 100 mph mark, covering one lap at 102 mph—the first time a car or three-wheeler had exceeded 100 mph in the Relay Races. However the pace could not last, and Rhodes came in with engine trouble to hand over to Laird. This year no work was allowed on cars in the paddock whilst the race was in progress, so Laird started with a cold engine. It was usual for the Morgans to run with just the high speed chain on, as the low gear chain would cause friction when running at high speed. They would thus chug round the bottom of the track until the engine built up speed and then join in the race. Laird was using a high top gear of 3.9 to 1 which made the start even more tricky, but despite this he soon began to lap at well over 90 mph, and put in one lap at 99.8 mph. At such high speed he found it virtually impossible to keep to the left of the black safety line at the Fork, receiving a reprimand from the officials. Laird's works engine was running on RDI fuel at 9.8 to 1 compression, with a 760 main jet in the single Amal carburettor.

After ten laps bumpy Brooklands took its toll, and Laird retired with a broken chassis tie bar, leaving Lones many more than his own thirty laps to cover. Soon he was cracking round, getting 95 mph from his 731cc engine—'the best engine JAPs ever produced' as he recently described it. By the seventieth of the ninety laps he lay third, just in front of Goodacre's supercharged Austin Seven and ten laps later he overtook Tuson's Fiat to take second place, which he held to the end, finishing behind Alan Hess's MG Magna. The Morgan team averaged 89.01 mph for the ninety laps, a speed only beaten by the supercharged 'dutch clog' Austin Seven team. This had been a gruelling race for Lones so soon after his Donington accident, and it is not surprising he had to rest up for several weeks afterwards.

In fifth place, just behind the Austin team, was McEvoy's team, the first 'mixed' team to finish, gaining the 'March Cup'. McEvoy himself managed around twenty fast laps, before Greaves took over. He also blew up, leaving John Hooper's old Morgan around fifty laps to cover. John hurtled on, with oil and water spraying back from the engine, and smoke belching out of the hot propshaft tunnel, but he held on to the finish. The team averaged 82.99 mph, Hooper's Morgan lapping not all that much slower than the works machines – a feat he was quite rightly proud of. Whilst driving to Brooklands for the event, Hooper's Aero broke its bevel box pinion and he had to send to Morgans for a replacement, spending all night with Bertie Le Man fitting it. Hooper had met McEvoy via Laird, and in fact his mechanic Bertie Le Man eventually went to work for him. It is interesting that John's passenger had thirty pebbles in his pocket with which to count off the laps: obviously he hadn't considered the possibility of having to do more.

As Laird had borrowed the air-cooled JAP for the Relay Race, he had to refit his water-cooled ex-Maskell engine for the August Bank Holiday Monday meeting at Donington. Using a compression of 8.3 to 1 and gears of 6.25 and 4.5 to 1 respectively, he finished second to Tozer's Norton outfit. John Hooper also entered his Aero, and Tom Rhodes his new 994cc JTOR engine, the sister to Fernihough's, but neither could make any impact. Laird's success was all the more praiseworthy in that he was driving with two broken ribs: when returning from a shopping trip in 'Yellow' he had turned over, trying to avoid a bus and an overtaking car.

Another Morgan driver making a name for himself at Brooklands was B Lambert, with a long stroke 1096cc air-cooled racing JTOR JAP-engined Morgan. Way back in

Donington Paddock: Hooper in 90, and Laird in 91. (Laird scrapbooks)

June he recorded 84.10 mph over the flying kilometre speed trials held before the races, and then finished third in one of the races behind Bickell's Bickell-JAP and Baragwanath's Brough Superior. At the end of July he finished second to Refoy's Excelsior JAP in the non-trade three-lap handicap. On 9th August he once again contested a three-lap non-trade handicap. Excellent handicapping saw an exciting battle between scratch man Bishop's Excelsior, Mobb's Velocette, Taylor's Cotton and Lambert's Morgan as they came off the Byfleet Banking for the last time. Lambert held on, to win by a mere 5 feet from Mobbs at 87.53 mph.

Back at Southport Tom Rhodes took his newly engined Morgan onto the sands for the 20-mile handicap on 12th August. Although starting with a favourable handicap he went onto one cylinder after three laps and thereafter stood no chance.

The following month the annual MCC High Speed Trials took place. All machines had to be in touring trim, less headlights. In one of the two-lap handicaps that preceded the 'hour blind', AL Hicks's 1096cc Morgan beat Maskell's 1096cc Super Aero by 300 yards, but his handicap had been 30 seconds compared to Maskell's 4. On scratch was George Brough in his banked sidecar outfit, fitted with a prototype JAP racing engine of 996cc. This was the 8/75, featuring no less than four oil pumps with twin magnetos. The cylinder barrels were partly buried in JAP 500cc style within the massive

Morgan Sweeps the Board

crankcase. Although looking very impressive the new engine tended to be too complicated and was not a great success.

The High Speed Trial itself saw Hooper and Laird gain first class awards, Hooper covering 79.74 miles, and Laird 63.08 miles. We suspect that Laird was using 'Yellow', his trials Morgan, for this event.

A silver medal was won by Jeffries, and a bronze by Hicks. Poor Maskell lost his low gear chain, which didn't help him when he tried to restart after stopping with engine trouble. He later retired after eight laps when the engine trouble proved incurable.

Also present was 'Joe' Huxham, though he didn't start in the High Speed Trial. He was, however, persuaded by Henry Laird to enter one of the relay teams for the Relay Race, held at the end of the meeting over just three laps. Just as he accelerated away from the start, the engine blew up! That evening poor 'Joe' was entertained most lavishly in the Hand and Spear by Henry Laird, who felt some moral responsibility for what had happened—this was the start of a life-long friendship. Laird's team, the 'Red' team, won the event at 72.18 mph, Laird driving 'Red', Hooper his Aero, and Bainbridge his Rudge motorcycle.

The International Six Days' Trial was based at Llandrindod Wells, and four Morgans entered as members of British Club teams. These were the two-speed twin rear wheel car of Cole, the factory three-speed twin rear wheel car, WP 2928 driven by Geoff Harris, Goodall in his MX2-powered GC 4, passengered by his son 'Jim', and Laird in 'Yellow', passengered as always for trials by his wife Barbara. Geoff Harris was wise to the scrutineering methods, whereby mechanical bits were marked with paint to prevent them being changed—he merely put his hand under the tent and acquired a tin!

Father and son Goodall storm Allt-y-Bady. (Motor Cycle)

The Three speeder Era

Geoff Harris on Dinas Rock. (Motor Cycle)

The Goodalls during the Donington Speed Test of the International. (Motor Cycle)

Morgan Sweeps the Board

Cole retired on the first day, and Laird didn't get much further as a centre pin sheered on the second. Harris and Goodall both completed the trial successfully without losing a single mark, gaining a gold medal each. This is not to say that they had no problems. Goodall fell behind time, and powered his way on trying to make it up. He succeeded, but knocked off both high level exhaust silencers on rocks on the way, these being handed back to him at the stage finish. Harris also had problems, for his dynamo packed up. He managed to get Charlie Curtis to leave a spare behind a hedge for him. This he painted with his tin of scrutineers' paint before fitting it and setting off on his way again!

The MCC Sporting Trial in October marked the last trial for Cole with the two-speed ex-factory twin rear wheel car. He took a silver medal while GB Brand took a bronze and Hooper retired.

In November Henry Laird borrowed the works three-speed twin rear wheel Morgan, WP 2928, to represent the East Midlands Centre in the ACU Team Trial. He emerged unpenalized along with the solos of Len Heath and Holdsworth, and also the Baughan-Python sidecar of Morris which had sidecar wheel drive, only to find that his team finished last after losing a total of 312.5 marks.

Both Laird and Harris had put up such excellent performances during the season that they earned themselves places in the British Expert's Trial, along with BSA three-wheeler expert GA Norchi. But then all three had their entries refused. The official reasons were that the Palmer Challenge Trophy was presented for and inscribed 'For the best sidecar performance', that several hills were unsuitable for tricars, and that there was a regulation restricting the drive to a single wheel. Whilst this ruled out Norchi's front wheel drive BSA, it did not rule out 'Yellow' or even the twin tyred single wheel of WP 2928 as used by Harris. But still the organizers were adamant that they should all use sidecar outfits. Henry was incensed by this, writing to the press to ask why he should compete all season with a Morgan, and then change to a sidecar for one event. He concluded by pointing out that 'Surely this is an open admission of the Morgan's superiority when competing against motorcycles and sidecars.'

The Olympia Motor Cycle Show in November brought modifications to the twin range of Morgans, but was especially notable for the introduction of the latest in the line of concession to the ordinary motorist—the four-cylinder Morgan three-wheeler. Way back in 1929 HFS had started work on producing such a vehicle, based upon a two-speed chassis. A later prototype did, however, have a redesigned chassis in which the centre backbone tube was retained and the side members produced as Z-shaped pressings with the body fixed to the top of the Z and the floor boards to the bottom limb. The engine was positioned behind the crosshead for the first time, with the radiator in front. Hence the steering track rod was now at the front of the car, to avoid the engine. The later of the two prototype four-cylinder Morgans was powered by a 750cc Coventry Climax side-valve engine and had a modified Family body with BSA-like radiator, but when the model was announced at the Motor Cycle Show it displayed a neat four-seater body fitted behind an inverted U-shaped radiator. Magna wheels were fitted instead of the two-speed type used on the prototype. Part of the delay in producing the model is thought to have been due to problems with the chassis suppliers,

An 'F' type, George Goodall's GC 4, Jim Goodall's Family and the Coventry Climax-engined prototype 'F' type at one of Huxham's rallies. (Harry Jones scrapbooks)

Rubery Owen, in tooling up for production. In fact this gave Morgan the chance to try another engine.

In October 1931 the Ford Motor Company had begun construction of vehicles at Dagenham, transferring production from Manchester. The timing was unfortunate, for sales of Ford's current range suffered with the onset of the depression, and the new plant soon faced financial disaster. Various British and French small cars had been shipped to the American Ford Company's factory at Dearborn, Michigan in 1930 for evaluation, and now Percival Perry, head of Dagenham, pleaded with Henry Ford for a small Ford to save the future of his factory. The result was the model Y, fitted with the 933cc Y type engine (56.6mm x 92.5mm) which produced 22 bhp at 4000 rpm, and was designed by Ford's chief engineer, Laurence Sheldric. This car, which was one of the last Fords that Henry Ford personally worked on, began production in August 1932. Morgans must have been quick off the mark in trying out the new Ford engine, which proved both more powerful than the Coventry Climax type, and was also cheaper to purchase. This was the engine that HFS chose to power his four-cylinder Morgan.

The twin-engined Super Sports Morgan had now been given a different body, resembling that of the Sports two-seater, except that the spare wheel was received into the tail instead of standing proud. This new 'barrel back' was in addition to the previous 'beetle back' style, which was also displayed at the Show. The new Morgan models now had two D-shaped cut-outs in the bonnet sides, the extra one being introduced in an attempt to improve the cooling of the side-valve Matchless engine. A works Sports model driven by Stuart Spring had proved quite troublesome in this respect, hence this modification.

A new Matchless engine was also introduced. This was the MX4, a water-cooled version of the MX2, with forked conrods instead of the side by side type. At 4800 rpm 42.1 bhp was claimed.

Other Morgan modifications included a new Family radiator, and a modified gearbox casing giving better worm wheel cooling and running on Castrol 'D' oil. The introduction of this gearbox caused the chassis numbers to change from R to D series; although the new gearbox was making its first show appearance, it had in fact been introduced in late 1932.

For the 1934 racing season JAPs announced the 8/75 engine as used by George Brough. The oiling system was dry sump and the additional Pilgrim pump fed the rocker boxes from one side, and annular grooves around the cylinder bases from the other. 14mm plugs were fitted, and deep spigots held each cylinder with maximum rigidity.

Once again the London-Exeter brought the year to a close. This year no Morgans took a premier award, although Goodall, Huxham, Laird, Campbell and Kelleher took silvers, and Aldington and Euston bronzes. 'Joe' Huxham was driving his new Morgan, LJ 8420, which had been delivered on 22nd October. This was a special Sports two-seater fitted with chassis number D589 and 2 inches longer than standard. The body had two scuttle mounted wind deflectors, a fold flat windscreen and a dummy radiator which contained a special petrol tank. It was painted black while the chassis and wheels were a dull red. The engine, MX2 505, was equipped with forked conrods and the optional high compression pistons ($7\frac{1}{2}$ to 1). Special 8 inch diameter brakes were fitted to the two-speeder-type front wheels.

At this year's Colmore Cup Trial, two events were to be run off, one for cars, and one for motorcycles, with Morgans competing against the motorcycles. Alterations in the rules made them eligible for the Colmore Cup itself though twin rear wheels were barred. Severe drizzle and fog made conditions very unpleasant. The Morgans found themselves considerably handicapped as there was little or no run up to many of the hills. In spite of this, Henry and Barbie Laird in 'Yellow' completed the course and lost only 57 marks, to take the Bayliss Cup for the best three-wheeler. John Hooper was driving the factory three-speed twin rear wheel car, WP 2928, but the chassis couldn't stand the pounding and he retired. The twin rear wheels had presumably been replaced by a single wheel, possibly of the type used by Harris later in the year which featured a special 16 inch Dunlop rim laced onto the special three-flange hub and fitted with an oversize tyre. The twin rear wheel set-up, although effective, was now to be increasingly restricted at mudplugger events. It went unmourned by many drivers, as its appalling road handling made the car very difficult to drive. One of the experts who still enjoyed it was Harry Jones.

The MCC had considered banning knobbly competition tyres from its trials events, causing many fierce arguments in the press. Curiously, Henry Laird disagreed with the ban, whilst his racing passenger and brother, Richard, approved it, as did George Goodall. For the London-Land's End Trial in March, Goodall drove on standard tyres to win a silver medal, in company with 'Jim' Goodall and Harry Jones. Jones was driving an MX4-engined three-speed Sports Model, fitted with twin rear wheels. The front wheels were Dunlop Magna and a spare was carried on the tail. This new twin rear wheel car was running on the old twin rear wheel registration UY 9862. Premier

Harry Jones with the new twin rear wheel three-speeder on Darracott. (Harry Jones scrapbook)

Morgan Sweeps the Board

awards were gained by FW 'Nobby' Clarke's JAP, and Tommy Coates's Matchless.

Two days later on Easter Monday, motor cycle racing returned to Donington Park. Over the winter the course had undergone alterations in the area around Starkey Hill and Starkey Corner, providing a flat-out straight about a mile long. This was the first motorcycle meeting to use the new circuit and it was an unusually cold day that greeted competitors and spectators alike. Laird entered 'Red' for the 1100cc sidecar and three-wheeler event, lowering the compression yet again, this time to 8.25 to 1. As usual Henry and Richard, his passenger, were up against Kim Collett's Norton, but this time they had the edge and forged ahead on the third lap to win easily at 55 mph.

On 14th April *The Motor Cycle* magazine sponsored one of their clubman's days at Brooklands, organized by the BMCRC for ordinary enthusiasts. In the flying kilometre events Euston's 1096cc JAP Morgan averaged 64.28 mph, whilst ER Jay's similar model averaged 61.12 mph.

25th April saw the first four-cylinder 'F type' Morgan leave the factory, chassis

Rhodes about to gain his Gold Star. (Wilson collection)

number FD 1, with Y type Ford engine number Y38054, and bound for the Birmingham agents of the Colmore Depot.

Although Tommy Rhodes had lapped Brooklands at over 100 mph in the last Relay Race, he needed to achieve this figure in a BMCRC race to qualify for a Gold Star. On 12th May he took his racer onto the track for the BMCRC 'Cup Day.' In the five-lap handicap for the Wakefield Cup, Tom won his heat from Muir's Norton, but in the final he just couldn't shake him off, in spite of lapping at over 100 mph, and the two cars crossed the finishing line neck and neck. Rhodes's fastest lap was 103.76 mph. This gave him the Morgan outer circuit lap record, previously held by Clive Lones at 102.48 mph, and also made sure of his Gold Star. Rhodes was the third Morgan driver to win one, the others being Lones and Jackson way back in 1930. Rhodes's Morgan was powered by his 996cc JTOR JAP engine tuned by Booker and Millington. It had a starred engine number, which signified that it was a special. The car had been modified for Brooklands racing during the previous winter by Charlie Curtis at the factory. A double dropped crosshead 'C' type chassis was fitted, further strengthened for Brooklands by replacing some of the chassis tubes with solid steel bars, and welding additional members between the two longitudinal chassis tubes running from the front to the rear of the car.

Five out of the six finishing Morgans in this year's London-Edinburgh gained premier awards, including Brand and Euston with their JAP engines, and 'Jim' Goodall and Harry Jones with Matchless. Harry Jones was driving the twin rear wheel Sports, UY 9862, now with an air-cooled MX2 engine, whilst 'Jim' had a standard Sports with a double D cut-out behind the MX2 engine, carrying the registration AB 16.

Henry Laird had, as usual, entered for the Bank Holiday Monday Donington meeting, held at Whitsun. In the 1100cc sidecar and three-wheeler race over the customary ten laps, 'Red' finished second to Bury's Douglas sidecar, despite a bad misfire on the first, second and tenth laps.

Down in Kent, the Kent and Sussex Light Car Club were running events on Race Hill at Lewes, as they had in the 1920s. The only Morgan present was the LTOW 'dog-eared' JAP-engined Super Aero of GEW Oliver. It proved much faster than during the previous trials on 12th May, putting in a time of 25.8 seconds and leaving a great deal of rubber on the track as it got under way.

Trials continued with Laird's 'Yellow' gaining a class award in the MCC's Llandudno trial held on 6th and 7th July. Interestingly enough the event finished with driving tests on the Conway Road which proceeded amidst the ordinary traffic!

At the Morgan factory HFS had been testing a 350cc Villiers two-stroke engine on the works pick-up. As expected, its performance was not adequate, and so before the Relay Race was held on 21st July it was replaced by a Matchless MX engine, Curtis being the factory mechanic in attendance.

Once again Rhodes was the 'A' driver, with Laird 'B' and Lones 'C'. Their cars were taken to Brooklands for preparation and tuning before being repainted with the Morgan colours of red with cream wheels. Rhodes's and Lones's cars were as last year, and Laird was again using a JAP factory JTOR engine on 'Red'.

As in the two previous Relay Races, one of the many mixed teams also contained a

Rhodes during practice for the Relay Race, with Lones's Morgan behind. (Syd Rhodes collection)

Rhodes's and Laird's Morgans await scrutineering. (Laird scrapbook)

'Joe' Huxham with customary refreshment and his Morgan. The factory pickup stands behind. (Laird scrapbooks)

Morgan entry. This was 'Joe' Huxham with his MX2-powered Sports, sporting regulation Brooklands silencers. He was running as the 'C' car in the West Hants LCC team behind an MG and a Crossley.

On the day Rhodes set off at high speed in the afternoon sunshine to try to overcome the heavy handicap once again set upon the team. After thirty fast laps he handed the sash over to Laird, who was passengered by his brother Richard. His JTOR engine was running on Lodge 14 mm plugs and Shell N4 fuel with Castrol R oil. The engine had a compression of 10.2 to 1 in the driver's side cylinder, and 9.8 to 1 in the passenger's side, both cylinders being supplied with fuel via a single Amal carburettor with 720 jet. This year he was running on a slightly higher top gear of 3.8 to 1. Like Rhodes, Laird had a trouble-free fast run and handed over to Lones after his allotted thirty laps. As Lones set off on the final leg with his water-cooled 731cc engine, the skies darkened and a torrential downpour began, soon flooding the track in places. Lones wasn't to be put off by such conditions and soon had the Morgan team in sixth place. By the eightieth lap he was in third, and this became second when Tuson's Fiat retired with a broken conrod. Victory went to the Austin team by 5 minutes, but the second-placed Morgans had averaged 90.91 mph for the ninety laps, faster than any other team in the race. Lones's 731cc engine had once again proved completely reliable in racing conditions

Morgan Sweeps the Board

and was now estimated to have around 11,000 racing miles under its belt in the various vehicles.

Finishing in ninth place was the West Hants team at 70.05 mph. 'Joe' Huxham accompanied the jubilant Morgan team for celebration afterwards in the Ship Hotel at Weybridge, no doubt also pleased with his own performance. Charlie Curtis, known as 'Fatty' Curtis to the racing lads, was also elated and managed to sing all 4(?) verses of 'The Muffin Man' balancing a full pint of beer on his head without spilling a drop.

Lones kept his Morgan in its Relay Race trim for record-breaking in August, when he captured eight 500cc class records using a 500cc rocker box JAP single. As usual Lones produced this engine from parts acquired from the JAP second-hand store, using many of the recent JAP speedway engine parts and some Freddie Dixon components such as the flywheels and conrod. Although Clive prefers not to rely on his memory at this late date, he believes it may have had a bronze crankcase.

When Laird appeared for the August Bank Holiday meeting at Donington he had once again installed the ex-Maskell 1096cc water-cooled JAP. The carburettor was a track type Amal, using a 250 main jet of his own manufacture, and his gear ratios were 6.25 and 4.3 to 1 respectively. In practice the misfiring Laird had experienced at the earlier Whitsun meeting recurred. He tried out various plugs and changed the magneto but with little effect, finishing the race unplaced. Afterwards both magnetos were found to be faulty. He used a 50/50 mixture of fuel (petrol and benzole) as was customary with this engine.

Back at Race Hill, Lewes, on 25th August, GEW Oliver's 'dog ear' JAP Super Aero, in full road-going trim, finished third in the 1100cc Super Sports Class, and second in the handicap. He achieved the fastest time of 25.8 seconds, identical to the time he clocked up in June.

Henry in the Fussen speed test. (Laird scrapbooks)

The Three-speeder Era

As Germany had won the 1933 International Six Days' Trial, she provided the Bavarian venue for the 1934 event in August. Three Morgans were entered, Henry Laird and Barbara in 'Yellow, Geoff Harris in a new factory car, and R C Mead driving the original 3-speed twin rear wheel factory car which he purchased as D360 on August 15th 1934, fitted with the MX4 561 instead of the LTOWZ. Harris's car, WP 6271, was an MX2-engined Sports model with shallow cranked front crosshead tubes. The car was built to take a twin rear wheel, but in fact ran with a special single rim laced onto the three-spoke flanges of the twin rear wheel hub, taking a wide 16 inch tyre. The three-speed gearbox and rear end were modified to take the extra large rear wheel set-up, presumably identical to those fitted to the previous works three-speed twin rear wheel Morgans. The rear fork trunnion on the offside was extended outwards, and fitted with a longer cross shaft. Specially fabricated forged fork arms extended from the rear fork trunnions to the rear wheel, and the rear springs were mounted further out from the gearbox to fit into the widened forks.

All went well for Harris until the final speed test when an inlet rocker broke, but he carried on on one 'pot' at 35 mph to complete the course. RC Mead failed on Ettaler Strausse on the third day and retired the following day, but Laird romped on with 'Yellow' to take a gold, even finding the 1 in 4¼ Ettalberg mountain an easy climb.

Back in England the MCC ran their annual High Speed Trial in September at Brooklands. 'Joe' Huxham's special MX 2 Sports earned a premier award by covering

Geoff Harris in WP 6271. (Wilson collection)

twenty-six laps at an average of 74 mph as did Maskell's JAP-engined Morgan which covered twenty-five laps. Poor RAV Dismore's Morgan seized up after just twelve laps.

Clive Lones continued his record breaking with eleven long-distance 500cc records, at speeds ranging from 68.06 mph for the 6 hours to 71.09 mph for 3 hours. Once again he was using his rocker box JAP single-cylinder engine.

On 15th September GEW Oliver took his 'dog ear' JAP-engined Super Aero down to Brighton for the famous Madeira Drive speed trials. He finished fourth in the passenger machine class after averaging 59.60 mph for the standing start half-mile.

Tommy Rhodes took his JAP-tuned JTOR-engined racer onto Southport sands for the Championship meeting at the end of the month. Despite a very damp track after early morning rain, Rhodes managed 95.60 mph for the flying kilometre, beating Lones's 1930 speed to become the fastest Morgan driver on the sands.

On 2nd November Lones returned once more to Brooklands for record breaking, this time using his 731cc water-cooled JAP twin engine. He covered the 5 kilometres at 101.16 mph, the first time a 750cc three-wheeler had lapped Brooklands at over 100 mph, and took records up to 10 miles at over 90 mph.

When the Olympia Motor Cycle Show opened in the late autumn none of the Morgans shown had JAP engines, signifying the end of a long association between HFS and the Tottenham concern. Gone too was the 'beetle back' Super Sports. All twins were fitted with the 990cc Matchless engines in side or overhead valve form, air- or water-cooled. The distributor rotor arms were replaced by a double-ended coil system, and the Ford engined model (F4) and the Super Sports model both had more rounded ends to their tails to give better accommodation to the spare wheel.

There were several Morgan entries in the London-Exeter Trial which started from Virginia Water on 28th December. Henry Laird was driving an 'F type' Morgan, fitted with a chain-driven Zoller supercharger. He proved unsuccessful on Fingle Bridge, succumbing to wheelspin. DC Campbell was using an MX4 Matchless engine with new hairpin valve springs on his barrel-back Super Sports, whilst another Morgan trials driver, KP Robert, drove a JAP Super Sports. He turned over on Ibberton Hill but was soon away again.

The Morgan factory was represented by George Goodall, his son 'Jim' and Harry Jones. As usual they were late setting off from the factory on their way to the start. Unfortunately, when Harry Jones braked hard for traffic lights in a town on the way, George Goodall ran into the back of him. The damage to George's car was extensive, with a front wheel pushed round the side, but Harry carried on with a buckled tail panel on the three-speed twin rear wheel Matchless Sports model, now carrying registration number AB 16.

Harry and 'Jim' started on time, but soon the rains came down. Harry's passenger spent most of the night standing up wiping the windscreen clear, whilst the twin rear wheels threw water high over the tail and down the back rest. Harry was a notoriously bad traveller on the overnight run. A favourite quip of one of the BSA three-wheeler drivers was to ask if he'd had breakfast. If the answer was yes, he would reply, 'Well, no doubt we'll be seeing it along the way!'

Fingle Bridge was reached and passed successfully, but then 'Jim' Goodall crashed

The Three speeder Era

Harry Jones on Ibberton, with the twin rear wheel three-speeder. (Motor Cycle)

into a stone wall, and number two of the Morgan team was out.

Simms Hill was the next hill, which Harry failed, even beginning to slide backwards. However, he did finish the course, the sole factory representative to do so.

The supercharger fitted to Laird's 'F type' in the Exeter was a direct result of Michael McEvoy becoming an agent for Zoller. It therefore came as no surprise that for the Colmore trial in February Henry should enter 'Yellow' with a type 4 Zoller. It was fitted to the nearside of the engine and chain-driven from a sprocket on the outside flywheel, supplying the rocker box LTOW JAP via a single induction pipe. Maximum boost pressure was 12 lbs/sq inch. The organizers insisted on standard rather than competition tyres, but Henry and Barbara failed to gain awards.

Laird in the Wye Valley Trial, with supercharger. (Laird scrapbooks)

'Yellow' was run in the same trim for the Victory Trial in March, and also in the Wye Valley Trial, but now with competition tyres back in place. 'Jim' Goodall also competed in the latter using WP 6271, the special single rear wheel Sports Morgan that he had now taken over from Geoff Harris. Straight crosshead tubes were now fitted in place of the shallow cranked ones.

Once again the amateur Morgan drivers turned up for the annual Motor Cycle Clubman's Day at Brooklands, held on 6th April. In the flying kilometre speed trials, Euston, now using a Matchless-engined barrel-back Super Sports, recorded 74.07 mph and RAV Dismore's 981cc JAP Morgan recorded 70.79 mph. In the clubman's passenger handicap Dismore came second to Bishop's Zenith JAP, but frightened spectators in the process by taking the Morgan to the very edge of the banking.

Once again George Goodall, 'Jim' Goodall and Harry Jones represented the Morgan factory in the April London-Land's End Trial. Harry Jones was driving a new Sports two-seater, WP 7592 with MX2 power, and George Goodall an 'F type' Morgan which had only two seats, a prototype F2 model.

The Three speeder Era

The Donington Park season commenced with the Easter Monday meeting when several interesting Morgans made an appearance. John Hooper now had another car for getting to and from work and had thus decided to purchase a proper racing Morgan for Donington, instead of using his Jack-of-all-trades Aero. In consequence he had been down to Brooklands to look at Robin Jackson's Beart-inspired special: Jackson had put this up for sale as pressure of work was restricting his racing activities. Jackson and Hatch had now completed the first of the air-cooled 1087cc vee twin Blackburne engines. Jackson had fitted this to his racer with a view to attempting the flying kilometre record, but had never got round to tuning it fully. He took Hooper out for two or three very fast laps around Brooklands and the deal was then completed. Hooper towed the racer to Walsall behind the car of his friend, Thompson Wilson, entering it for the Easter Monday meeting after lowering the compression ratio to allow it to run on petrol.

Henry Laird had transferred his Zoller supercharger from 'Yellow' to 'Red' for this meeting, with McEvoy in attendance for advice and help.

A newcomer to Morgan racing was Cyril Hale, known as 'Charlie'. Way back in 1934 he had watched a Morgan race at Donington but had not been very impressed by the speeds they had achieved. He had then ordered a Colmore Special Morgan Super Sports with MX4 Matchless engine from the Colmore Depot. He took the car to Morgans and told them he wanted to race it, whereupon George Goodall threatened to help—sending the engine back to Matchless and working on the chassis at Malvern. The black barrel-back Morgan sported twin carburettors on the Matchless engine for this, 'Charlie's' first race.

Practice soon showed John Hooper that his ex-Jackson racer was completely unsuited to Donington's twisting circuit, being all 'go' and no 'stop'. Not only was the

Jackson's special as entered by Hooper for the Donington Easter meeting. (Hooper collection)

Morgan Sweeps the Board

chassis wrong but the special Jackson engine repeatedly oiled the plugs. In desperation he called in at Laird's pit and borrowed some special plugs from McEvoy, returning to the track in a now rather aggressive state of mind. Unfortunately a solo motorcycle cut across in front of him as he approached Starkey Corner, throwing him completely off his line. He turned a complete somersault before landing on three wheels again. The chassis tie bar was broken and his passenger badly knocked about. Still undaunted, Hooper repaired it with an old brake cable, borrowed one of Laird's friends as a passenger, and was thus able to compete in the afternoon race.

Cyril Hale was confident that he had a good chance of winning, thinking he was really doing everything right when he had cornered on two wheels. But when the ten-lap passenger race started, there was no-one to touch Laird, who finished miles ahead of Taylor's Norton to set a new ten-lap record speed of 56.05 mph. Poor 'Charlie' finished right at the back, though he did have to repair a plug lead, for which purpose his passenger extracted a safety pin from his underwear.

Action returned to Donington on 18th May. Henry Laird once again started in a

Henry and brother Richard with 'Red' at the May Donington meeting. (Laird scrapbooks)

'Jim' in WP 6271 on Wrynose in the London-Edinburgh Trial. (Goodall scrapbooks)

fantastic style with his blown ex-Maskell engine on 'Red'. After being last at the start of the 10-mile race, he finished the first lap in front, and was streets ahead on lap two. Unfortunately the rear main bearing then collapsed and he had to retire at the end of lap three. During the race he achieved one lap at 60.19 mph and in practice one at 62.02 mph. The race was won by Taylor's Norton sidecar, which broke Laird's ten-lap record at 56.16 mph. Laird's 'Red' had been fitted with a three-speed and no reverse gearbox by the Morgan factory, and he used overall ratios of 9.1, 6.5 and 4.1 to 1. He may well have had this same gearbox in 'Red' at the earlier Easter meeting. The Zoller supercharger was supplying 50/50 mixture at a theoretical 18 lbs./sq. inch boost from a $1^{5}/_{16}$ inch choke TT Amal carburettor fitted with 1200 main jet. It was driven by sprockets of 22/33 tooth ratios. The compression of the driver's side cylinder was 6.1 to 1, and that of its sister 5.6 to 1.

Tommy Rhodes took his Booker and Millington tuned JTOR-engined racer to Brooklands on 25th May for the BMCRC 'Cup Day'. He demonstrated that he was still a force to be reckoned with when he finished third in the three-lap outer circuit handicap, and won the ten-lap outer circuit handicap at 98.62 mph. It is possible that his car was also fitted with the racing three speed and no reverse gearbox for this meeting—this was certainly the case by July.

7th June saw the start of the annual London-Edinburgh Trial. Once again the

George Goodall in the 'F' type on Summer Lodge, passing the recovery equipment. (Goodall scrapbooks)

Morgan factory were represented by the two Goodalls and Harry Jones, and all took premier awards. As in the Land's End, George Goodall drove a prototype F2, registration BGO 8, to which he had fitted an Amal downdraught carburettor. 'Jim' drove WP 6271, and Harry WP 7592. Euston and Hunting took silver medals with Matchless Morgans.

On 10th June the action returned to Donington. For the 25 mile passenger handicap, Laird had to give the rest of the field 100 seconds start. The blown Maskell engine was run as in May, but with a repaired rear main bearing. Unfortunately oil leaked onto the clutch plate from the flywheel spigot bearing, forcing his retirement on the third lap. He made a note not to oil it in future.

On 26th June Laird took his supercharged 'Red' to Brooklands for his first race on the Mountain Circuit. Passengered by Bill Clarke of HRD Vincent fame, he found that a 4.1 to 1 top gear was too high for the circuit but he did finish fourth in the ten-lap event. The engine was set up as at Donington.

For this year's Relay Race, however, Laird did change his engine. He had managed to aquire a special long stroke (80mm x 107mm) JTOR with bronze crankcases. When tuned to give 70 bhp or so the JTOR engine's weak point was its crankcase, and Baragwanath is believed to have cast a few sets out of bronze for increased strength and rigidity. Way back in 1931 Ron Horton had used a highly modified long stroke bronze crankcase JTOR in his Shelsley special—'The Horton Special'—built by him and Robin Jackson from GN bits. It is possible that Laird had acquired this engine. Prior to installing the engine into the chassis it was checked over by Bill Ayrton, Morgan's tuner. When testing the big-end he asked Derek Evans, a young apprentice, for his opinion and finding some up and down movement in the conrods, Derek thought that a replacement was needed. "No", said Bill, "that's just about right, I like a bit of play

The Three speeder Era

for racing." For practice Laird used twin track type 1 1/8 inch Amals, with 800 jet in the driver's side and 900 in its sister. He ran the car on Shell N4 fuel, using compression ratios of 10.2 and 9.8 to 1. For the event itself, in which he was the 'A' car, he reverted to a single system, possibly using different cylinder heads.

The 'B' car was Tom Rhodes's three-speed racer with its usual Booker and Millington tuned 996cc JTOR on the front. Clive Lones drove the 'C' car using his favourite engine, the watercooled 731cc—still in two-speed form as he didn't like the three-speed system. As usual George Goodall, 'Fatty' Curtis, a JAP mechanic and Davenport from Amals were on hand for help and advice.

Two other Morgans were entered in mixed teams, those of 'Joe' Huxham and Martin Soames. 'Joe's' friendship with Henry Laird had persuaded him to fit a Zoller supercharger in a similar position to that used on 'Red', to feed the MX2 engine on his special Sports model. During practice, the passenger-side piston holed and welded itself to the cylinder bore after a mere two laps. Poor 'Joe' and his partner Tom Bryant worked like mad trying to solve the problem, fitting extra oil leads, boring out jets, and so on. Sammy Lee of Martlet's kept turning up new pistons with more clearance than the last and a great deal of help was given by Minnie and Granville Grenfell. Alas, the same thing happened in the race itself, after only two laps: 'Joe' was running as the 'B' driver behind Hartwell's MG and in front of Hendy's Singer. He had to leave the Morgan by the Hawker sheds, running back with the sash to the pits to hand over to

'Red' with a new bronze crankcase long stroke JAP in practice for the Relay Race. (Laird scrapbooks)

Hendy. When he arrived at the pits, he was so winded he was unable to avail himself of the liquid refreshment his pit staff had kindly anticipated that he would need.

The Martin Soames car, running as 'B' in another mixed team, was a Super Aero chassis M 107, supplied by Morgan with a JTOR engine, number JTOR/W 68175/S. It had in fact been exhibited on the 1930 Olympia show stand before going to Beart's agency. Soames, an apprentice at Leyland Motors, had bought the car from its original owner and used it on the road for two years before modifying it for racing. He was able to lighten the car to 5 cwt 14 lb, a saving of 28 per cent. Baragwanath tuned the engine, Robin Jackson produced a new propeller shaft (possibly with an ash inset) and Dunlop built some very light front wheels to take 3.25 x 19 inch ribbed tyres, dished inwards by 1¼ inches. Unfortunately for Soames the 'C' car in his team, an Aston Martin, broke a timing gear in practice. This meant that his team was unable to compete, as each team's 'C' car had to finish the race. Soames had lapped at over 90 mph running on RD1 fuel with a single carburettor. He believed that well over 100 mph would have been achieved with two.

The first Morgan to take to the track was Laird, who was soon lapping at 94 mph. This proved to much for the bronze sliders which both broke, forcing his retirement after seventeen laps. In future Laird was to use specially made steel sliders. Rhodes then took over and reeled off the rest of Laird's laps and his own thirty, lapping in the late 90s before handing over to Lones.

One of the weak points of Lones's 731 engine was the front timing shaft, which was liable to break whilst the engine accelerated. Sure enough, this happened after just five laps, putting the Morgan team out of the race. In later events Clive eventually overcame the problem by fitting a much larger shaft, modifying the crankcase to suit. Forked con rods were used on this engine, which did not have the power of Lones's JTOR.

On 5th August racing returned to Donington for the Bank Holiday Monday meeting. 'Red' retained the bronze crankcase (80mm x 107mm) JAP, and the Zoller supercharger was fitted once more, supplying the two cylinders by separate feed pipes. In the unlimited passenger handicap Laird started with a handicap of 100 seconds and really flew for two laps, doing a standing lap at 2 minutes 40 seconds, but then the passenger-side piston seized due to Pilgrim pump oil failure. Laird was using compressions of 6.2 and 5.65 to 1, and special Martlet pistons machined to give clearances of .012 inches on skirt, .024 inches on top land, and .016 inches below bottom ring. The Amal carburettor had a 1100 main jet and ran on 50/50 mixture (petrol/benzole). Gear ratios were 10, 6.25 and 3.9 to 1.

John Hooper had also entered for this race with his ex-Jackson car, which he had now lowered by double cranking the front crosshead to make it more suitable for Donington's corners. Unfortunately he once again broke the chassis after the tie rod broke. John had registered the Morgan for the road on 29th July as CDH 127.

As we have previously mentioned, the 60 degree LTOWZ engine introduced in 1931 was really a concession to the ordinary motorist, rather than a sporting proposition. This is not to say that some enthusiast did not try to tune it into a racing engine. Two young enthusiasts, Rupert Watkins-Pitchford and his cousin Paul Willson, even tried to capture Tommy Rhodes's Morgan outer circuit Brooklands lap record of 103.76

Hooper's ex-Jackson car after Donington, its damaged chassis braced by wire. (Hooper collection)

mph with one during the summer of 1935. They modified the former's 1934 'beetle back' Super Sports by stripping it right down to get it as light as possible. The compression was raised on the LTOWZ engine, and the coil ignition replaced by the optional magneto type using a Bosch product. Finally they visited Eric Fernihough, now a well known motorcycle tuner, at his premises at Weybridge. 'Ferni' was as meticulously clean as ever with his motorcycle preparation, even to the extent of brushing off the tyres before wheeling machines into his workshop. He referred them to his assistant, Richard Chapman. Twin Bowden carburettors of the type preferred by 'Ferni' himself were purchased, and Richard machined up some manifolds for the Morgan out of solid steel section, using a 3 inch treadle-driven Drummond round bed lathe. The sections were then welded together and ground out to a curved taper with the

Twin Bowden carburettors on the Watkins-Pitchford Morgan. (R Chapman)

big flexible drive machine used for machining heads. Despite all this the Morgan would still lap no faster than 98 mph so they never did attack the record. Nevertheless it *was* exciting. Paul Willson remembers that they had to make the Morgan into a single-seater as he was literally thrown from driver to passenger seat by the bumps on Brooklands.

Incidentally, 'Ferni' would often remove a carefully set-up carburettor after an event and hang it up with a label attached, giving details of when it was used and all the relevant information. Never was a plug changed or a jet altered without the fullest details being written into a notebook.

Now that Laird had the bronze crankcase engine for 'Red', he transferred the ex-Maskell 'dog-ear' engine to 'Yellow'. For the International Six Days' Trial in Bavaria, which started on 9th September, Henry put the supercharger installation back in 'Yellow'. He became the only British passenger machine to finish, in spite of spending 59 minutes replacing a broken slider after a ditching accident, and losing the use of his

The Three-speeder Era

front wheel brakes. 'Yellow' sported a new body for this event, fitted by Morgans who were no doubt embarrassed by the state of his old one. The new body was similar to that of the early 32 Sports two-seater, though its bonnet had a double D cut-out. When 'Red' became a three-speeder, Laird was able to transfer the old two-speeder rear fork assembly and shock absorber set up to 'Yellow', using it for the first time in this trial. At the same time, he equipped Red with Hartford shock absorbers to the side of each three-speed rear fork blade.

At the MCC High Speed Trial at Brooklands on 14th September, 'Joe' Huxham tried once again for high speeds with the blown MX2, now fitted with a special streamlined tail. He was lapping at around 95 mph when the front cross tubes flexed so much that they knocked off the exhaust pipes, and he was flagged off for excessive noise. Also competing was 'Jim' Goodall in WP 6271, covering 67.75 miles. WP 6271 was fitted with an MX2 engine, number 619, which featured hairpin valve springs and the forked conrods of the MX4.

On 22nd October Henry took 'Red' to Brooklands for world records. His bronze crankcase engine was unchanged from the August Donington meeting, except for compression ratios of 6.3 and 5.8 to 1 and an Amal carburettor main jet enlarged to

Hectic work by the Lairds in Oberstdorf paddock. (Laird collection)

'Red' the record-breaker. (Laird scrapbooks)

1400. Gear ratios were 10, 7, and 4.3 to 1 and the stripped Morgan weighed 996 lb. Passengered by Barbara, Henry took the standing start kilometre and mile at 72.28 and 81.56 mph respectively. His pit personnel were his friends 'Joe' Huxham and Tom Bryant.

On the following day was the final BMCRC Brooklands meeting of the year. Henry contested the five-lap mountain handicap, this time passengered by Tom Bryant, and won in record time at 63.44 mph.

At the Motor Cycle Show this year Morgans introduced the two-seater version of the 'F' type – the F2, and made optional the new larger bore Ford 'C' engine (1172cc, 63.5mm x 92.5mm). This claimed 30.1 bhp at 4000 rpm and had been introduced by Ford for their 10 hp Ford in late 1934.

The twenty-first London-Exeter Trial on Boxing Day saw HFS return to trials driving, this time in the veteran class. He had competed in the very first trial in 1910. As if to celebrate this anniversary he chose to enter the very first production four-wheeler Morgan, with which he won a premier award. This was the very first true 4/4 (4 wheels, 4 cylinders) though this same Coventry Climax engined car had in fact appeared at Brooklands in July with preproduction bodywork. The prototype four-wheeler that preceded it was a modified F type to which a car type rear axle had been fitted, probably in 1934. It was on this earlier four-wheeler that Peter Morgan learnt to drive in the grounds of his father's home. Both carried the registration WP 7490.

Three-wheelers were represented by five Morgans, including 'Jim' Goodall, Henry Laird and 'Joe' Huxham in his supercharged Sports. Laird retired, but 'Jim' and 'Joe' both gained silvers, 'Joe' also winning a Simms Hill Trophy award.

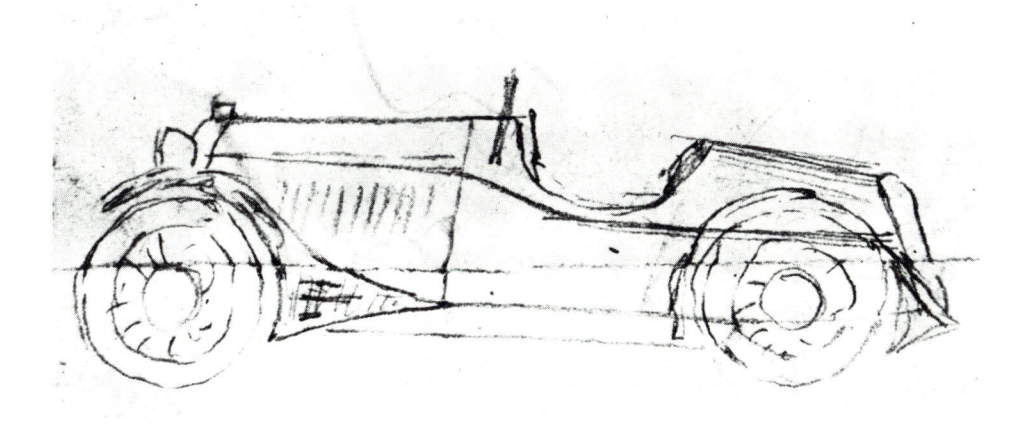

The Four-Wheeler Era

Now that Morgans had introduced the four-wheeler, the factory naturally began to support four-wheeler events, though 'Jim' Goodall remained faithful to the three-wheeler when he left his employment at the local power station to join the Morgan factory in 1936.

1935 was the last year of racing for Tom Rhodes, who eventually took a public house in Wales. Clive Lones was to join the four-wheeler Morgan drivers in 1936, not with one of the new 4/4s, but by modifying his three-wheeler racer to take a GN back axle with radius arms running into the bevel box. He called this car 'Tiger Cat', and raced it with his famous 731cc engine in the popular sprint venues of the day. Jan Breyer's four-wheeler, the converted Aero 'Salome', was also proving successful in these meetings. The KTCY engine had now received a set of special internal flywheels and conrods from JAPs, giving 10mm extra stroke and bringing the capacity up to 1096cc. Together with special Martlet pistons, this improved the performance considerably.

Henry Laird continued to battle on with his two three-wheelers. In the Bemrose trial he took the Syston Cup with 'Yellow' for the second best passenger machine after losing just 10 marks.

On 28th March Henry and Barbara took 'Yellow' through the Wye Valley Trial to collect a first class award after an amazing display of driving. Indeed, reporters doubted whether he was ever on three wheels at any one time as he literally leapt from rock to rock. Laird was using an Aero screen on his side of the scuttle of 'Yellow'. 'Jim' Goodall in WP 6271 wasn't so lucky, for he burst both front tyres and then bent back a front crosshead and retired.

By 10th April, 'Jim's' Morgan had been repaired and he was able to enter the

Goodall corrects a tail slide on Beggars Roost. (Motor Cycle)

London-Land's End, which this year included a new version of the Bluehills Mine hill. He was the only three-wheeler Morgan driver to gain a premier award, although Darken, Price and Hunting gained bronzes, the latter driving a smart MX4 barrel-back Super Sports, WP 7098.

During the winter, Henry Laird's 'Red' was ferried to Morgans for modifying for the forthcoming season. He was unhappy with the position of the Zoller supercharger, low down on the nearside of the front crosshead and had it moved to immediately behind the engine. This improved the performance of the large carburettor which now sat in the current of warm air passed by the engine, but meant that the bonnet had to be redesigned in order to accommodate it. At the same time the chassis had been 'tuned', and was now much more deeply cranked at the front crosshead with double tie rods supporting it. The width between centre pins was now $46\frac{1}{4}$ inches at the top and $46\frac{1}{2}$ inches at the bottom. The top tubes sloped back to give better handling, an improvement also discovered by Jackson.

The new 'Red' made its debut at the Donington meeting on 13th April in the ten-lap sidecar handicap event, in which Henry had to give 60 seconds to the 500cc sidecar outfits. He went well for five laps, and looked like winning, when an oil pump failed on the bronze crankcase engine. Henry was using compression ratios of 6.2 and 5.7 to 1 and running on the 50/50 mixture he normally used when supercharged.

On 25th April *The Motor Cycle* once again held its Clubman's Day at Brooklands. Euston was the only Morgan driver to take part with his Matchless barrel-back Super Sports, recording 70.79 mph over the flying kilometre, but being unplaced in the two-lap passenger handicap. This was not altogether surprising as the start was with dead engines with passengers seated inside the vehicles. Once the flag dropped the passenger

The Four wheeler Era

had to dash out to hand start the engine before they could set off.

When 'Red' next appeared in May for the Brooklands Meeting, it sported special cylinder heads made out of Boronia bronze, this material improving cooling in the important valve seat area. Unfortunately, despite Baragwanath's help and advice, the Morgan retired after just 1½ laps with a broken passenger side piston. Shell 50/50 fuel was used as usual.

This year the Light Car Club ran their Relay Race much earlier than usual, holding it in May. Although it was now open to cars of more than 1500cc, to the consternation of true light car enthusiasts, only eleven teams competed, and this year there was no factory Morgan team. Only one Morgan took part, the blown MX2 Sports of 'Joe' Huxham, which was entered in team 9 in company with Whitelock's Wolseley and Kitson's MG. Only eight teams finished and team 9 came in sixth at 74 mph.

'Jim' Goodall continued his trials success with WP 6271 when he took a premier home from the London-Edinburgh, whilst bronzes were collected by Euston and Darken.

Back at Donington on 1st June for the Whit Monday Meeting, Cyril Hale appeared

'Joe' Huxham gets instructions from Tom Bryant before starting in the Relay Race. (Motor Sport)

Morgan Sweeps the Board

with his MX4 racer. It had now been rebodied with a slimmer beetle-back body which he had removed from a recently purchased second-hand side-valve JAP-engined Super Aero, and the whole car was now painted a very smart white.

For the 25-mile handicap for passenger vehicles up to 1100cc, Henry Laird joined Cyril Hale as one of the eight starters. Despite the prospect of a great battle with 'Kim' Collett driving his JTOR Brough Superior sidecar, poor Henry, after starting well, had to retire after one lap when the supercharger drive chain broke a linkage. 'Charlie' pressed on, however, and came home a well deserved second after Collett's Brough had turned over. Hale's cornering had impressed the reporters, showing up the Morgan in a very favourable light.

On 27th June MH Bradshaw-Jones took to the Southport sands with his beetle-back ohv JAP three-speed Super Sports, which he had named 'Jabberwock', reviving the old McMinnies name. He won the 1100cc passenger 1 mile event, and cornered on two wheels in the longer distance events.

The power of the Morgans had upset the organizers of the Donington Park Meetings, so for their big August Bank Holiday Monday meeting they restricted the engine capacity for the passenger event to 750cc. Now that Clive Lones was four-wheeler racing this effectively barred all the current racing Morgans. However, Henry Laird decided that Morgans should not give in and managed to acquire a 60 degree 500cc (60 x 80mm) vee-twin Blackburne engine for 'Red', as used by Jackson in the 1920s and possibly even one of the very same units. Henry geared down to give a 5.5 to 1 top gear (16 tooth gearbox sprocket), but was still rather slow off the mark.

On his eighth lap he missed a gear change and this broke the engine's main shaft, forcing his retirement. Subsequently, the shaft was found to have a flaw in it anyway. Henry ran the engine with a compression of 7.2 to 1 and fed 50/50 mixture through new 15/16 inch choke Amal TT carbs, with 240 jet in the driver's side cylinder and 310 in the passenger's.

The following day Henry replaced his super-charged 'bronze' engine for the 25-mile passenger handicap and put on a 20 tooth gearbox sprocket, giving a 3.9 to 1 top when using a 4.50 x 19 inch rear tyre. Once again he fed 50/50 mixture into the Zoller Z4 supercharger, via a 1½ inch Amal carburettor with 1400 main jet. Compression ratios were 6.2 and 5.63 to 1. Henry came third at 58.43 mph off scratch, despite brake fade. On the last lap he pulled back 5 seconds on the winner (Taylor's 600cc Norton) and used full throttle down the Starkey straight for the first time. Two days later Henry stripped the engine, and found it to be in excellent condition.

The International Six Days' Trial started on 17th September in Bavaria. Henry and Barbara entered 'Yellow', fitted with a Zoller supercharger low down on the left-hand side of the ex-Maskell engine as before, but with the carburettor sitting on top of the supercharger casing as in the Wye Valley Trial earlier in the year. Unfortunately, big end failure made itself apparent on the second day following an oil pipe breakage, and Henry retired to make repairs in Stuttgart.

The MCC ran their annual High Speed Trial at the beginning of October. All the Morgans motored round effortlessly to gain premier awards, apart from Maskell who had mechanical problems. Maskell was driving Clive Lones's 731cc racer, fitted with lights and mudguards to make it road legal. 'Jim' Goodall was fastest with WP 6271,

'Red' with Blackburne engine at Starkey corner. (Laird scrapbooks)

covering 72.32 miles, whilst Tanner covered 71.96. Hunting also gained a premier using his usual trials barrel-back MX4.

On 10th October, Henry Laird and his brother Dick took 'Red' to Brooklands for the classic BMCRC Hutchinson Hundred, a handicap event over thirty-seven laps of the outer circuit. 'Red' had been modified for the longer distance with an extra fuel tank on the floor under the passenger's legs. A hand pump was provided for the passenger to pump fuel from this into the main tank. Henry removed the supercharger, and ran the bronze engine with Boronia heads atmospherically, using dirt tract pistons with .010 inch clearance on the skirt. The compression ratio was raised to 11 to 1 and Shell fuel (80 per cent methanol, 20 per cent benzole) fed via two track type Amals with jets of 840 and 900 for the driver's and passenger's side cylinders respectively. Ignition timing was advanced 45 degrees and a top gear of 3.7 to 1 was used.

Only ten finished out of thirty-six starters, Henry covering the thirty-seven laps at an average of 87.99 mph to finish eighth. He took the first thirty laps at about 99 mph, but then a carburettor came adrift on the driver's side cylinder, causing the piston to melt. He covered three laps at 100.61 mph, for which he won a Gold Star. Richard Laird had another reason to remember this race. Over-zealous pumping of fuel into the main tank caused it to spill out of the overflow and straight into his lap. The effect of the alcohol on certain parts of his anatomy caused him considerable discomfort for several days afterwards.

Shortly after the event Henry returned to the track for private trials. The compression was raised from 11 to 1 to 12.9 to 1 on the driver's side, and to 12.4 to 1 on the passenger's. The fuel was changed to Shell racing Ethyl, necessitating larger jets

(1500s), but the spark plugs showed that the mixture was still too weak and so twin float chambers were fitted to each carburettor. Laird was trying for the lap record held by Tommy Rhodes at 103.76 mph, and hoped to use a maximum of 5400 rpm with a top gear ratio of 3.7 to 1, having calculated that a lap average of 5000 rpm using a 3.7 top gear would give 106 mph. Unfortunately, a strong head wind along the Railway Straight meant that the gear was too high, but he did two laps at 103 mph.

On the other side of the world, in Australia, Peter Griffiths had taken delivery of a Morgan from the Malvern factory. To avoid the high import duty on bodies, just the mechanical parts were sent over, unfortunately in two shipments as the radiator and fuel tank were omitted in the first chest. With the Morgan built up, Pete Griffiths and his friend Frank Pratt, a noteworthy sidecar rider, turned their attention to the forthcoming South Australian Centenary Grand Prix and TT Races to be held on Boxing Day at Victor Harbour, not far from Adelaide. The compression on the Matchless MX4 engine was raised to around 10 to 1 and new tulip valves were fitted. Pete duly entered the combined handicap scratch race over seven laps of the 7¾ mile bitumen circuit, with two 2¼-mile-long straights. His passenger Len Willets hand cranked the motor and they set off at the back of the field, but by the end of the first lap they were in sixth place. Retirements pushed him up the field and he finished third at 63 mph, behind winner Badger's Ariel sidecar. His last lap was much slower than the others as an exhaust valve broke, causing havoc with the piston and waterjacket, but he managed to patch up the Morgan to make the 500 mile journey back home on one cylinder.

There was no London-Exeter Trial in 1936, as it was held on 1st and 2nd January 1937. Competitors could choose whether to start from Stratford-on-Avon, Penzance or Virginia Water. 'Jim' Goodall was, as usual, in WP 6271 and he put up a clean ascent of Windout Hill, included in the trial for the first time, but failed on Simms Hill. Brewster was driving a Ford 'C'-engined 'F' type, but failed to finish. As George Goodall had discovered in 1935, the Ford engine, whilst ideal for the road, hadn't got the low down torque of the vee twin that was so essential for trials. Amongst the four-wheeler drivers was 'Joe' Huxham who had switched to four wheels to support the new Morgan 4/4, selling his MX2 Sports, less blower, to a policeman. 'Joe' had not confined his Sports Morgan to Brooklands and trials, but had also entered it in grass track meetings, removing the passenger door to give free vent to the acrobatics of his passenger Tom Bryant. They never won a race, but managed one or two seconds and thirds, and never once turned over, even when Tom fell off on a bumpy left-hand sweep at Blackmore Vale. This was not the only Morgan they used for grass track racing, as Tom Bryant had used a LTOWZ-powered bare chassis for some earlier meetings.

WP 6271 and 'Jim' Goodall appeared again at the London-Land's End on 26th March, putting up the sole clean ascent of Bluehills Mine and gaining a bronze, together with JF Hayes's Matchless Morgan. The two F types entered, Brewster's 'C'-engined model and Kessel's 'Y'-engined, both failed to gain awards.

On 29th March Henry Laird and 'Red' returned to Donington, travelling from their new home in Kenilworth. During practice the supercharger picked up on the blades so it was stripped and reassembled to give greater clearance. RR59 alloy pistons were now fitted to the engine. Henry started 40 seconds late, but tore through the field,

Grass track racing with 'Joe's' blown MX2. (Bryant collection)

Bryant racing the bare chassis. (Bryant collection)

Henry at the Easter Donington. (Laird scrapbooks)

overtaking everyone except Taylor's Norton, to finish second at 58.37 mph, passengered by Michael Faraday.

On 3rd April Henry and Barbara took 'Yellow' to the Wye Valley Trial. With the acrobatic Barbara lying over the tail, Henry struggled through to a second class award, whilst poor 'Jim' Goodall was unsuccessful in WP 6271.

Cyril Hale visited Brooklands on 17th April for his one and only Brooklands event, but was unplaced. He retained the Brooklands silencers for the Whit Monday Donington meeting on 17th May, which Laird also entered with 'Red' set up as at the March meeting, and with Faraday once again as passenger. Laird gave 40 seconds start to the motorcycles, and 30 seconds to Hale and Bate, driving a white LTOWZ-engined Super Sports.

Unfortunately, he set off on one cylinder and had to stop, but once he got going again he went very quickly, breaking the lap record at 61.20 mph. The strain must have been too much for the magneto, for the mounting bolts sheared on the fifth lap forcing his retirement. Bate also retired when his motor went phut at Starkey's, but Hale,

'Red' at the Whitsun Donington. (Laird scrapbooks)

despite bad misfiring, carried on to finish third.

The International Six Days' Trial in July was based at Llandrindod Wells in Wales. Prior to this event 'Jim' Goodall's WP 6271 had received a strengthened front crosshead of heavier gauge tubing, and double tie rods. All seemed well until the Tuesday when he noticed a rocker box moving. It transpired that a rocker box bolt had sheared. He tried to unscrew it with a piece of wire, but unfortunately it wouldn't come out. Without more ado they tipped the Morgan over to get out the offending bolt, and replaced it with a borrowed longer bolt, packed with washers to give the right length. Goodall's efforts were in vain, however, for he retired on Wednesday with a broken propshaft.

Morgan Sweeps the Board

Henry Laird and Barbara in 'Yellow', now run without the supercharger on the Maskell engine, had better luck, winning a gold.

Sir Malcolm Campbell was at Brooklands on 16th July for the first motorcycle meeting over the new circuit named after him. RC Rowland, a Brooklands motor tuner and friend of Eric Fernihough, was driving the ex-Horton ex-Jackson Blackburne Super Aero, but failed to feature in the results.

Sunny weather graced the Donington August Bank Holiday meeting. Four Morgans and six sidecars entered the five-lap sidecar event. Laird was the last to start with 'Red' because of a grouchy engine, but he roared his way through the field to finish second. Passengered by his friend Rodney Bainbridge, Henry was using the bronze engine minus supercharger and fitted with JAP pistons. Cyril Hale finished fourth, while poor Bate overturned his 1084cc Morgan at Coppice corner. WE Brown's Morgan, although a valiant trier, never managed better than last place.

Later in the meeting Henry entered the ten-lap passenger Grand Prix, leading the field for seven laps until an oil pipe broke and a piston started to sieze.

11th September saw Henry at Brooklands for the Hutchinson 100, although this

Henry and Barbara celebrate their gold in the International (Laird scrapbook)

RC Rowland on the test hill hairpin on the Campbell Circuit. (Autocar)

time his brother Richard wisely left the passengering to Bill Clarke of HRD Vincent fame! This year nothing went right, and he retired after eleven laps, unable to lap above 90 mph and suffering from misfiring thought to be due to the magneto. This was Henry's last race, for he now joined the magazine *Motor Cycling* as Midlands editor. 'Red' and 'Yellow' passed to the capable hands of Tom Bryant, 'Joe' Huxham's business partner at Bournemouth.

For the 1937 show Morgans discontinued the MX engine and Family model, relying on the MX2 and MX4 for the Sports and Super Sports. A new F type made an appearance—the F Super, a cross between the front half of the F2 and the vee twin Super Sports model. Fitted with the 'C' type engine and twin type wings, the new Morgan claimed over 70 mph. Girling brakes were introduced on the new F Super, the foot pedal now operating on all three wheels. Whilst JAPs no longer supplied Morgans with any production engines, they still produced the best racing engines, and in late 1937 they introduced their latest, the JTOS or 8/80, based on the engine that had proved so successful in Fernihough's Brough Superior. 'Ferni' had developed the engine in conjunction with Stanley Greening at JAPs, and had fitted two speedway 500cc single barrels and heads onto a highly modified 50 degree JTOR crankcase. It wasn't a true twin in the old JAP style as both exhausts came off the same side of the engine, making twin carburettors essential instead of the single inlet T pipe of the true vee twin. Twin magnetos were fitted and the cylinder and heads had remarkably shallow finning. The capacity was the same as the JTOR and 8/75 JAP racing engines (80 x 99mm: 996cc).

'Jim' Goodall on 'Pumpkins' in the Wye Valley Trial. (Goodall scrapbooks)

1938 opened with the London-Exeter Trial, but the best Morgan performances resulted only in bronze medals, one won by a Matchless Morgan, one by a JAP and two by Ford 'C' type-engined Morgans.

Despite precipitating his passenger out of WP 6271, 'Jim' Goodall finished the Wye Valley Trial to win the WVAC Cup for the best three-wheeler up to 1100cc.

Now that Laird had retired, 'Jim' was the only serious Morgan trials driver still competing, but he deserted to four-wheeler Morgans later in the year, selling WP 6271 to Mr IH Steer in November.

On 2nd April, *The Motor Cycle's* Clubman's Day at Brooklands saw Wren's Matchless Morgan record 68.20 mph over the flying kilometre. In the two-lap passenger machine handicap Wren was slow to get away, though not as slow as Day whose self starter failed on his Matchless.

An interesting return to Donington on 18th April was that of the ex-Hooper ex-Jackson special Blackburne racer, CDH 127. John Hooper had parted with this in 1936 when he got married. It had been purchased from a Brownhills Garage by a young Vincent racer named Phil Heath, just for domestic use. However, he soon realized that it was a very special Morgan and decided to try his luck racing it. As purchased, it still had the special Jackson engine of 1087cc with the twin track type Amal carburettors, each with twin float chambers. Each chamber had its own fuel supply line with a separate tap. Engine lubrication was by a battery of hand pumps on the dash, and a foot throttle was fitted.

Phil and his passenger Rob Buxton completed practice successfully, but incorrect carburettor settings caused a piston to melt during the event itself.

The Four-wheeler Era

'Charlie' Hale was also entered, with a new engine on his Morgan—no less than a new 8/80 JAP, obtained from the Tottenham concern for £60, with the help of a note from George Goodall. Although the new engine was very fast, Hale had trouble with piston seizure.

This was the first Morgan race to use the Donington Circuit since it had been extended to 3 miles 220 yards for the 1937 RAC TT meeting held the previous September. The new circuit carried straight on at Starkey's corner, dropping down the hill to a new hairpin bend called Melbourne corner before rejoining the old circuit.

April marked the tragic death of Eric Fernihough during an attempt to take the world's motorcycle speed record with his 8/80 near Budapest. One of those with 'Ferni' at the time of the attempt was Morgan driver RC Rowland.

On 14th May Phil Heath took CDH 127 to Brooklands for the BMCRC meeting on the Campbell circuit. On the first practice lap Phil messed up a gear change and broke all the bolts holding the top gear sprocket to the rear wheel, bending the liberally drilled sprocket oval in the process. Luckily, Thomson and Taylor, one of the track tuning firms, obliged with replacements. In the race itself he only got as far as the first bend before spinning on a patch of oil and hitting the bank, damaging the magneto mounting.

Henry Laird passengered George Brough in his Brough Superior sidecar for the London-Edinburgh Trial on 3rd June, whilst Barbara passengered AG D'A Sugden in his 1938 beetle-back MX2 Super Sports with two-speed front wheels.

Phil Heath returned to Donington with CDH 127 for the Whit Monday meeting on 6th June. After starting from scratch in the 25-mile sidecar and three-wheeler race, he put up a phenomenal speed to finish third at 57.38 mph. Phil and his passenger, Rob Buxton, were lucky to finish, for as they crossed the line the top gear chain fell off. 'Charlie' Hale with his 8/80 and HC Bate both failed to show their true potential. In the last race Heath went faster still until he developed mechanical trouble. Harold Bate, a one-legged ex-motorcyclist, had rebuilt his Morgan with a wider chassis and lowered the body. The LTOWZ now boasted a compression ratio approaching 12 to 1.

Phil Heath and Rob Buxton ahead of 'Charlie' Hale. (Heath collection)

Hayes at Donington with his 'F' Super. (Motor Cycling)

On 24th June the MCC ran a race meeting at Donington for the first time. The second race, a five-lap handicap, was won by Bill Clarke on a big Vincent twin, but two Morgans also took part, the F Super of JF Hayes, and the MX2 barrel-back Super Sports of HE Gower-Fox. The Morgans held early leads before the motorcycles passed them, Gower-Fox demonstrating some spectacular cornering on two wheels.

Phil Heath and 'Charlie' Hale were back at Donington on 2nd August for the traditional Bank Holiday meeting. Phil was going faster than ever at the approach to McCleans corner, so much so that Rob Buxton over-anticipated when to pull on the hand brake for the front two wheels (there was a foot brake on the rear only). The Morgan skidded before turning a full somersault, fracturing Rob's collar bone and giving Phil a cut over the right eye. As a result Phil decided to go back to racing on two wheels, considering this to be much safer.

'Charlie' Hale had also entered with his 8/80. Although the first race was of only four laps, he was given his usual eight-lap race handicap. None of the other entrants thought this to be fair, but their complaints to Fred Craner, who administered the racing at Donington, went unheeded. Poor 'Charlie' had to push the car to the first corner before it started. He then set off hell for leather, breaking the sidecar and three-wheeler lap record on the third lap at 62.09 mph. With just one sidecar to overtake for victory, the engine seized once more and he coasted down to Melbourne corner, stopping on the hill on the other side. This was the third or fourth time that the engine had seized along the Starkey straight. As the Pilgrim oil pump could not be opened up any more without oiling the plugs, Cyril later added a hand pump to feed the dry cylinder. This finally cured the trouble. When the seizing point was approached a few strokes of the hand pump were all that was required to keep the engine going.

On 27th August Hale returned to Donington for the Dunlop 50th Anniversary

The Four-wheeler Era

Meeting. His special lubrication system proved satisfactory, as he finished third at 59.88 mph in the five-lap passenger machine race.

During the the year Robin Jackson had approached Phil Heath and eventually persuaded him to sell back the special engine fitted to CDH 127. Jackson was involved with David Fry and Dick Caesar—whose first special we described in Chapter 3 (1926 and 1927)—in the tuning of a rear-engined hill climb special. Based on a GN chassis, its front suspension was from an old Morgan three-wheeler, and the first engine, an Anzani, had also been from a Morgan. This car was built by Fry and Caesar in the mid 1930s and named the 'Freikaiserwagen'. For 1937 it acquired a much more powerful engine, namely the second of the special air-cooled 1087cc Blackburne engines produced by Jackson and Hatch, but tuned to run on two Bowden carburettors with a bit of help from Eric Fernihough. On $10\frac{1}{4}$ to 1 compression, 70 bhp was anticipated.

As we have mentioned earlier, Jackson and Hatch began construction of the air-cooled engine as a replacement for the KMB series in 1927. Unfortunately, only two were ever built. The only standard Blackburne parts were the 500cc barrels and one cylinder head, the sister cylinder's mirror image heads being machined from three special castings. Six special crankcases were cast, but only three machined, with the help of Alfred Fairn at 'Birmal'. Jackson himself machined one set of Zillwood (Sinbad) Milledge-designed conrods, whilst Chater-Lea's helped with another. Now that Jackson had both engines in his possession he could begin to tune for yet more power, and the car's great heyday was to come postwar.

At the 1938 Motor Cycle Show just three Morgan models were shown, the Super Sports ohv Matchless twin and two Ford-engined models, the F4 and F Super. All models now had the compensated Girling braking system introduced at the previous year's Show on the F Super Sports.

1939 started with the MCC insisting on standard tyres for the London-Exeter Trial. In the Land's End Trial, Peter Garnier drove his 1932 LTOWZ JAP Super Sports, which he had purchased second-hand for £37 10 0d in 1936, but failed on the restart test on Bluehills Mine.

Cyril Hale started from scratch in the eight-lap passenger machine race at *Motor Cycling* magazine's Donington Meeting on 6th May, giving 40 seconds to the 600cc

Hale at Melbourne corner at the Motor Cycling *meeting.* (Motor Cycling)

Morgan Sweeps the Board

sidecars. Despite this he sped through the field to finish second at 60.26 mph to A Horton's Norton.

On 16th May EB Ware, one of the great Morgan pioneers, died at the age of fifty-four. He had started building his first motorcycle including the engine in his own workshops at the age of seventeen, finishing it two years later and driving it to Brighton and back to London without mishap. In 1912 he had inaugurated the Experimental Department at JAPs and become an authority on the chemistry of combustion. As well as racing motorcycles and Morgans, he also found time to design and fly JAP-engined aeroplanes in the pioneer aeroplane era. Few did so much for Morgans in the early years as EB Ware with his special JAP Morgans.

Racing returned to Donington on 27th May, when at last the handicapping system was altered so that Morgans and the 600cc sidecars were both on scratch. Tom Bryant was making his debut with the ex-Laird 'Red', running it without a supercharger. In the first eight-lap sidecar race he moved into second place on the second lap, and held this position to the end, despite scraps with first A Horton and then Taylor with Nortons, finishing the eight laps at a record speed of 62 mph.

Later in the afternoon, the second sidecar race saw Bryant handicapped to give 64 seconds to Burke's 996cc Morgan. Bryant again went all out but could make no impression on the Taylor and Horton Nortons, and finished fourth after spinning at Melbourne. Cyril Hale failed to make any impression; it was thought that there was probably insufficient fuel drop height to supply enough fuel to the carburettors.

Sodergren's Morgan leads Walker's Norton and Gill's Rudge at Woods Hairpin, Cadwell Park. (Motor Cycling)

The Four wheeler Era

On the same day Morgans also made their first appearance at the delightful Cadwell Park circuit near Louth. Both Morgans entered were outclassed by the sidecars, although Sodergren's 'dog-ear' JAP Super Aero proved faster than Bate's Morgan, now KTOR engined, which several times took to the grass on the Mountain turn.

Racing returned to Cadwell on 5th August for the Bank Holiday Monday Meeting, once again clashing with the Donington Meeting, and splitting the Morgan ranks. Sodergren had entered his JAP Super Aero in the three-wheeler passenger handicap and made a gallant effort until the wobble of the nearside front wheel caused his retirement. His passenger was more out of the Morgan than in it, and straddled the tail, standing on a foot rest on either side.

At the Donington meeting Tom Bryant entered 'Red' in the first sidecar race, but made a bad start with the atmospheric bronze engine. He gradually made up ground and passed Horton at half-distance. These two then pulled out all they knew. Horton eventually repassed Bryant but left his braking too late at Red Gate and had to take to the sliproad. This left Bryant on his own to finish in second place at 61.96 mph. In the

Tom Bryant with 'Red' at Donington. (Motor Cycling)

223

Morgan Sweeps the Board

Hale uses a scuttle-mounted fuel tank. (Motor Cycling)

second sidecar race, Tom suffered brake trouble and was unplaced.

'Charlie' Hale's Morgan had been sent back to the factory in a bid to sort out the fuel feed problems, and at George Goodall's suggestion a streamlined fuel tank had been fitted actually on top of the scuttle. Thus equipped, and running painted in primer, the Morgan made a bad start in the scratch race for sidecars. Cyril had to make a pit stop to change a plug, only getting going again when the sidecars were on their third lap and thus standing no chance of a place. Tom Bryant was the other entry with 'Red' but he also made a bad start after backfiring and coasted in to retire after one lap.

War was on the horizon now: it was to stop racing for over six years. It was also to bring to an abrupt conclusion the development of an interesting engine for Jan Breyer's 'Salome'. This was a 1500cc vee twin air-cooled engine which used specially produced JAP crankcases developed from rear 8/80 crankcases machined to fit back to back. The cylinders and rotary valve heads were specially designed by Roland Cross of Bath, and it was estimated that it would produce at least 100 bhp at 6500 rpm.

The past four years had seen one Morgan make a considerable name for itself in Jersey. We have previously referred to GEW Oliver's LTOW JAP Super Aero which competed successfully in sprint meetings at Lewes Hill and Brighton in 1934 and had also been raced by him on Brooklands. In 1935 he had taken this red Super Aero to

224

The Four wheeler Era

Jersey for the 50-mile sand race, and after the event it was purchased by a Jerseyman, George Goldsmith. As purchased it was still in sand racing trim, the tuned engine running on 'dope' (PMS2), with a welded shield fitted in front of the engine to protect it from sand and spray. George Goldsmith used this car at sand racing events at St Ouens Bay, and also at the famous Bouley Bay hill climb with some success. The LTOW JAP engine was highly tuned, and the cast iron cylinder barrels proved unreliable under such stress, twice breaking off at the base. George's cure caused much amusement at the time: the barrels were pulled down over the cylinder heads and fastened with motorcycle chain to the crankcase. Of course, the LTOW JAP wasn't really the ideal engine for very high compression; the proper JAP racing engines (KTOR, JTOR, etc) were fitted with high tensile bolts holding the heads to the crankcases.

George was also unhappy about the cone clutch arrangement, replacing it with a much lighter Borg and Beck unit. In an effort to prevent the internal flywheels shifting when he applied full power, he tightened up the crankpin nuts to the limit, but this merely caused the cast iron flywheels to crack at the taper at the next event. Thus a special set of steel flywheels were fitted and well tightened up—a complete cure.

Running on 'dope' meant using cold racing plugs. These invariably oiled whilst the car was kept waiting at the starting line, so he returned the heads to the London firm of Barimar, who fitted an extra plug hole opposite the existing one. To supply the extra plug an extra magneto was fitted on the other side of the timing case mounted on a platform attached to the chassis, driven from the existing bevel drive. This made a tremendous improvement, and also gave more power.

The two-speed transmission wasn't really adequate for sand racing, as the long

Goldsmith on the beach at St Ouens Bay. (Goldsmith collection)

straights were invariably into the wind in one direction, and against it in the other. To help rectify this he fitted a three-speed Austin Seven gearbox in the chassis backbone, so that he now had six forward speeds (and, incidentally, two reverse!).

Thus modified, the car proved very successful, seeing off most of the opposition. The Morgan had a considerable advantage in sand races at the chicane. The fairly direct geared steering allowed George great accuracy in placing the car close to the first barrel, and the absence of a rear axle meant that he could drive straight on between the next two barrels. For cornering, a speedway style broadside proved advantageous as well as exciting.

In common with all British racing events, George's competition days were brought to an abrupt end in the autumn of 1939 by the onset of the Second World War. George himself left the Morgan in Jersey whilst he returned to England.

War once again stopped the production of Morgans, but unlike the 1914-1918 War, that of 1939-1945 was to have many long-reaching effects on the Morgan three-wheeler. Pre-war racing drivers who failed to see victory included Henry Laird, killed in a motorcycle accident whilst returning to Home Guard Duty, and Martin Soames who lost his life in the RAF. Martin's father sold his son's Morgan to RC Rowland, the Brooklands racing car tuner. In 1943 it was acquired by George Fairburn of Newcastle, who reduced the compression ratio to 7 to 1 to run on the pool petrol he expected to be available after the War. He looked forward to using the Morgan on Donington when it re-opened.

Unfortunately, the War also took its toll of racing circuits, for Donington became a military transport depot, and was retained by the War Department for many years afterwards. Not only had Donington gone, but the most famous racing circuit in the world, Brooklands, had been sacrificed in the cause of aircraft production at the adjacent Vicker's factory.

The War did produce one notable Morgan success, however, and that was the formation of the Morgan Three-Wheeler Club, as a result of correspondence in *Motor Cycling*. Its inaugural General Meeting was held in September 1945, attended by over fifty members.

When Morgans announced their post-war models in December 1945, only Ford-engined models were shown, as Matchless did not resume production of their big twin engines. Two models were available, the 'Y'-engined F4 and the 'C'-engine F Super. Twelve Matchless MX4-engined Super Sports models were produced by Morgans, probably using up their pre-war stock of engines, of which more later.

The first post-war road race meeting was held at the pre-war Cadwell Park circuit on Good Friday and Easter Monday 1946. Competing in the Monday meeting was George Fairburn with his detuned ex-Soames car. They survived two eight-lap heats but then the top gear dogs stripped. Petrol rationing at this time was severe, and poor George had saved up his coupons for months, driving down surrounded by several 2-gallon cans of petrol.

The difficulties of post-war road racing caused many people to turn to hill climbs and sprinting for their motor sport. Clive Lones was already doing just that. On 22nd September 1946, he ran his four-wheeler 'Tiger Cat' at Prescott hill climb, gaining first place in his class with a time of 51.35 seconds, and being the third fastest of the

The Four-wheeler Era

George Fairburn at Cadwell Park. (Fairburn collection)

unsupercharged cars. Clive was using an 8/80 JAP engine, which was obviously fast, but Clive himself still believes that his JTOR engine was better, and that the 731cc was the best JAP engine ever produced.

Clive was soon to construct a 500cc TT JAP-engined hill climb special called 'Tiger Kitten', featuring an inverted Austin Seven chassis and front axle although this was later changed to Morgan independent front suspension. With this he proved very successful as one of the pioneers of 500cc racing. Another Morgan driver was soon to climb to fame in this class of racing—none other than Stirling Moss, who learnt some of his driving techniques with his Matchless MX4 Super Sports.

Before the War, Cec Warren, a wealthy Australian racing driver, had become fascinated by the Morgan three wheelers that he had seen in England in the early 1930s and tried unsuccessfully to import them. After the War, however, he teamed up with Ron Edgerton to form Edgren Motors of Melbourne and initiated the import of nine of

Cec Warren at Ballarat aerodrome (G Thomas)

the twelve post-War Matchless Super Sports models. They were despatched in two batches, chassis numbers D1884-D1887 arriving in September, and D1888-D1892 leaving Malvern in November. Incidentally, the last Matchless car, D1894, was despatched to Colmore Depot in Liverpool on 2nd January 1947. Cec himself claimed D1884, fitted with MX4 942 and entered it for Victoria's first post-War road races at Ballarat aerodrome. The course was over a 3.2-mile lap with four right-hand and two left-hand bends. Cec came second in the under 1500cc 6-lap Wendourel handicap to an MG TC.

On the very same day another of the Australian batch, D1885, engine number MX4 944, was being raced at Marsden Park near Sydney by a National Airlines pilot, Henry Warlow-Davies. Marsden Park was another aerodrome, but this time the race track was just up and down the runway with two straights of nearly a mile a piece. 5000

The Four-wheeler Era

Warlow-Davies at Marsden Park. (B Gunther)

spectators saw Harry come second in the six-lap championship scratch race for cars up to 1500cc, behind McLachlan's TA MG. Harry was able to brake later than the field of MGs and corner faster, but McLachlan's was the only MG able to take the lead on the long straights.

On 27th March, aerodrome racing for Morgans began in England. Bill Sharma'n, passengered by Bill Lee, entered his 1933 LTOWZ beetle-back Super Sports with 50,000 miles on the clock for the Blackburn Aircraft Welfare MC event at Brough Aerodrome near Hull. The first event was for club members only, being an eight-lap handicap race for solos and sidecars. Running on pool petrol and using a 17 tooth gearbox sprocket, Bill off 5 seconds gained third place behind Wooley's Ariel Square Four on scratch and Harrop's 350cc BSA off 15 seconds.

Morgan Sweeps the Board

The eight-lap sidecar scratch race saw Sharman make a bad start, but he soon picked up and began duelling with Walker's Norton for the lead, gaining it on the third lap at the hairpin. Unfortunately, on the seventh lap he missed a gear change, letting Walker back into the lead which he held to the end.

In the sidecar handicap, Sharman once again duelled with Walker, but was unable to catch him. Sharman's competitiveness was due to his complete dominance over the sidecars on cornering, which in turn was due to the agility of Bill Lee, who, as passenger, never once used the passenger seat. Bill would sit on the tail and transfer to a running board on the offside for right-hand bends, leaning out and hanging onto a grab handle on the tail and a steel hoop attached to the bonnet. For left-hand bends he leant over the tail, whilst the driver, Bill Sharman, moved his weight over into the passenger compartment.

Bill also ran his Morgan at the later Brough meetings in June and October before rebuilding the Morgan with an attractive lightweight body. He intended to fit the ex-Clive Lones racing KMB Blackburne engine to this, having acquired it from Clive in 1946, but he never completed this project.

Bill Sharman and Bill Lee at Brough. (Sharman collection)

The Four-wheeler Era

Back in Australia, on 23rd March George Gosse took another of the last batch of Morgans, chassis D1892, engine MX4 940, onto Gawler Aerodrome. He was the scratch car in the up to 14 hp 'Stock Car' three-lap event, but performed badly and made no impression. In the second event for cars under 1500cc, Gosse rapidly ran through the field to finish first, but was disqualified for exceeding the lap time upon which his handicap was based (derived from the earlier event in which he hadn't been running well).

Harry Warlow-Davies appeared at Foley's Hill hillclimb on 15th May to finish fifth in 25.6 seconds in the under 1500cc class. His cornering was just as exciting as at Marsden Park, for he rose onto two wheels at the hairpin and motored into the bush, but lost little time.

Cec Warren continued to campaign D1884. On 15th April he failed to make much impression at Killara Park, but on 17th May he beat everything of less than 3 litres, except the Ford Frontenac-powered Innis Special, at speed trials held on Pakenham airstrip.

Cec had hoped to take part in the New South Wales Grand Prix at Nowra in June, but the organizers barred him from entering on the grounds that the Morgan was a three-wheeler. Correspondence at the time reveals that competition rules in Australia stated that three-wheelers, in general, were subject to control by motorcycling clubs. However, the Australian Automobile Association accepted the Sporting Club of NSW's recommendation that three-wheel cyclecars should be brought under the control of their four-wheeler car clubs.

Back in England, two Morgan Three-Wheeler Club members entered the Chester Motor Club Speed Trials at Queensferry. Stan Withers, the Club chairman, recorded 35.1 seconds for the standing half-mile with his tuned F4, and Les Bolton clocked $32\frac{3}{5}$ seconds with his specially built JAP-engined racer. This latter time beat a supercharged Bugatti and gained Les a win in the three-wheeler class. This was Les's second Morgan, a KTOR-engined Super Aero that he had purchased at the beginning of the War. He had first noticed it alongside some tents at a campsite some years earlier, but was unable to persuade the owner to part with it at that time. Les had the ambition of taking a world record with a Morgan, and was to produce many specials over the years with this aim in view, although he never got round to making an attempt. To produce his first special, he had removed the Super Aero body and replaced it with a lightweight special body painted British racing green. The 'wide B' chassis was heavily braced and a home-made face cam drove a petrol pump from the engine magneto drive.

In November Cec Warren was back in action with his Morgan, this time on the $1\frac{1}{8}$ mile D-shaped grass circuit at Nar Nar Goon. The green Morgan had already been nicknamed 'the Grasshopper'. It turned out to be quite at home on the grass and was unlucky not to gain an award.

This event at Nar Nar Goon had been only a minor grass track meeting and consequently little attention was probably given to the rules governing the racing together of three- and four-wheelers in Australia. However, it was a different matter for the Light Car Club of Australia's important Australian Grand Prix meeting held on 26th January 1948 at Point Cook Aerodrome. But despite the legalities, or otherwise, Cec Warren found his entry accepted and obtained a place in the field for the 10 lap 24 mile scratch race for 1500cc cars, finishing sixth, just in front of King's four-wheeler 4/4 Morgan.

With a temperature of 98°F in the shade, Cec Warren set off from his 18-minute handicap in the 100-mile Australian Grand Pix. But the heat proved too much and he failed to complete the distance.

22nd August 1948 saw Les Bolton, the Morgan Three-Wheeler Club's North-West Group Organizer, competing in the Wirral 100 Club's sprint meeting at the Shell-Mex refineries near Chester. The 8/80 engine fitted to the front of his special suffered from fuel starvation, and he was beaten by Stan Withers with his F4, which now sported a Marshall supercharger.

On 22nd October, Cyril Hale entered his pre-War racer for the Antelope MCC's event at Ansty Aerodrome near Coventry. After leading the second heat of the sidecar races, Hale retired, allowing Jack Surtees victory.

1948 also saw a new posting for Harry Hatch, the pre-War Blackburne engine designer, who joined Matchless, now known as AMC Ltd, as research and development engineer. Following the closure of Blackburnes Harry had been involved with the design of the Excelsior Mechanical Marvel—which won the lightweight TT in 1933, the Francis-Barnett Stag, the triple ohc 349cc AJS and George Brough's 'Dream'. During the War he had also worked on the development of air-cooled aircraft engines.

In April 1949 the uprooted BMCRC staged its first meeting at Haddenham Aerodrome in Buckinghamshire, which it hoped would replace Brooklands as its new home. The width of 18 feet was a trifle narrow for sidecar racing around the 2.2-mile perimeter circuit. This meant that once Cyril Hale had leapt into the lead at the fall of the flag, he was safe for the three laps despite Jack Surtees's 998cc Vincent outfit being hot on his tail.

Cyril Hale leads Jack Surtees in a 998cc Vincent-HRD. (Motor Cycle)

Wally Wannacott climbs Beggars Roost. (Wannacott collection)

Wally Wannacott had been competing with his second-hand 1938 MX2 Super Sports, registration FAE 107, in trials since the 1947 London-Land's End Trial. For the 1949 event at Easter he devised a three-speed twin rear wheel set-up by widening the near-side rear fork blade by 4¼ inches to take two three-speed rear wheels on a modified hub. A 43 tooth rear wheel sprocket was used, and each rear wheel was provided with 6lb/square inch tyre pressure for hills, this being upped to 12 lb for road sections. For hairpin bends a longer steering drop arm gave extra lock.

'Charlie' Hale returned to Haddenham in May but retired on the second lap after lying second. He had better luck on 3rd September, when Blandford Army Camp became the unlikely venue of road races, finishing third in the sidecar race. Also making a reappearance was Tom Bryant with 'Red', but he suffered from mechanical trouble.

Once again, just two Morgan models were shown at the 1949 Motor Cycle Show, these being the F4 and F Super. Comfort was improved by fitting longer and stiffer front coil springs, using redesigned chassis lugs. In October 1949 Peter Morgan joined the Morgan Board of Directors. In the same month Cyril Hale did well at Brough, gaining one third and a fourth place behind 600cc Nortons.

In March 1950 the Morgan Three-Wheeler Club South-East Group held a hill climb at Telegraph Hill, Herts. Ray King, driving a Super Sports, achieved fastest time. This

Morgan Sweeps the Board

Morgan was originally powered by a Matchless engine, and then by two Scott engines fitted at Brooklands by Granville Grenfell. By 1950 this system had been replaced by a Ford 'C' engine slung out at the front.

The BMCRC switched to the RAC's new racing circuit at Silverstone for their April meeting. In the three-wheeler race, Cyril Hale retired when in fourth place. One week later, on 29th April, the ACU ran an international race meeting at Blandford Army Camp, Dorset. Tom Bryant entered 'Red' on twin carburettors and after starting on the last of the three-row grid, drove through the field to win at 67.7 mph from the Nortons of Taylor and Cyril Smith. 'Charlie' Hale managed fifth place. When racing was first held at Blandford in 1948 the course was hailed as the best circuit in England since Donington as it provided racing on real roads rather than 'artificial' tracks such as Aerodromes.

June brought great news, with the end of petrol rationing in Britain. At long last drivers could enjoy competitive motoring without first having to count up their valuable petrol coupons.

A new JAP range of racing vee-twin engines was announced in August 1950, the Mark I 996cc (80 x 99mm) and 1097cc (84 x 99mm) engines. Unlike the 8/80, these Stanley Greening designed engines were 'real' twins, having inlet ports adjacent to one another in the centre of the vee. Dry sump lubrication, electron crankcases, light alloy cylinder barrels with cast iron liners and light alloy cylinder heads all featured on the Mark I units.

Tom Bryant at Blandford. (Bryant collection)

The Four-wheeler Era

Another engine achieving remarkable power output was the air-cooled Blackburne in the 'Freikaiserwagen'. Jackson's continued development had now produced a very flexible unit giving around 120 bhp via two stage Roots supercharging, and producing very usable power from 2500 rpm up to 7500. Linered aluminium cylinder barrels were now in use on this engine.

On 20th August the Bugatti Owners' Club invited the BMCRC to the Prescott hill climb. One of those invited to enter was Cyril Hale. During practice he skidded on the last bend and went through the hedge, bending the crosshead back into the body. He straightened this out with the aid of planks of wood and had the car ready for the sidecar and three-wheeler class, but as he got to the starting line the 8/80 went onto one 'pot'. However, he continued up the hill and took fourth place with 73.84 seconds.

In an attempt to reduce weight, Cyril constructed an aluminium pannelled body which was enlarged in the cockpit area so that his passenger Fred Hadley could get behind the driver for right-hand corners. A streamlined cowl was fitted and possibly the new set of closer ratio gears that had been made especially for Cyril, to replace his pre-War set of close ratio gears made earlier by Harpers and Beans. Cyril entered the new body at the Ashton Combine's newly opened Thruxton Aerodrome circuit near Andover, one week after Prescott, but was unplaced in the eight-lap handicap. He may also have been using this same body at the earlier Prescott meeting.

For the 1951 London-Exeter Trial three Morgan Three-Wheeler Club members entered. Fred Willis had trouble with oil on the clutch of his F Super, and Paddy O'Shea's Matchless Super Sports dropped a valve, but Wally Wannacott's twin rear wheel Super Sports went through to take a second class award.

Cyril Hale returned to Thruxton for the 1951 Easter Monday race meeting. He made a sluggish start in the three-wheeler race, and then spun on the first lap as he tried to pull back some of the half-mile lead of the others. When he did get going once more, he rapidly overtook several competitors, but had insufficient time to challenge the leaders.

In May 1951 Morgans returned to Madresfield for the Morgan Three-Wheeler Club's sprint meeting over a standing $\frac{1}{4}$ mile. The two 8/80 machines of Les Bolton and Cyril Hale contested for fastest time of the day. Bolton's impressive skids probably lost him time when compared with Hale's smoother approach, and indeed Cyril won with 30.9 seconds. The standard ohv class was won by MB Skirrow's LTOWZ JAP Super Sports with 36.6 seconds, whilst R Small's was the fastest side-valve Morgan in 44.2 seconds. Watching the racing were George Goodall and Sammy Davis, to whom it brought back very fond memories.

Bad news for Les Bolton came at the June Chester Speed Trials, for he blew up his 8/80 in a most comprehensive way, only one cylinder head being salvageable. Cyril Hale, however, clocked 27.9 seconds, whilst an XK 120 Jaguar just beat him with 27.8 seconds.

On 23rd June Cyril was back on Thruxton race track for the eight-lap sidecar and cyclecar event. Once again he made a bad start, but recovered to finish third.

6th August 1951 saw Tom Bryant back in action with 'Red', at Thruxton again, this time for the ACU International Road Race meeting. He finished second to Cyril Smith's Norton in the eight-lap passenger event.

In February 1952, plans were prepared by an official of the Sheffield and

Hallamshire Motor Club for enlarging the Cadwell Park circuit, by adding what is now called the Goose Neck extension which forms the current club circuit.

The Morgan Motor Co did not wish to stop production of three-wheelers, but unfortunately company policy could not be dictated by preference alone. In the troubled post-War period, steel was in very short supply and allocations were largely dependent upon export potential. To a large extent this ruled out the poor three-wheeler, which did not enjoy the British road fund licence tax advantage over the four-wheeler abroad. Thus the decision was made to cease production of the three-wheeler and concentrate on the four. In any event, it cost more to make the rear end of the three-wheeler than to purchase the ready-made back axle of a four. On 29th July 1952, F1301, fitted with Ford engine number C611562, brought production to an end, leaving for Bennets of Southampton.

Happily, the Morgan Three-Wheeler Club refused to let them die, and racing continued under the leadership of Cyril Hale and Les Bolton, now both Vice Presidents of the Club. Cyril's 8/80 JAP was regularly overhauled at the JAP factory, where it gradually underwent a metamorphosis into one of the Mark 1 engines. The founder of JAPs, John Alfred Prestwich, died on 28th November 1952 at the age of seventy-eight, one of the pioneers of a great era of British supremacy in racing. President of the Morgan Three-Wheeler Club until his death in 1959, at the age of seventy-seven, was the man who started it all, HFS Morgan. Happily his son took over the position, the close link with the factory greatly benefiting the club over the ensuing years.

Into the future with Cyril Hale. The engine has now 'changed' into a Mark I JAP (Wilson collection)

Records Held by Morgans 1912-1930

Record	Date	Driver	Engine & No of Cyls	B & S	CC	Time or Distance	MPH
1912 Standing at December							
British Records							
Cyclecars							
fs kilo	9.11.12	HFS Morgan	JAP-2	90 x 77.5	986	37.95s	58.94
fs mile	9.11.12	,,	,,	,,	,,	1m 1.16s	58.86
50 miles	23.11.12	,,	,,	,,	,,	50m 28⅗s	59.43
1 hour	23.11.12	,,	,,	,,	,,	59ml 1123yd	59.63
1914 Standing at August							
Class J—Cyclecars not exceeding 750cc							
fs kilo	25.7.14	EB Ware	JAP-2	76 x 82	744	34.4s	65.10
fs mile	25.7.14	,,	,,	,,	,,	57.06s	63.09
fs 5 miles	25.7.14	,,	,,	,,	,,	4m 53.8s	61.22
10 miles	25.7.14	,,	,,	,,	,,	10m 5s	59.50
50 miles	28.3.14	,,	,,	,,	,,	1hr 3m 7.8s	47.52
1 hour	28.3.14	,,	,,	,,	,,	47ml 457yd	47.26
1920 Standing at December							
Class J—Cyclecars not exceeding 750cc							
fs kilo	25.7.14	EB Ware	JAP-2	76 x 82	744	34.4s	65.10
fs mile	25.7.14	,,	,,	,,	,,	57.06s	63.09

Morgan Sweeps the Board

Record	Date	Driver	Engine & No of Cyls	B & S	CC	Time or Distance	MPH
fs 5 miles	25.7.14	EB Ware	JAP-2	76 x 82	744	4m 53.8s	61.22
10 miles	25.7.14	,,	,,	,,	,,	10m 5s	59.50
50 miles	28.3.14	,,	,,	,,	,,	1h 3m 7.8s	47.52
1 hour	28.3.14	,,	,,	,,	,,	47ml 457yd	47.26

1921 Standing at December
Class K—Cyclecars not exceeding 1100cc

fs kilo	17.11.21	EB Ware	JAP-2	85.7 x 95	1090	26s	86.04
ss 10 miles	29.10.21	,,	,,	,,	,,	7m 54.14s	75.92

1922 Standing at December
Class J1—Single-seater cyclecars not exceeding 750cc

10 miles	25.7.14	EB Ware	JAP-2	76 x 82	744	10m 5s	59.50

Class J2—Two-seater cyclecars not exceeding 750cc

50 miles	28.3.14	EB Ware	JAP-2	76 x 82	744	1h 3m 7.80s	47.52
1 hour	28.3.14	,,	,,	,,	,,	47ml 457yd	47.26

Class H2—Two-seater cyclecars not exceeding 1100cc, max weight 772 lb

fs kilo	25.11.22	WD Hawkes	Anzani-2		1078	23.73s	86.94
fs mile	25.11.21	EB Ware	JAP-2		1090	43.80s	82.19

World Records

5 miles	23.11.22	WD Hawkes	Anzani-2		1078	3m 31.40s	85.14
10 miles	23.11.22	,,	,,		,,	7m 20.60s	81.70

1923 Standing at December
Class J1 Single-seater cyclecar: not exceeding 750cc
British Records

10 miles	25.7.14	EB Ware	JAP-2	76 x 82	744	10m 5s	59.50

Class H1—Single-seater cyclecars not exceeding 1100cc, max weight 772lb
World Records

fs 1 mile	11.9.23	WD Hawkes	Anzani-2	85 x 95	1078	40.20s	89.54
ss kilo	13.9.23	,,	,,	,,	,,	34.35s	65.122
ss mile	13.9.23	,,	,,	,,	,,	49.86s	72.20
fs 5 miles	13.9.23	,,	,,	,,	,,	3m 22.26s	88.99
ss 10 miles	13.9.23	,,	,,	,,	,,	6m 56.09s	86.52

Class H2—two-seater cyclecars not exceeding 1100cc, max weight 772lb
World Records

fs kilo	6.11.23	GN Norris	Blackburne-2	85 x 96.8	1098	24.63s	90.823
fs mile	6.11.23	,,	,,	,,	,,	40.08s	89.82
fs 5 miles	20.10.23	,,	,,	,,	,,	3m 21.4s	89.36
ss 10 miles	20.10.23	,,	,,	,,	,,	6m 59.66s	85.78

Records Held by Morgans 1912-1930

Record	Date	Driver	Engine & No of Cyls	B & S	CC	Time or Distance	MPH

1924 Standing at December
Class H1—Three-wheel cyclecars, without passenger, not exceeding 1100cc
British Records

fs kilo	11.9.23	WD Hawkes	Anzani-2	85 x 95	1078	24.27s	92.17
fs mile	6.11.24	H Beart	Blackburne-2	85 x 96.8	1098	36.99s	97.32
ss kilo	13.9.23	WD Hawkes	Anzani-2	85 x 95	1078	34.32s	65.18
ss mile	13.9.23	,,	,,	,,	,,	49.17s	73.21
fs 5 miles	13.9.23	,,	,,	,,	,,	3m 22.26s	88.99
fs 10 miles	13.9.23	,,	,,	,,	,,	6m 56.09s	86.52

Class H2—Three-wheel cyclecars, with passenger, not exceeding 1100cc
British Records

fs kilo	20.10.24	H Beart	Blackburne-2	85 x 96.8	1098	23.2s	96.33
fs mile	20.10.24	,,	,,	,,	,,	38.07s	94.50
fs 5 miles	17.10.24	,,	,,	,,	,,	3m 10.82s	94.33
ss 10 miles	17.10.24	,,	,,	,,	,,	6m 40.50s	89.88
50 miles	21.7.22	EB Ware	JAP-2	85.5 x 95	1090	38m 57.29s	77.01

1925 Standing at December
Class J1—Three-wheel cyclecars, without passenger, not exceeding 750cc
World Records

fs 5 miles	25.7.14	EB Ware	JAP-2	76 x 82	744	4m 53.8s	61.27
ss 10 miles	25.7.14	,,	,,	,,	,,	10m 5.0s	59.50

Class J2—Three-wheel cyclecars, with passenger, not exceeding 750cc
World Records

fs kilo	6.7.24	M Dhôme	Darmont-2	68 x 94.5	687	28.56s	78.32
fs mile	6.7.24	,,	,,	,,	,,	49.11s	73.30
ss kilo	6.7.24	,,	,,	,,	,,	42.38s	52.78
ss mile	6.7.24	,,	,,	,,	,,	1m 1.29s	58.73
50 miles	28.3.14	EB Ware	JAP-2	76 x 82	744	1h 3m 7.80s	47.52
1 hour	28.3.14	,,	,,	,,	,,	47ml 457yd	47.26

Class H2—Three-wheel cyclecars, with passenger, not exceeding 1100cc
World Records

fs kilo	19.8.25	H Beart	Blackburne-2	85 x 96.8	1098	21.64s	103.37
fs mile	19.8.25	,,	,,	,,	,,	35.07s	102.65
ss kilo	7.10.25	R Jackson	,,	,,	,,	34.93s	64.04
ss mile	7.10.25	,,	,,	,,	,,	50.68s	71.03
fs 5 miles	24.7.25	H Beart	,,	,,	,,	3m 0.58s	99.67
ss 10 miles	24.7.25	,,	,,	,,	,,	6m 20.37s	94.64
50 miles	18.9.25	,,	,,	,,	,,	33m 0.69s	90.87
100 miles	18.9.25	,,	,,	,,	,,	1h 5m 32.68s	91.54
fs 5 kilos	24.7.25	,,	,,	,,	,,	1m 51.40s	100.40
ss 10 kilos	14.7.25	,,	,,	,,	,,	4m 1.94s	88.78
50 kilos	18.9.25	,,	,,	,,	,,	20m 42.74s	89.99
100 kilos	18.9.25	,,	,,	,,	,,	40m 56.17s	91.07
1 hour	18.9.25	,,	,,	,,	,,	91ml 847yd	91.48

Morgan Sweeps the Board

Record	Date	Driver	Engine & No of Cyls	B & S	CC	Time or Distance	MPH

1926 Standing at December
World Records
Class 1—Three-wheel cyclecars, with passenger, not exceeding 500cc

Record	Date	Driver	Engine	B & S	CC	Time/Distance	MPH
fs kilo	12.10.26	R Jackson	Blackburne-2	60 x 88	497	30.88s	72.44
fs mile	30.6.26	EC Fernihough	JAP-1	86 x 85	494	50.20s	71.71
fs 5 miles	31.3.26	,,	,,	,,	,,	4m 6.16s	73.12
ss 10 miles	31.3.26	,,	,,	,,	,,	8m 36.86s	69.65
50 miles	23.10.26	,,	,,	,,	,,	48m 50.39s	61.42
200 miles	31.8.26	,, and Miss Butler	,,	,,	,,	3h 27m 58.12s	57.70
fs 5 kilos	31.3.26	EC Fernihough	,,	,,	,,	2m 32.45s	73.37
ss 10 kilos	31.3.26	,,	,,	,,	,,	5m 17.90s	70.37
50 kilos	1.10.26	,,	,,	,,	,,	28m 53.44s	64.52
100 kilos	23.10.26	,,	,,	,,	,,	1h 0m 38.03s	61.49
1 hour	23.10.26	,,	,,	,,	,,	61ml 830yd	61.48
3 hours	31.8.26	,,	,,	,,	,,	173ml 92yd	57.68
4 hours	31.8.26	,, and Miss Butler	,,	,,	,,	232ml 800yd	58.11
5 hours	31.8.26	,, ,,	,,	,,	,,	288ml 436yd	57.65
6 hours	31.8.26	,, ,,	,,	,,	,,	297ml 98yd	49.51

Class K—Three-wheel cyclecars, with passenger, not exceeding 1100cc

Record	Date	Driver	Engine	B & S	CC	Time/Distance	MPH
fs kilo	19.8.25	H Beart	Blackburne-2	85 x 96.8	1098	21.64s	103.37
fs mile	19.8.25	,,	,,	,,	,,	35.07s	102.65
ss kilo	7.10.25	R Jackson	,,	,,	,,	34.93s	64.04
ss mile	7.10.25	,,	,,	,,	,,	50.68s	71.03
fs 5 miles	24.7.25	H Beart	,,	,,	,,	3m 0.58s	99.67
ss 10 miles	24.7.25	,,	,,	,,	,,	6m 20.37s	94.64
50 miles	18.9.25	,,	,,	,,	,,	33m 0.69s	90.87
100 miles	18.9.25	,,	,,	,,	,,	1h 5m 32.68s	91.54
fs 5 kilos	24.7.25	,,	,,	,,	,,	1m 51.40s	100.40
ss 10 kilos	24.7.25	,,	,,	,,	,,	4m 1.94s	88.78
50 kilos	18.9.25	,,	,,	,,	,,	20m 42.74s	89.99
100 kilos	18.9.25	,,	,,	,,	,,	40m 56.17s	91.07
500 kilos	27.10.26	,,	JAP-2	85.7 x 95	1096	5h 7m 8.55s	60.69
1 hour	18.9.25	,,	Blackburne-2	85 x 96.8	1098	91ml 847yd	91.48
2 hours	23.10.26	,,	JAP-2	85.7 x 95	1096	127ml 486yd	63.68
4 hours	27.10.26	,,	,,	,,	,,	243ml 854yd	60.87
5 hours	27.10.26	,,	,,	,,	,,	303ml 826yd	60.69
6 hours	27.10.26	,,	,,	,,	,,	362ml 811yd	60.41
7 hours	27.10.26	,,	,,	,,	,,	421ml 728yd	60.20
8 hours	27.10.26	,,	,,	,,	,,	475ml 1589yd	59.50

Records Held by Morgans 1912-1930

Record	Date	Driver	Engine & No of Cyls	B & S	CC	Time or Distance	MPH
1927 Standing at December							
World Records							
Class 1—Three-wheel cyclecars, with passenger, not exceeding 500cc							
fs kilo	1.10.26	R Jackson	Blackburne-2	60 x 88	497	30.88s	72.44
fs mile	6.9.27	M Dhôme	1 cylinder	85 x 88	499	47.86s	75.23
fs 5 miles	31.3.26	EC Fernihough	JAP-1	86 x 85	494	4m 6.16s	73.12
ss 10 miles	31.3.26	,,	,,	,,	,,	8m 36.86s	69.65
50 miles	25.10.27	R Jackson	Blackburne-2	60 x 88	497	45m 20.22s	66.17
100 miles	26.10.27	EC Fernihough	JAP-1	86 x 85	494	1h 36m 24.56s	62.23
200 miles	26.10.27	,,	,,	,,	,,	3h 14m 42.48s	61.63
fs 5 kilos	31.3.26	,,	,,	,,	,,	2m 32.45s	73.37
ss 10 kilos	31.3.26	,,	,,	,,	,,	5m 17.90s	70.27
50 kilos	3.5.27	R Jackson	Blackburne-2	60 x 88	497	28m 19.00s	65.83
100 kilos	25.10.27	,,	,,	,,	,,	56m 3.70s	66.50
1 hour	25.10.27	,,	,,	,,	,,	66ml 933yd	66.53
2 hours	26.10.27	EC Fernihough	JAP-1	86 x 85	494	124ml 1297yd	62.37
3 hours	26.10.27	,,	,,	,,	,,	184ml 1260yd	61.57
4 hours	31.8.26	,, and Miss Butler	,,	,,	,,	232ml 800yd	58.11
5 hours	31.8.26	,, ,,	,,	,,	,,	288ml 436yd	57.65
6 hours	31.8.26	,, ,,	,,	,,	,,	297ml 98yd	49.51
Class J—Three-wheel cyclecars, with passenger, not exceeding 750cc							
World Records							
100 miles	20.9.27	JJ Hall	JAP-2	74 x 85	731	1h 26m 41.20s	69.40
200 miles	20.9.27	,,	,,	,,	,,	2h 56m 47.72s	67.87
1 hour	20.9.27	,,	,,	,,	,,	68ml 956yd	68.54
2 hours	20.9.27	,,	,,	,,	,,	135ml 1143yd	67.82
3 hours	20.9.27	,,	,,	,,	,,	203ml 1005yd	67.86
Class K—Three-wheel cyclecars, with passenger, not exceeding 1100cc							
World Records							
fs kilo	19.8.25	H Beart	Blackburne-2	85 x 96.8	1098	21.64s	103.37
fs mile	19.8.25	,,	,,	,,	,,	35.07s	102.65
ss kilo	7.10.25	R Jackson	,,	,,	,,	34.93s	64.04
ss mile	7.10.25	,,	,,	,,	,,	50.68s	71.03
fs 5 miles	24.7.25	H Beart	,,	,,	,,	3m 0.58s	99.67
ss 10 miles	24.7.25	,,	,,	,,	,,	6m 20.37s	94.64
50 miles	18.9.25	,,	,,	,,	,,	33m 0.69s	90.87
100 miles	18.9.25	,,	,,	,,	,,	1h 5m 32.68s	91.54
200 miles	20.9.27	JJ Hall	JAP-2	74 x 85	731	2h 56m 47.72s	67.87
fs 5 kilos	24.7.25	H Beart	Blackburne-2	85 x 96.8	1098	1m 51.40s	100.40
ss 10 kilos	21.7.25	,,	,,	,,	,,	4m 1.94s	88.78
50 kilos	18.9.25	,,	,,	,,	,,	20m 42.74s	89.99
100 kilos	18.9.25	,,	,,	,,	,,	40m 56.17s	91.07
500 kilos	27.10.26	,,	JAP-2	85.7 x 95	1096	5h 7m 8.55s	60.69
1 hour	18.9.25	,,	Blackburne-2	85 x 96.8	1098	91ml 847yd	91.48

Morgan Sweeps the Board

Record	Date	Driver	Engine & No of Cyls	B & S	CC	Time or Distance	MPH
2 hours	10.11.27	R Jackson	Blackburne-2	85 x 96.8	1098	136ml 1692yd	68.48
3 hours	20.9.27	JJ Hall	JAP-2	74 x 85	731	203ml 1005yd	67.86
4 hours	27.10.26	H Beart	JAP-2	85.7 x 95	1096	243ml 854yd	60.87
5 hours	27.10.26	,,	,,	,,	,,	303ml 826yd	60.69
6 hours	27.10.26	,,	,,	,,	,,	362ml 811yd	60.41
7 hours	27.10.26	,,	,,	,,	,,	421ml 728yd	60.20
8 hours	27.10.26	,,	,,	,,	,,	475ml 1589yd	59.50

1928 Standing at December
Class I—Three-wheel cyclecars, with passenger, not exceeding 500cc
World Records

fs kilo	12.10.26	R Jackson	Blackburne-2	60 x 88	497	30.88s	72.44
fs mile	6.9.27	M Dhôme	1	85 x 88	499	47.86s	75.23
50 miles	30.10.28	R Jackson	Blackburne-2	60 x 88	497	42m 5.34s	71.27
100 miles	26.10.27	EC Fernihough	JAP-1	86 x 85	494	1h 36m 24.56s	62.23
200 miles	26.10.27	,,	,,	,,	,,	3h 14, 42.48s	61.63
50 kilos	30.10.28	R Jackson	Blackburne-2	60 x 88	497	26m 21.06s	70.74
100 kilos	30.10.28	,,	,,	,,	,,	52m 13.34s	71.38
1 hour	30.10.28	,,	,,	,,	,,	71ml 713yd	71.40
2 hours	26.10.27	EC Fernihough	JAP-1	86 x 85	494	124ml 1297yd	62.37
3 hours	26.10.27	,,	,,	,,	,,	184ml 1260yd	61.57
4 hours	31.8.26	,, and Miss Butler	,,	,,	,,	232ml 800yd	58.11
5 hours	31.8.26	,, ,,	,,	,,	,,	288ml 436yd	57.65
6 hours	31.8.26	,, ,,	,,	,,	,,	297ml 98yd	49.51

Class J—Three-wheel cyclecars, with passenger, not exceeding 750cc
World Records

fs kilo	25.8.28	A Darmont	Darmont-2	70 x 96.5	743	23.62s	94.70
fs mile	25.8.28	,,	,,	,,	,,	38.19s	94.26
fs 5 miles	2.9.28	,,	,,	,,	,,	3m 25.61s	87.54
ss 10 miles	2.9.28	,,	,,	,,	,,	7m 8.96s	83.92
50 miles	6.11.28	H Beart	JAP-2	74 x 85	731	36m 20.33s	82.56
100 miles	7.11.28	,,	,,	,,	,,	1h 12m 46.80s	82.45
200 miles	9.11.28	,,	,,	,,	,,	2h 37m 44.24s	76.07
fs 5 kilos	2.9.28	A Darmont	Darmont-2	70 x 96.5	743	2m 2.69s	91.16
ss 10 kilos	2.9.28	,,	,,	,,	,,	4m 19.99s	86.04
50 kilos	6.11.28	H Beart	JAP-2	74 x 85	731	22m 46.98s	81.82
100 kilos	7.11.28	,,	,,	,,	,,	45m 22.74s	82.16
1 hour	7.11.28	,,	,,	,,	,,	82ml 675yd	82.38
2 hours	9.11.28	,,	,,	,,	,,	152ml 386yd	76.11
3 hours	9.11.28	,,	,,	,,	,,	207ml 908yd	69.17

Class K—Three-wheel cyclecars, with passenger, not exceeding 1100cc
World Records

ss kilo	7.10.25	R Jackson	Blackburne-2	85 x 96.8	1098	34.93s	64.04
ss mile	7.10.25	,,	,,	,,	,,	50.68s	71.03

Records Held by Morgans 1912-1930

Record	Date	Driver	Engine & No of Cyls	B & S	CC	Time or Distance	MPH
50 miles	18.9.25	H Beart	Blackburne-2	85 x 96.8	1098	33m 0.69s	90.87
100 miles	18.9.25	,,	,,	,,	,,	1h 5m 32.68s	91.54
200 miles	9.11.28	,,	JAP-2	74 x 85	731	2h 37m 44.24s	76.07
50 kilos	18.9.25	,,	Blackburne-2	85 x 96.8	1098	20m 42.74s	89.99
100 kilos	18.9.25	,,	,,	,,	,,	40m 56.17s	91.07
500 kilos	27.10.26	,,	JAP-2	85.7 x 95	1096	5h 7m 8.55s	60.69
1 hour	18.9.25	,,	Blackburne-2	85 x 96.8	1098	91m 847yd	91.48
2 hours	9.11.28	,,	JAP-2	74 x 85	731	152ml 386yd	76.11
3 hours	9.11.28	,,	,,	,,	,,	207ml 908yd	69.17
4 hours	27.10.26	,,	,,	85.7 x 95	1096	243ml 854yd	60.87
5 hours	27.10.26	,,	,,	,,	,,	303ml 826yd	60.69
6 hours	27.10.26	,,	,,	,,	,,	362ml 811yd	60.41
7 hours	27.10.26	,,	,,	,,	,,	421ml 728yd	60.20
8 hours	27.10.26	,,	,,	,,	,,	475ml 1589yd	59.50

1929 Standing at December
Class H—Three-wheel cyclecars, with passenger, not exceeding 350cc
World Records

Record	Date	Driver	Engine & No of Cyls	B & S	CC	Time or Distance	MPH
ss mile	18.10.29	HC Lones	JAP-1	70 x 90	346	1m 12.57s	49.60
fs 5 miles	23.11.29	Mrs G Stewart	,,	,,	,,		74.01
ss 10 miles	23.11.29	,,	,,	,,	,,		69.87
50 miles	4.10.29	HC Lones	,,	,,	,,	45m 6.29s	66.51
100 miles	4.10.29	,,	,,	,,	,,	1h 33m 37s	63.85
fs 5 kilos	23.11.29	Mrs G Stewart	,,	,,	,,		74.07
ss 10 kilos	23.11.29	,,	,,	,,	,,		68.28
50 kilos	4.10.29	HC Lones	,,	,,	,,	28m 3.88s	66.42
100 kilos	4.10.29	,,	,,	,,	,,	55m 56.43s	66.85
1 hour	4.10.29	,,	,,	,,	,,	66ml 1190yd	66.68
2 hours	4.10.29	,,	,,	,,	,,	113ml 907yds	56.75

Class I—Three-wheel cyclecars, with passenger, not exceeding 500cc
World Records

Record	Date	Driver	Engine & No of Cyls	B & S	CC	Time or Distance	MPH
fs mile	6.9.27	M Dhome	1	85 x 88	499	47.86s	75.23
fs 5 miles	1.9.29	Mrs G Stewart	JAP-1	80 x 99	498		80.34
ss 10 miles	1.9.29	,,	,,	,,	,,		77.61
50 miles	15.11.29	,,	,,	,,	,,		76.81
100 miles	15.11.29	,,	,,	,,	,,		77.07
200 miles	24.7.29	HC Lones	,,	,,	,,	3h 8m 30.03s	63.66
fs 5 kilos	1.9.29	Mrs G Stewart	,,	,,	,,		80.59
ss 10 kilos	1.9.29	,,	,,	,,	,,		76.09
50 kilos	15.11.29	,,	,,	,,	,,		76.07
100 kilos	15.11.29	,,	,,	,,	,,		77.08
1 hour	15.11.29	,,	,,	,,	,,		77.24
2 hours	15.11.29	,,	,,	,,	,,		65.71
3 hours	24.7.29	HC Lones	,,	,,	,,	194ml 56yd	64.68

Morgan Sweeps the Board

Record	Date	Driver	Engine & No of Cyls	B & S	CC	Time or Distance	MPH
4 hours	31.8.26	EC Fernihough and Miss Butler	JAP-1	86 x 85	494	232ml 800yd	58.11
5 hours	31.8.26	,,	,,	,,	,,	288ml 436yd	57.65
6 hours	31.8.26	,,	,,	,,	,,	297ml 98yd	49.51

Class J—Three-wheel cyclecars, with passenger, not exceeding 750cc
World Records

Record	Date	Driver	Engine & No of Cyls	B & S	CC	Time or Distance	MPH
fs kilo	25.8.28	A Darmont	Darmont-2	70 x 96.5	743	23.62s	94.70
fs mile	25.8.28	,,	,,	,,	,,	38.19s	94.26
ss kilo	25.8.29	M Dhôme	,,	,,	,,	33.71s	66.35
ss mile	25.8.29	,,	,,	,,	,,	50.40s	71.42
fs 5 miles	17.5.29	Mrs G Stewart	JAP-2	74 x 85	731	3m 12.88s	93.32
ss 10 miles	17.5.29	,,	,,	,,	,,	6m 50.33s	87.73
50 miles	21.5.29	,,	,,	,,	,,	35m 31.19s	84.45
100 miles	16.8.29	,,	,,	,,	,,	1h 8m 26.76s	89.84
200 miles	20.10.29	,,	,,	,,	,,	2h 24m 58.22s	82.77
500 miles	25.10.29	,,	,,	,,	,,	7h 2m 50.69s	70.94
fs 5 kilos	17.5.29	,,	,,	,,	,,	1m 59.73s	93.41
ss 10 kilos	17.5.29	,,	,,	,,	,,	4m 18.91s	86.39
50 kilos	21.5.29	,,	,,	,,	,,	22m 16.66s	83.67
100 kilos	21.5.29	,,	,,	,,	,,	45m 52.92s	84.95
500 kilos	20.10.29	,,	,,	,,	,,	3h 51m 44.19s	80.44
1 hour	16.8.29	,,	,,	,,	,,	87ml 466yd	87.26
2 hours	20.10.29	,,	,,	,,	,,	164ml 1598yd	82.45
3 hours	20.10.29	,,	,,	,,	,,	242ml 316yd	80.72
4 hours	20.10.29	,,	,,	,,	,,	319ml 1488yd	79.96
5 hours	25.10.29	,,	,,	,,	,,	353ml 1496yd	70.77
6 hours	25.10.29	,,	,,	,,	,,	423ml 740yd	70.57
7 hours	25.10.29	,,	,,	,,	,,	496ml 897yd	70.93
8 hours	25.10.29	,,	,,	,,	,,	568ml 1267yd	71.09
9 hours	25.10.29	,,	,,	,,	,,		63.20
10 hours	25.10.29	,,	,,	,,	,,		56.88
11 hours	25.10.29	,,	,,	,,	,,		51.71
12 hours	25.10.29	,,	,,	,,	,,		47.40

Class K—Three-wheel cyclecars, with passenger, not exceeding 1100cc
World Records

Record	Date	Driver	Engine & No of Cyls	B & S	CC	Time or Distance	MPH
ss kilo	12.11.29	HC Lones	JAP-2	85.7 x 95	1096	32.59s	68.63
ss mile	12.11.29	,,	,,	,,	,,	47.84s	75.25
fs 5 miles	10.11.29	Mrs G Stewart	JAP-2	80 x 99	996	2m 49.32s	106.30
ss 10 miles	10.11.29	,,	,,	,,	,,	5m 54.54s	101.54
50 miles	7.9.29	,,	,,	,,	,,		100.95
100 miles	7.9.29	,,	,,	,,	,,		101.79
200 miles	25.3.29	,,	,,	,,	,,		83.68
500 miles	25.10.29	,,	JAP-2	74 x 85	731	7h 2m 50.69s	70.94
fs 5 kilos	10.11.29	,,	JAP-2	80 x 99	996	1m 45.06s	106.45

Records Held by Morgans 1912-1930

Record	Date	Driver	Engine & No of Cyls	B & S	CC	Time or Distance	MPH
ss 10 kilos	10.11.29	Mrs G Stewart	JAP-2	80 x 99	996	3m 45.13s	99.36
50 kilos	7.9.29	,,	,,	,,	,,		99.99
100 kilos	7.9.29	,,	,,	,,	,,		101.23
500 kilos	20.10.29	,,	JAP-2	74 x 85	731	3h 51m 44.19s	80.44
1000 kilos	12.9.29	,, and WD Hawkes	JAP-2	80 x 99	996		66.98
1 hour	7.9.29	Mrs G Stewart	,,	,,	,,		101.53
2 hours	25.3.29	,,	,,				83.03
3 hours	20.10.29	,,	JAP-2	74 x 85	731	243ml 316yd	80.72
4 hours	20.10.29	,,	,,	,,	,,	319ml 1488yd	79.96
5 hours	16.9.29	,,	JAP-2	80 x 99	996		71.19
6 hours	16.9.29	,,	,,	,,	,,		72.15
7 hours	20.10.29	,,	JAP-2	74 x 85	731	496ml 897yd	70.93
8 hours	20.10.29	,,	,,	,,	,,	568ml 1267yd	71.09
9 hours	12.9.29	,, and WD Hawkes	JAP-2	80 x 99	996		67.26
10 hours	12.9.29	,, ,,	,,	,,	,,		67.17
11 hours	12.9.29	,, ,,	,,	,,	,,		66.39
12 hours	12.9.29	,, ,,	,,	,,	,,		66.70

1930 Standing at December.
Class H—Three-wheel cyclecars, not exceeding 350cc

fs 5 kilos	23.11.29	Mrs G Stewart	JAP-1	70 x 90	346		73.78
10 kilos	23.11.29	,,	,,	,,	,,		68.28
ss mile	18.10.29	HC Lones	,,	,,	,,		49.60
fs 5 miles	23.11.29	Mrs G Stewart	,,	,,	,,		74.01
10 miles	23.11.29	,,	,,	,,	,,		69.88
50 kilos	4.10.29	HC Lones	,,	,,	,,		66.42
100 kilos	4.10.29	,,	,,	,,	,,		66.65
50 miles	4.10.29	,,	,,	,,	,,		66.51
100 miles	4.10.29	,,	,,	,,	,,		64.09
1 hour	4.10.29	,,	,,	,,	,,		66.68
2 hours	4.10.29	,,	,,	,,	,,		56.76
3 hours	20.5.30	,,	,,	,,	,,		52.43

Class I—Three-wheel cyclecars, not exceeding 500cc

ss kilo	4.6.30	HC Lones	JAP-1	80 x 90	498		55.81
fs 5 kilos	1.9.29	Mrs G Stewart	,,	,,	,,		80.59
ss 10 kilos	1.9.29	,,	,,	,,	,,		76.09
fs mile	6.9.27	M Dhôme			499		75.23
ss mile	4.6.30	HC Lones	JAP-1	80 x 90	498		62.95
fs 5 miles	1.9.29	Mrs G Stewart	,,	,,	,,		80.34
10 miles	1.9.29	,,	,,	,,	,,		77.61
50 kilos	15.11.29	,,	,,	,,	,,		76.08
100 kilos	15.11.29	,,	,,	,,	,,		77.09
50 miles	15.11.29	,,	,,	,,	,,		76.81

Morgan Sweeps the Board

Record	Date	Driver	Engine & No of Cyls	B & S	CC	Time or Distance	MPH
100 miles	15.11.29	Mrs G Stewart	JAP-1	80 x 99	498		77.08
200 miles	24.7.29	HC Lones	,,	,,	,,		63.66
1 hour	15.11.29	Mrs G Stewart	,,	,,	,,		77.24
2 hours	15.11.29	,,	,,	,,	,,		65.71
3 hours	24.7.29	HC Lones	,,	,,	,,		64.68
4 hours	31.8.26	EC Fernihough and Miss Butler	JAP-1	86 x 85	494		58.11
5 hours	31.8.26	,, ,,	,,	,,	,,		57.65
6 hours	31.8.26	,, ,,	,,	,,	,,		49.51

Class J—Three-wheel cyclecars, with passenger, not exceeding 750cc

Record	Date	Driver	Engine	B & S	CC		MPH
fs kilo	24.8.30	Mrs G Stewart	JAP-2	74.5 x 85	741		99.11
ss kilo	25.8.29	M Dhôme	-2	70 x 96	741		66.35
fs 5 kilos	31.8.30	Mrs G Stewart	JAP-2	74.5 x 85	741		100.64
10 kilos	9.2.30	,,	JAP-2	74 x 85	731		88.46
fs mile	24.8.30	,,	JAP-2	74.5 x 85	741		98.33
ss mile	25.8.29	M Dhôme	-2	70 x 96	741		71.43
fs 5 miles	9.2.30	Mrs G Stewart	JAP-2	74 x 85	731		95.52
10 miles	9.2.30	,,	,,	,,	,,		91.07
50 kilos	3.3.30	,,	,,	,,	,,		90.02
100 kilos	3.3.30	,,	,,	,,	,,		92.16
500 kilos	30.4.30	,,	JAP-2	74.5 x 85	741		85.19
1000 kilos	9.4.30	WD Hawkes and Mrs G Stewart	JAP-2		728		69.76
50 miles	3.3.30	Mrs G Stewart	JAP-2	74 x 85	731		91.79
100 miles	3.3.30	,,	,,	,,	,,		92.28
200 miles	30.4.30	,,	JAP	74.5 x 85	741		84.58
500 miles	15.4.30	WD Hawkes and Mrs G Stewart	JAP	74 x 85	731		73.52
1 hour	3.3.30	Mrs G Stewart	,,	,,	,,		92.42
2 hours	3.3.30	,,	,,	,,	,,		85.50
3 hours	30.4.30	,,	JAP-2	74.5 x 85	741		84.94
4 hours	30.4.30	,,	,,	,,	,,		85.26
5 hours	15.4.30	WD Hawkes and Mrs G Stewart	JAP	74 x 85	731		73.69
6 hours	15.4.30	,, ,,	,,	,,	,,		73.70
7 hours	15.4.30	,, ,,	,,	,,	,,		73.64
8 hours	15.4.30	,, ,,	,,	,,	,,		73.83
9 hours	9.4.30	,, ,,	JAP-2		728		69.81
10 hours	9.4.30	,, ,,	,,		,,		70.27
11 hours	9.4.30	,, ,,	,,		,,		69.97
12 hours	9.4.30	,, ,,	,,		,,		68.09

Records Held by Morgans 1912-1930

Record	Date	Driver	Engine & No of Cyls	B & S	CC	Time or Distance	MPH

Class K—Three-wheel cyclecars, not exceeding 1100cc

Record	Date	Driver	Engine & No of Cyls	B & S	CC	MPH
fs kilo	24.8.30	Mrs G Stewart	JAP-2	80 x 108	1086	115.66
ss kilo	24.8.30	,,	,,			70.43
fs 5 kilos	6.8.30	,,	JAP-2	80 x 108.5	1091	113.52
10 kilos	7.8.30	,,	,,			102.72
fs mile	24.8.30	,,	JAP-2	80 x 108	1086	114.83
ss mile	24.8.30	,,	,,			80.70
fs 5 miles	7.8.30	,,	JAP-2	80 x 108.5	1091	107.51
10 miles	7.8.30	,,	..			102.82
50 kilos	12.9.30	,,	JAP-2	80 x 96	965	103.43
100 kilos	12.9.30	,,	,,			102.48
500 kilos	27.3.30	,,	JAP-2	80 x 108.5	1091	83.89
1000 kilos	2.4.30	WD Hawkes and Mrs G Stewart	JAP-2	80 x 99	996	80.51
1500 kilos	15.5.30	SCH Davis and Mrs G Stewart	JAP-2	80 x 109	1096	72.58
2000 kilos	15.5.30	,, ,,	,,		,,	71.79
2500 kilos	15.5.30	,, ,,	,,			71.66
50 miles	12.9.30	Mrs G Stewart	JAP-2	80 x 96	965	102.64
100 miles	7.9.29	,,	,,	80 x 99	996	101.79
200 miles	5.11.30	,,	JAP-2	80 x 108	1086	88.82
500 miles	27.3.30	,,	JAP-2	80 x 99	996	82.11
1000 miles	15.5.30	SCH Davis and Mrs G Stewart	JAP-2	80 x 109	1096	72.67
1500 miles	15.5.30	,, ,,	,,		,,	71.53
1 hour	7.9.29	Mrs G Stewart	JAP-2	80 x 99	996	101.55
2 hours	5.11.30	,,	JAP-2	80 x 108	1086	88.61
3 hours	21.3.30	,,	JAP-2	80 x 108.5	1091	83.14
4 hours	21.3.30	,,	,,		,,	84.09
5 hours	21.3.30	,,	,,		,,	82.74
6 hours	27.3.30	,,	JAP-2	80 x 99	996	82.10
7 hours	27.3.30		,,		,,	80.98
8 hours	2.4.30	WD Hawkes and Mrs G Stewart	,,		,,	80.63
9 hours	2.4.30	,,	,,		,,	81.04
10 hours	2.4.30	,,	,,		,,	80.60
11 hours	2.4.30	,,	,,		,,	73.86
12 hours	15.5.30	SCH Davis and Mrs G Stewart	JAP-2	80 x 109	1096	72.72
24 hours	15.5.30	,, ,,	,,		,,	64.85

Morgan Sweeps the Board

Brooklands Gold Stars

11.10.1930	HC Lones	996cc	Morgan-JAP	102.48 mph
11.10.1930	RR Jackson	1098cc	Morgan-Blackburnes	101.85 mph
12. 5.1934	TA Rhodes	996cc	Morgan-JAP	103.76 mph
10.10.1936	H Laird	1096cc	Morgan-JAP	100.61 mph

Brooklands
51 laps Mountain Course Times

7. 5.1932	HC Lones	996cc	JAP	5m 49.2s	
12.10.1935	H Laird	1096cc	JAP	5m 31.8s	63.44 mph

Brooklands
Outer Circuit Records

11.10.1930	HC Lones	996cc	JAP	102.48 mph
12. 5.1934	TA Rhodes	996cc	JAP	103.76 mph

Index

Aero model, 34, 42, 164
  AB 16, 71, 114
  modifications (1920), 49
  new model (1922), 60
  ohv JAP-engined, 110
  round-tailed, 69
  special at Motor Cycle Show (1926), 108
  twin rear wheels, 155
aerodrome racing, 229
Allard, Sydney
  JAP Super Aero, 134, 138, 148, 152, 159
  trials special, 174
Anzani engines, 101, 118
  CC type, 53, 118
  8-valve air-cooled, 54
  prototype ohv, 98
  water-cooled 8-valve ohc, 66
Aston, Reg, 34
Australian racing, 131, 212, 228, 231
Auto-Cycle Union
  Six Days' Trial: (1911) 16, (1919) 41-2, (1921) 51, (1922) 58, (1923) 67
  Stock Machine Trials: (1920) 50, (1922) 53, (1923) 61, (1924) 72, (1925) 90, (1927) 112, (1928) 121
Baragwanath, 'Barry', 169-70
Barker, ER, 59
Beart, Harold, 52, 74
  Aero-Blackburne, 66, 68, 75
  construction of special, 83-4
  cranked chassis special, 127
  end of apprenticeship, 71
  Kingston-upon-Thames agent, 95
  speed trial successes (1925), 93-4
  trials with KMB engine, 106
Blackburn, J, 27, 28
Blackburne engines
  KM series, 59
  KMB, 120, 153
  special KMB racing engines, 80
  KMC, 109
  used in 'Freikaiserwagen', 235
Blake, Bob, 73
Blumfield engines

8 hp, 19
670cc, 21
991cc sv, 21
Boddington, Frank, 47, 50, 51, 62
Bolton, Les, 231, 235
Breyer, Jan, 167, 207, 224
Bristol MCC Speed Trials, (1913) 28, (1914) 34
British Experts Trial (1933), 184
British Motor Cycle Racing Club
  Brooklands meetings (1922) 54-5
  Combined Services race (1914) 38
  first Haddenham meeting (1949), 232
  first 3-wheeler championship (1923), 69
  hour trial (1912), 18-19
  100-mile handicap race (1932), 173
  100-mile high speed trial (1914), 31-2
  international scratch race (1912), 17-18
  joint meetings with Essex MC, (1919) 42, (1920) 50, (1922) 59, (1923) 63
  six-hour scratch race (1913), 27
  ten-lap 3-wheeler handicap (1930), 152
  track championship (1924), 80
Bryant, Tom, 222, 233, 234-5
Bullough, John Miles, 66, 77, 99, 108
  'Creeping Jane', 89
Burbridge, Richard, 15
Busby, Vernon, 21, 30, 37

C-type chassis, 154
Cadwell Park, (1939) 223, (1946) 226, (1952) 236
Caesar, RD (Dick), 45
  Blackburne Aero special, 111
Carr, Bill, 62
Churchwood, GC, 13
Cole, RJ, 174
Colmore Cup Trials, (1913) 19-20, (1922) 53, (1924) 70, (1926) 98, (1927) 110, (1928) 119, (1929) 132, (1930) 143, (1931) 155, (1932) 166, (1933) 175, (1934) 186, (1935) 195
Commercial model, 118
Cowley, George, 65-6

Cox, FG, 28, 34
Creed, Lionel, 121, 122, 155, 173
  Blackburne Super Aero, 134
Cross, Roland, 224

Davis, 'Sammy', 144-5
Day, Geoffrey, 23, 39
Dean, William, 13
De Luxe model, 63
  improved version, 130
  redesigned, 95
Denley, H, 39
Donington Park, (1932) 172, (1933) 177, (1934) 188, 189, 192, (1935) 197, 198, 202, (1936) 209, (1937) 212, 216, (1938) 218-20, (1939) 222

Elce, Billie, 49, 50, 51
Eldridge, Ernest, 130
English Six Days' Trial, (1913) 28, (1914) 34, (1925) 93

F-type Morgans, 188-9
  F2 prototype, 200
  F4, 221, 226, 233
  F Super, 217, 221, 226, 233
Fairburn, George, 226
Family model
  development, 39
  introduction, 42
  modifications to gearbox and radiator, 186
  redesigned (1932), 173
  two-seater, 164
Family Aero model, 106
  at Olympia Show, 108
Fernihough, Eric, 63, 203, 219
  special built-on racing chassis, 96-8, 103
Ford engines, 185
four-cylinder model, 184
French Grand Prix, (1913) 21, (1921) 51
Frazer-Nash, Archie, 45, 49, 58, 118

Goldsmith, George, 225

Index

Goodall, George, 53, 61, 62, 65
   Aero Blackburne (Jim), 72, 74, 76, 86, 115, 161
   flat-sided Aero, 62
   Sports Family, 145
   Sports with Magna wheels, 178
Goodall, 'Jim', 209, 215, 218
Grand Prix model, 33-4, 40
   displayed at 1913 Show, 28
   special for Chris Richards, 34, 37
Green Precision engine, 24
Griffith, George, 30, 35
Griffiths, Peter, 212

Hale, Cyril, 197, 209, 219-21, 235
Hall, Jim, 41-45, 47, 50, 117, 121-2
Harris, FLM, 158
Harris, Geoff, 80, 162
   JAP Aero ML1 142, 114, 143, 160, 168
   JTOR-engined Super Aero, 170
   MX2-engined Sports, 193
Hawkes, W Douglas, 40, 41, 55
   'Flying Spider', 56, 58, 63, 66
   JAP-engined MEB, 130
   MAG-engined TT ('Land Crab'), 42, 44, 45-6, 48-9, 51, 58
   modified flat-sided Aero, 68
   single-seater special, 143, 149
   special for 1922 JCC 200-mile race, 56, 60
Heath, Phil, 218
Holder, NF, 21, 24, 26
Holmes, Harold, 49, 61
Hooper, John, 182
   ex-Jackson special, 197, 202, 218
Horrocks, 45, 50, 59
   'Kettle', 66
Horton, Ronald Tooms, 70, 89-90, 111
   Blackburne Aero, 89
   JAP Aero, 132
Hughes, HV, 59, 66
Huxham, EP 'Joe', 172, 174
   'Huxham's Rallies', 178
   special Sports 2-seater, 186, 201, 209, 212

International Six Days' Trial, (1926) 103, (1927) 114, (1928) 127, (1933) 182, (1934) 193, (1935) 204, (1936) 210, (1937) 215
Intervarsity Trials, (1926) 98, 109, (1927) 110, (1932) 166-7

Jackson, Robin, 74, 76, 94
   aluminium-bodied special, 103, 110, 123, 144
   Blackburne Aero, 81
   construction of special, 101-3, 108, 147
   ex-Horton Blackburne Super Aero, 157, 164
   KMB-engined Aero, 153, 157
   rear-engined hill climb special, 221
   steering problems, 136-7
James, Billie, 34, 53
James, Freddie, 41, 47, 53, 143
   Family Aero, 106, 133
   Grand Prix ('Kango'), 45
JAP engines
   4 and 8 hp Runabouts, 15, 16
   8/75 engine, 186
   90 degree air-cooled, 63
   731cc ohv special, 117
   750cc racing, 22
   976cc in Aero, 42
   1082cc, 37
   1087cc water-cooled sv, 40-1
   1090cc water-cooled ohv, 77
   introduction of aluminium pistons, 52
   JTOR 996cc, 69-70; production, 116
   JTOS or 8/80, 217, 219
   KT, 43, 50; redesigned, 95
   KTC, 52
   KTOR 976cc, 77
   KTR twin camshaft 976cc, 69
   LTOW, 95; 1096cc modifications, 141; variants, 109
   LTOWZ 1096cc, 163, 202; modifications, 173
   LTZ 1096cc, 163
   Mark 1 racing vee-twins, 234
   modified side-valve engine, 28

Jay, Cecil, 118
  Blackburne Aero ('Jim'), 138, 147
Jones, Harry, 177, 186
Junior Car Club, 40
  General Efficiency Trials, (1922) 53, (1923) 61
  Spring Meeting, (1922) 54, (1923) 62
  200-mile race, (1921) 51-2, (1922) 56, (1923) 68, (1924) 77

Laird, Henry, 158, 162, 172, 182, 217, 226
  'Johnny Red', 177, 180, 199, 202, 205, 208, 210
  'Johnny V' (later 'Yellow'), 186, 196, 207, 216
Light Car Club, 143
  Brooklands meeting (1930), 145
  90-lap relay, (1931) 160, (1932) 169, (1933) 178, (1934) 189-91, (1935) 200, (1936) 209
London-Edinburgh Trial, (1911) 16, (1913) 22, (1928) 121-2, (1929) 134, (1930) 145, (1931) 159, (1932) 168, (1933) 178, (1934) 189, (1935) 199-200, (1936) 209
London-Exeter Trial, (1910) 16, (1912) 19, (1920) 49, (1922) 61, (1923) 70, (1924) 80, (1925) 95, (1926) 109, (1927) 119, (1928) 130, (1930) 155, (1931) 164, (1933) 186, (1934) 194, (1935) 206, (1937) 212, (1938) 218, (1939) 221, (1951) 235
London-Gloucester Trial, (1912) 19, (1921) 52, (1930) 155, (1931) 164
London-Land's End Trial, (1923) 62, (1924) 72, (1925) 90, (1927) 112, (1928) 121, (1930) 143, (1931) 158, (1932) 167-8, (1933) 176, (1934) 186, (1935) 196, (1936) 208, (1937) 212, (1939) 221, (1949) 233
Lones, H Clive, 191-2
  Blackburne Aero, 92, 94
  Blackburne-engined Grand Prix, 65
  cranked chassis Aero, 112, 119-20
  JTOR engine, 134, 161, 169

Jackson's aluminium-bodied special, 144, 145
  lowered chassis Super Aero ('Bob'), 124, 135, 138, 140, 145, 153, 158, 177
  LTOW-engined Morgan, 103
  special built on 'C' type chassis, 166, 167
  'Tiger Cat', 207, 226
  'Tiger Kitten', 227
Longden, Eric, 41, 50
  JAP-engined Grand Prix, 42, 43

'M' type chassis, 141-2
McCarthy, Stanley, 49, 50, 61
McMinnies, W Gordon, 17, 20, 24-8, 32, 34
Madresfield Speed Trials, (1921) 51, (1923) 65, (1924) 74, (1925) 92, (1927) 115, (1928) 122, (1929) 135, (1930) 145, (1931) 161, (1951) 235
MAG engines, 35
  1078cc, 37
  water-cooled, 39
Martin, Harry, 18, 54-5, 56
Maskell, Arthur, 161, 177
  Anzani Grand Prix, 62
  Family Aero special, 100
  'M' type Super Aero, 161, 177, 181
Matchless engines, 194
  MX 990cc, 176-7
  MX2, 178
  MX4, 185-6
Merrill, EW, 41
Morgan, Dorothy, 19, 22, 23, 35
Morgan, Henry Frederick Stanley, 13, 18, 236
  Aero AB16, 71
  Anzani-engined wide-track Aero, 65
  JAP-engined Grand Prix, 61
  ohv 90 bore JAP for hour race (1912), 18
  return to trials driving, 168
Morgan, Hilda Ruth (née Day), 18
Morgan Motor Company
  factory opened in Malvern, 42

Index

three-wheeler production ended, 236
Morgan Three-Wheeler Club, 226, 236
Moss, Stirling, 227
Motor Cycle Club
  High Speed Trial, (1925) 95, (1926) 109, (1929) 141, (1930) 153, (1931) 161-2, (1932) 172-3, (1933) 181-2, (1934) 193-4, (1935) 205, (1936) 210
  light car handicap (1914), 35-6
  Sporting Trial (1933), 184
Motor Cycle Show, (1910) 15, (1911) 17, (1919) 42, (1920) 49, (1921) 52, (1922) 60, (1923) 69, (1926) 108, (1927) 117, (1928) 130, (1929) 141-2, (1930) 154, (1931) 163, (1932) 173, (1933) 184, (1934) 194, (1935) 206, (1937) 217, (1938) 221, (1949) 233
Motor Cycling Cyclecar Trophy (1912), 18, 19

New Cyclecar Club, 114
  Brooklands Meeting, (1928) 123, (1929) 137-8
Norris, Norman, 53, 58, 62, 63, 68, 109
  driver for Lea Francis, 80
  MAG-engined Standard, 61

Oliver, GEW, 192, 194, 224
Oliver RD, 23, 28, 30, 35

Prestwich, John Alfred, 19, 52, 236
  see also JAP engines
propshaft modification, 149
Prowse, Keith, 91

Quadrant engines, 30-1

'R' chassis, 163
Rhodes, Tommy, 114, 115, 169, 180, 207
  Blackburne Aero, 124, 138
  JTOR Super Aero, 172, 177, 189, 199
Runabout, 15, 115
Russell BBF
  saloon-bodied Aero ('Newt'), 112

Scottish Six Days' Trial, (1913) 27-8, (1914) 34, (1920) 50, (1923) 63, (1924) 75, (1925) 93, (1926) 103, (1927) 114, (1928) 122, (1929) 134, (1930) 144, (1931) 160, (1932) 168
Silverstone, 234
Smith, RD, 61, 145
South, WD, 24, 28, 37
Southport, (1921) 50, (1923) 66, (1924) 77, 80, (1926) 95-6, 99, 101, 107, (1927) 110, 111, 114, 115, (1928) 119-20, 127, (1929) 132, 141, (1930) 153, (1931) 161, (1932) 173, (1933) 181, (1934) 194, (1936) 210
Speed trials ban, 85-6
Speedway tracks, 132
Sports Family, 144, 145, 154, 164
Sports model
  incorporating spare wheel, 173
  twin rear wheel with LTOWZ engine, 175
Standard model, 31, 44
Stephenson-Peach, W, 14
Stewart, Gwenda, 130, 140-1, 142-4, 154
  single-seater special, 149
  Super Aero with JTOR engine, 132
Super Aero
  body improvements, 130
  'M' type chassis, 142
  'R' type chassis, 163
  rear spring mounting, 133
Super Sports model
  'barrel back' body, 185
  Matchless MX4 engine, 226, 227, 231
  ohv Matchless twin, 221
Super Sports Aero model, 117, 164
Swift, GE, 119
  3-speed Super Sports, 167
Sylvester, Jack, 34
  Blackburne Aero AB16, 73
  KMA Aero, 76-7
  MAG-engined Standard, 44

Thruxton circuit, 235
TT model, 37, 38, 41

twin rear wheel development, 155

Victory Cup Trial, (1919) 39, (1923) 61, (1924) 70, (1925) 84, (1926) 98, (1927) 110-11, (1929) 132, (1933) 175, (1935) 196

Ware, Edward Bradford, 30, 31-2, 35-6, 51, 222
  experimental 90 degree JAP engine, 63
  Family with special JAP 1087cc engine, 40-1
  final JCC 200-mile race, 78
  Grand Prix with JAP 90 bore ohv, 48
  modified single-seater, 42-3
  narrow-bodied 2-seater (JAP II), 46-7, 48-9, 50, 52, 53, 56, 68
  Standard with KTC engine, 61
  wide-track flat-sided Aero, 77
Welch, Dennis, 174
Whatley, Charles L, 62
  Anzani Grand Prix, 64
Woodhouse, Jack, 30
World World War I, 37-8
World War II, 224, 226
Wye Valley Trial, (1932) 168, (1933) 175, (1935) 196, (1936) 207, (1937) 214, (1938) 218

Zoller supercharger, 195, 197, 199, 208